TAKEOVER IN TEHRAN

Takeover In Tehran

The Inside Story of the 1979 U.S. Embassy Capture

Massoumeh Ebtekar

as told to Fred A. Reed

Talonbooks

2000

Talonbooks
P.O. Box 2076
Vancouver, British Columbia, Canada V6B 3S3
Tel.: (604)444-4889; Fax: (604)444-4119; Internet: www.talonbooks.com

Typeset in Adobe Garamond and printed and bound in Canada by Hignell Book Printing.

Second Printing: March 2001.

Canadian Cataloguing in Publication Data

Ebtekar, Massoumeh, 1960-
Takeover in Tehran

ISBN 0-88922-443-9

1. Iran Hostage Crisis, 1979-1981. 2. Iran--Politics and government--1979-1997. 3. United States--Foreign relations--Iran. 4. Iran--Foreign relations--United States. I. Reed, Fred A., 1939- II. Title.
E183.8.I55E27 2000   955.05'4   C00-910759-2

The publisher gratefully acknowledges the financial support of the Canada Council for the Arts; the Government of Canada through the Book Publishing Industry Development Program; and the Province of British Columbia through the British Columbia Arts Council for our publishing activities.

In the Name of God, the Merciful, the Compassionate.

The special dedication of this book goes to those who settled for nothing less than the vision of God, and to the martyrs of the Muslim Students Following the Line of the Imam.

This book is less the work of an individual than the fruit of a collective commitment to produce an account faithful to the facts and spirit of Iran's "Second Revolution." For this reason my thanks go first to my family and friends, who shared their thoughts and ideas with me as I developed the concept of the book. I owe special gratitude to my husband Mohammad for his constant encouragement and support, and for his thoughts and memories of events that became an integral part of the story I tell in these pages.

My sincere thanks go to Hassan Abdulrahman as well, for his dedication to the project over the past seven years. Without his strategic contribution, we would simply have been unable to succeed. I would also like to thank Fred A. Reed, whose efforts helped bring this work to life.

Finally, I have discussed many of the ideas central to this book with Hojjatoleslam Seyyed Mohammad Mousavi Khoeiniha, who was kind enough to devote much of his precious time to those conversations. I am grateful for his support.

Massoumeh Ebtekar
Tehran, July, 2000

CONTENTS

CHRONOLOGY OF EVENTS LEADING TO THE ISLAMIC REVOLUTION AND THE TAKEOVER OF THE UNITED STATES EMBASSY IN TEHRAN

1891-92   Revolt led by Shi'ite religious dignitaries against the tobacco monopoly granted by Shah Naser al-Din Qajar to British interests. Concession repealed following a national boycott.

1901   First petroleum concession granted to William Knox d'Arcy.

1906   Popular movement led by a coalition of West-influenced intellectuals, merchants and Shi'ite clerics leads to establishment of Iran's first Majlis (Parliament). Adoption of Iran's first constitution.

1907   St. Petersburg Accords between Russia and Great Britain divide Iran into zones of influence.

1908   Oil discovered at Masjid-e Soleiman.

         Majlis bombarded, autocracy restored. Constitutionalist revolt in Tabriz.

1909   Creation of the Anglo-Persian Oil Company (APOC).

         Conquest of Tehran by the constitutionalists; restoration of constitutional government.

         Public execution of anti-constitutionalist clergyman Sheikh Fazlollah Nouri, who had earlier militated for an Islamic parliament.

         Inauguration of the second Majlis.

1911   Morgan W. Schuster, an American-appointed Treasurer General of Persia, arrives in Tehran.

         Northern Iran occupied by Russian troops, constitutional reforms aborted.

         Second Majlis dissolved; Schuster dismissed.

1914   British Admiralty becomes majority shareholder of APOC. Winston Churchill later described the deal, which fueled the victory of the Entente in the First World War, as a "prize from fairyland far beyond our brightest dreams."

1920   Iranian Communist Party founded at Anzali, northern Iran.

1921   Headed by Reza Khan, a peasant from Mazandaran, the White Russian-trained Cossack Brigade occupies Tehran.

         Irano-Soviet Treaty.

1922	Arthur C. Millspaugh, an American, appointed by the Iranian government to reorganize state finances.
1923	Reza Khan appointed prime minister.
1925	Abolition of the Qajar Dynasty. After assuming full command of the armed forces, Reza Khan crowned Shahanshah ("King of kings") by military-controlled Majlis. Inauguration of Pahlavi Dynasty.
1925-1941	Reign of Reza Shah Pahlavi.
1928	Reza Shah ends foreign capitulations.
1934	Reza Shah visits Kemalist Turkey.
1935	Women ordered to unveil.
1941	Invasion of Iran by Soviet and British troops. Pro-German Reza Shah deposed, sent into exile; his son Mohammad-Reza assumes the throne.
1943	Tehran Conference (Churchill, Roosevelt, Stalin).
1945	Proclamation of Soviet-occupied Autonomous Republic of Azerbaijan.
1946	Proclamation of the pro-Soviet Kurdish Republic of Mahabad. Iranian forces re-occupy Azerbaijan and Kurdistan.
1951	Majlis votes to nationalize Iran's oil industry; Mohammad Mossadegh appointed prime minister. AIOC (Anglo-Iranian Oil Company, formerly APOC) ceases production.
1953	July 6, clandestine arrival in Iran, as "James F. Lochridge," of Kermit Roosevelt, high-ranking CIA officer. August 1, public arrival in Tehran of General Norman Schwartzkopf. August, Operation Boot/Ajax (a joint British-American plan to overthrow the Mossadegh government and reverse oil industry nationalization) set in motion, coordinated by Roosevelt and Schwartzkopf. Mossadegh refuses to abandon prime ministership. August 16, Shah Mohammad-Reza Pahlavi leaves Iran for Italy. Rioting in Tehran, by street gangs funded and organized by Roosevelt.

August 19, military coup d'état.

Mossadegh forced to flee his residence; arrested.

August 22, shah returns to Iran.

1957   Creation, in consultation with CIA, of Iran's secret police, SAVAK. Primary targets: Iranian Communist Party, Islamic groups.

1963   January, Plebiscite on White Revolution, a wide-ranging program including land reform and female suffrage.

June 5, Ayatollah Khomeini denounces White Revolution.

Thousands killed in massive anti-shah demonstrations throughout Iran.

1964   Khomeini criticizes immunity accorded to American military personnel in Iran. Expelled to Turkey; relocates to Najaf, Iraq.

1971   Mohammad-Reza Shah Pahlavi celebrates 2500 years of empire at Persepolis.

1973   Closing of Hosseiniyeh Ershad, Tehran religious institution made popular by Dr. Ali Shariati.

1973   OPEC meets in Tehran. Crude oil prices increase from $2.90 to $11.60/barrel. Oil shock in West.

1976   Iran abandons solar Hegira (Islamic), adopts imperial calendar.

1977   Shah visits Washington, to massive protests by Iranian students.

Death of Dr. Ali Shariati in London.

1978   January 7, publication of an article insulting Imam Khomeini in *Etala'at* newspaper; rioting in Qom violently repressed.

February 18, rioting in Tabriz.

August 11, martial law declared in Isfahan.

August 19, pro-shah provocateurs burn Rex Cinema in Abadan; more than 400 die.

September 7, martial law declared in 11 cities.

September 8, Black Friday massacre in Jaleh Square, Tehran. Thousands shot.

September 10, U.S. President James Carter calls shah from Camp David to express personal support and friendship.

November 4, violent repression of student demonstrations at Tehran University.

November 6, general strike declared.

November 9, United States ships riot control equipment to Iran.

November 10, millions demonstrate on Ashura, anniversary of the death of Imam Hossein at Karbala.

November 30, President Carter reaffirms full confidence in shah.

December 25-20, President Carter, State Secretary Cyrus Vance dispatch General Robert Huyser to Iran.

December 26, strikers close down oil production.

December 31, shah names Shapour Bakhtiar prime minister.

1979   January, Guadaloupe Summit (U.S., Great Britain, W. Germany, France) seals fate of shah.

January 4, General Robert Huyser arrives in Tehran to convey American support for the military, encourage Iranian generals to stage a coup d'état if Bakhtiar government falls.

January 16, Shah Mohammad-Reza Pahlavi flees into exile in Egypt. Millions of Iranians take to the streets to demonstrate their joy.

January 22, Imam Khomeini receives Ramsay Clark at Neuphle-le-Château.

February 1, triumphal return of Ayatollah Khomeini to Tehran, where he is welcomed by huge crowds.

February 10, mass uprisings bring down the remains of the Pahlavi regime. Imam Khomeini appoints Mehdi Bazargan Islamic Iran's first prime minister.

February 14, leftists attack and capture U.S. Embassy, hold Ambassador Sullivan and more than 100 staff hostage for two hours before being dispersed.

February 18, Yassar Arafat first foreign dignitary to visit the revolutionary state.

Iran severs diplomatic relations with Israel.

February 26, total nationalization of the oil industry.

March, violent clashes in border regions between revolutionary guardsmen and Kurdish, Turkoman rebels.

April 1, Proclamation of the Islamic Republic of Iran following a national referendum.

April 7, execution of Amir Abbas Hoveyda, Court Minister under the shah.

May 1, assassination of Ayatollah Morteza Mottahari by *Forqan*, an extremist anti-clerical group.

May 17, United States Senate condemns Iran for executions.

May 25, assassination attempt on Ali Akbar Hashemi Rafsanjani, later Majlis Speaker, President of the Islamic Republic.

August 23, Kurdish insurgency against the Islamic regime.

September 9, death of Ayatollah Mahmoud Taleghani.

October 22, Mohammad-Reza Pahlavi admitted to the United States.

November 1, provisional government official Ibrahim Yazdi meets U.S. National Security Advisor Zbigniew Brzezinski in Algiers.

November 4, occupation of the United States Embassy by Muslim Students Following the Line of the Imam.

November 6, Bazargan government resigns.

November 14, U.S. government freezes Iranian assets.

December 2-3, Iranians ratify the Constitution of the Islamic Republic, instituting the *Velayat-e Faqih* (Mandate of the Jurisprudent).

December, students begin release of documents revealing U.S. intelligence activities in Iran.

1980   January 1, U.N. Secretary General Kurt Waldheim arrives in Tehran, meets members of the Revolutionary Council.

January 2, Soviet invasion of Afghanistan.

January 17, U.S. aircraft carrier *Nimitz* enters Persian Gulf.

February, Turkoman rebellion in Northeast Iran.

Five-member U.N. special commission established.

March, U.N. commission leaves Tehran without obtaining release of hostages.

April 7, President James Carter breaks diplomatic relations with Iran.

April 23, Cultural Revolution closes all universities, research centers.

April 25, U.S. hostage rescue mission fails in the desert at Tabas.

July 27, Mohammad-Reza Pahlavi dies in Cairo.

September 12, military coup d'état in Turkey.

September 22, Iraq invades Iran, starting a war that was to last eight years.

1981   January 20, 52 American hostages released, after 444 days of captivity.

Inauguration of U.S. President Ronald Reagan.

American clergymen shown with Massoumeh Ebtekar and
hostages Katherine Koob and Elizabeth Swift. Christmas, 1979.

FOREWORD

THIS BOOK PRESENTS for the first time an Iranian eye-witness account of the capture, on November 4, 1979, of the United States Embassy in Tehran by Iranian students, and of the 444-day hostage crisis that it touched off. Massoumeh Ebtekar, then a freshman at Tehran Polytechnic Institute, was an active participant in the political movement that planned, organized and carried out the action. Its impact was to shatter relations between the United States and Iran, and propel Iranian religious radicals, under the leadership of Ayatollah Ruhollah Khomeini, to the fore as the country's dominant political force. *Takeover in Tehran* tells the story of this group of students, their supporters, the Iranian revolutionaries, and the 61—and ultimately 52—American hostages, and how they became caught up in events that mushroomed into a major international issue and ultimately eluded their control.

It is a book that promises to become one of the keys to confronting a troubled and controversial past, both in Iran and in the United States. Massoumeh Ebtekar, like several of her fellow-students, has gone on to hold positions of responsibility in Islamic Iran. She is currently vice-president in charge of the Department of the Environment, a close political advisor to President Seyyed Mohammad Khatami, and one of the founders of the Islamic Iran Participation Front (IIPF). This was the broad coalition that won more than 70 percent of the votes in the Majlis (parliamentary) elections of February 18, 2000 which pried control of the country's legislative branch from the country's ultra-conservative political faction.

Ms. Ebtekar's generation, which came to precocious maturity during the first days of the Islamic Revolution, is now, twenty years later, emerging as Iran's new political elite. Mohammad-Reza Khatami, the

British-trained nephrologist, younger brother of President Khatami and IIPF leader, was among the student activists who seized the embassy on that fateful November 4, 1979. On a more sombre note, so was Sa'id Hajjarian, wounded in a failed assassination attempt by a Revolutionary Guard Corps intelligence operative loyal to the defeated clerical faction, as he was arriving to attend a Tehran City Council meeting several days after the election. Mr. Hajjarian is generally regarded as the architect of the strategy that led the reform coalition to victory, and was formerly a high-ranking official in the Information Ministry, a position that had given him privileged access to the inner workings of the Islamic state's intelligence apparatus, and to detailed files on all leading figures of the regime.

Another former student who has gone on to win a reputation as a combatant for Iran's emerging civil society is Abbas Abdi, the investigative journalist whose reports exposed the direct involvement of the security services in the brutal "chain murders" of secular nationalist opposition politicians in November, 1978. Mr. Abdi's hard-hitting, chillingly documented reports appeared several months later in the radical daily *Salâm*, published by Hojjatoleslam Mousavi Khoeiniha, who twenty years earlier had acted as spiritual and political advisor to the occupying students. Mr. Abdi was subsequently imprisoned, and *Salâm* shut down by Iran's clerical-dominated judiciary system in June, 1999.

The emergence of the one-time student militants as reform activists committed to an Islamic civil society, democratic pluralism and cultural dialogue has been seen by some as a paradox. Others interpret their rise to prominence as a ruse perpetrated by a putative monolithic Shi'a clerical establishment. Still others see it as an implicit disavowal by the one-time students of the errors and excesses of their past. If nothing else, this apparent paradox calls into question conventional views of the hostage crisis itself, and about the society created by the massive, inchoate upheaval known as the Islamic Revolution.

For twenty years, the prevailing "globalized" version of the embassy capture has cast the students as, at best, well-intentioned but naive young people manipulated by a Machiavellian hierocracy, and at worst, as irresponsible extremists. They are seen not as initiators of events, but as agents of the mollahs.

"It now seems certain," writes James Bill in his authoritative account of U.S.-Iran relations, "that the militants had plans to move on the American Embassy in Tehran long before November 4 and that they put their plans into action when anti-American rhetoric and feeling began to peak in the first three days of that month."[1]

Ms. Ebtekar's account of the events leading up to the seizure of the embassy supplies some of the key detail lacking in Bill's rather sweeping assessment. In fact, several student groups, of widely varying political allegiances, had been contemplating such action, and had even invaded the embassy grounds for brief periods prior to November 4. The Islamic students were, she demonstrates, the first to act, a decision persuasively explained by widespread indignation at a specific action by the United States: the Carter administration's decision to admit the ailing Mohammad-Reza Pahlavi, Shah of Iran, to American soil on "humanitarian grounds" less than two weeks previously.

Sa'id Amir Arjomand, an author hostile to the clerical regime, sets the events of November, 1979, against an almost exclusively Iranian political background. "Following the taking of hostages by an Islamic student group at the American Embassy on November 4, 1979, the Bazargan government fell, and the clerical coup d'état took place, in the form of a direct takeover of the state by the clergy-dominated Revolutionary Council."[2]

Well before then, by August of that year, argues Arjomand, the clerical party had already shown its true colors, by clamping down on press liberties which had flourished in the months immediately following the fall of the shah's dictatorship. It also began, he says, to attack organizations like the National Democratic Party, the Marxist-oriented Feda'iyan, the Mujahideen Khalq Organization (MKO) and the Tudeh (Communist) Party. All of these political factions, however, continued to function throughout the embassy occupation. Moreover, as Massoumeh Ebtekar's account makes clear, each one sought to profit from the extraordinary popularity of the students' initiative among ordinary Iranians by both endorsing it, and seeking to join it.

That the clerical party maneuvered cleverly, aggressively and often brutally in pursuit of its declared aims—to undo a century of Western influence in Iran and to establish an Islamic state as conceived by Ayatollah Ruhollah Khomeini—is beyond dispute. To posit it as the sole architect of events strains the imagination. Iranians of almost all social backgrounds could have been forgiven for seeing in the American handling of the fall of the shah in 1979 a potential replay of the events of 1953.

It was then that the government of Mohammad Mossadegh, which had nationalized the Iranian oil industry, to the dismay of Great Britain and the United States, had been overthrown by a coup directly organized and financed by the CIA, as part of which the *New York Times* was handed the responsibility of destroying the late Dr. Mossadegh's character by depicting him as under Soviet influence. Confirmation of the fact by U.S. Secretary of State Madeleine Albright in March, 2000, forty-seven years later, offered cold comfort to Iran, which had been strong-armed into a quarter-century of tyranny at the hands of the Pahlavi regime.

Secretary Albright's admission was accompanied by a major *Times*[3] article purporting to reveal hitherto unknown details of the coup that overthrew Dr. Mossadegh. The information was drawn from a "secret history" allegedly written by Dr. Donald N. Wilbur, an expert in Persian architecture who is described as one of the leading planners. Wilbur was, however, no expert in analyzing the behavior of those whom he was charged to influence, referring to the "recognized incapacity of Iranians to plan or act together in a thoroughly logical manner."

That the *Times* would obtain this previously classified material only hours after Ms. Albright's near-admission of American guilt can be viewed as coincidence only by the credulous. Best described as politically motivated spin, the document details the agency's "limited success" in using the American press in the months leading up to the American-planned military coup. It avoids, however, using the words "no success," and quotes the now-deceased *Times* reporter in Tehran, Kennett Love, as admitting to being "responsible, in an impromptu sort of way, for speeding the final victory of the royalists," all the while being fed information by a CIA operative masquerading as the American Embassy's press officer.

In fact, it is generally accepted in Tehran that Love was on the agency payroll, and that his reports were instrumental in preparing American public opinion for the impending coup.

The thesis that the students were manipulated by the clerical party in 1979 fails on another, more serious count. It is predicated upon an assumption of inability on the part of the unaffiliated Islamic students who captured the embassy to draw conclusions from their own social, political and ideological environment, and from their country's recent history, and then to act independently on those conclusions. At the same time, it hastens to confer a spurious legitimacy on the myriad other ideologically driven groups struggling for public support and recognition in the flood tide of revolutionary upheaval, suggesting that because of their pro-West, secular, liberal or Marxist credentials, their grasp of events was somehow more firm or enlightened. However, this book confirms, in its eye-witness account of the Iranian public's response to the takeover, the immense popularity enjoyed by the students. Their assessment of public awareness had been acute and it had been accurate. No serious account of those politically-charged events has ever concluded anything less.

Jean-Pierre Digard, Bernard Hourcade and Yann Richard, in their comprehensive overview of Iran in the twentieth century argue that "the existence, within its ranks, of a 'third-worldist, leftist' trend at logger-heads with the traditionalist, 'right wing' clergy, reminds us of how mistaken it would be to reduce the Islamic Republic to some kind of medieval theocracy or caliphate, and to what extent it continues to be marked by the popular revolution upon which it is based." [My translation.][4]

Seen from such a perspective, the students can be understood as articulate representatives of the "third worldist" trend that has always existed within the Islamic Republic, though until recently in a minority position. Ms. Ebtekar's narrative provides ample evidence of their original and ongoing commitment to the democratic ideals that are now gaining currency in Iran, twenty-one years later, under the deft guidance of President Khatami. Certainly they could not have been accused of complacency then. Judging by their actions, the political activists, journalists and public figures they have become cannot be so accused today.

Far from an accident, the ascendancy of the student "radicals" as reformers committed to a program of civil society within an Islamic framework, reflects the maturing of one of the two dominant aspects of the Islamic Revolution: its democratic structures and high degree of representativity. The other of these two aspects is the theocratic structure that derives its legitimacy from the doctrine of the *Velayat-e Faqih* (Rule of the Jurisprudent), propounded to accommodate the extraordinary personality of Ayatollah Khomeini.

Inescapably, the process of reappraisal that is accompanying the emergence of an Islamic civil society in Iran has also focused new, critical attention on the past. Once beyond all criticism, even the Khomeini legacy is itself being questioned. Such articles of faith as obligatory *hijab* (modest Islamic dress, taken to include head covering) are being challenged by outspoken women. The role of the country's leadership in the eight-year war against Iraq is being submitted to close re-examination. The battle for reinterpretation that is part and parcel of any process of political renewal has been joined, and Massoumeh Ebtekar's account can be taken as a part of that ongoing engagement.

In keeping with the new spirit of frankness at large in Iranian society, some voices—notably that of dissident philosopher Abdolkarim Soroush[5]—argue that the embassy capture, occupation and hostage taking should be seen as a mistake. The former students who are today assuming positions of influence in society are, in his view, best understood to be striving, through positive, non-violent political action, to expiate past wrongs. It would seem indisputable that awareness of the excesses that occurred during the first years of the Islamic Revolution would attempt to work itself out in many ways. Active or near-overt forms of self-examination, regret or even repentance cannot be ruled out, and may well extend to Dr. Soroush himself, one of the principal architects of Iran's Cultural Revolution of 1980-1981, which closed the universities, dismissed professors on ideological grounds, and recast curricula along strict Islamic lines.

The Iran-Iraq war, which began while the students still held the embassy, was a human catastrophe for which those who prolonged it, due in part to the acquisition, via Israel, of sophisticated American weapons systems, may eventually be called to account. Shortly after the end of hostilities, Ayatollah Hossein-Ali Montazeri, then successor-designate to Khomeini, declared: "We must realize that we have voiced slogans, many of which have contributed to our isolation in the world; slogans for which there were wiser ways, but we closed our eyes and ears and cried: 'It is as we say!', and later found out we were wrong. We must understand our mistakes and admit our errors before God and the nation."[6]

A few days after making this statement, Montazeri was stripped of his title, and is still being held under house arrest in Qom. But he has retained and even increased his influence among devout Iranians as a religious authority.

A powerful factor motivating the students' action, argues Ms. Ebtekar, was the slanted if not hostile coverage of events in Iran by the international, and primarily the American, media establishment. In their determination to explain the wrongs committed in and against Iran by a succession of United States governments and intelligence agencies, the students sought to address the American people directly. The capture of the embassy and the sequestering of its diplomatic and intelligence staff would give them, they believed, both an ideal platform and the necessary leverage to do so. It was here, if anywhere, that they could have been criticized for naiveté.

Though transnational ownership of the mainstream press and radio-television outlets of the early seventies was less concentrated than it is today, American media shared the same characteristics then as now. These included unwavering fealty to a well-defined "national interest" and systematic denigration of any views or information that might challenge a centrally originated and agreed-upon version of facts, persons and events. This the Iranian students were to certify. The description of their doing so is one of the most touching and eloquent parts of Ms. Ebtekar's book.

The U.S. government had learned a bitter lesson in Vietnam. This was the conflict that was alleged to have been "lost" as a result of allowing American print and electronic journalists access to the front lines which later proved damaging to the political and military objectives of the United States. A study of television coverage of the war,[7] however, revealed that the media could not have been held responsible for the American people's disaffection with their country's political and military objectives in the region. Nearly half of all broadcast information dealt with the operations of the American ground and air forces; official statements by Washington and the U.S. puppet government in Saigon accounted for another 12%. The "enemy" viewpoint was reflected in less than 3% of coverage.

Never again would Washington and the media owners make the same mistake. Even three percent was too much. Television coverage may have been unable to conceal the clouds of tear-gas wafting across the White House lawn when Shah Mohammad-Reza Pahlavi visited the American capital in 1977 at the invitation of President James Carter, nor the tears it brought to the eyes of the visiting royalty and their hosts. But two years later, when the Muslim students seized the American Embassy to protest the admission of the shah to the United States, they would first be portrayed as wild-eyed fanatics and fundamentalists, then dismissed outright, and their ideas and ideals ridiculed.

That the primary spokesperson for the students was an articulate young woman with fluent English named "Mary"—author Massoumeh Ebtekar—would prove no obstacle to Betty Mahmoody's tendentious and inventive *Not Without My Daughter* later becoming the accepted Western description of the plight of all Iranian women.

As the Gulf War, and the NATO aerial campaign against Serbia over Kosovo in support of Albanian separatist guerrillas were to confirm, the lessons of the role of the media in Vietnam have since been applied with cybernetic precision. Outrages have been manufactured to shape public opinion; claims of genocide in the tens of thousands have fallen lightly from the lips of State Department spokespersons. CNN retained the services of active-duty United States Army psychological warfare specialists to buttress the battlefront reporting of Christiane Amanpour, the spouse of State Department spokesman James Rubin.

On another, less controversial level, this story is one of youthful audacity leavened by humor and anecdote, related in a way that throws new, revealing light on the ideas and the powerful belief that motivated the student rebels. Massoumeh Ebtekar depicts the American hostages, their would-be Iranian rescuers among the moderate political forces, the students' friends, families, and all those who attempted to use and manipulate them for political ends, in new depth and perspective. In this book we have an articulate, detailed account of a "third world" crisis not from the point of view of Washington, but from that of the "third world."

Massoumeh Ebtekar presents a fast flowing, day-by-day, blow by blow account of the planning of the embassy seizure, introduces us to several of the key student leaders, and takes us behind the scenes into the complex world of religious and political conflict that raged in the aftermath of the Islamic Revolution, the flood tide of popular frustration and resentment that swept away the imperial regime, then brought down Iran's first post-revolutionary government, clearing the way for what long seemed unrestricted rule by Iran's traditional Shi'ite clergy, the *ulama*.

Hers is also an account that wears its heart on its sleeve. We meet young men and women like the narrator, moved by a powerful combination of offended national pride and religious dedication, as they experience a situation of growing complexity. We encounter people who, as the occupation draws on, are overtaken by forces beyond their control, and that will ultimately take control of them. Finally, the "October Surprise," having sealed Jimmy Carter's political doom, would lead to the negotiated release of the hostages on the day of Ronald Reagan's inauguration. We gain insight into the complexities of Islamic Iran, into the power of Ayatollah Khomeini to shape and guide events, and into his complex and ambiguous legacy of theocratic absolutism and grass-roots democracy.

Islamic Iran, in all its contradictions, has always been anything but dull or predictable. Massoumeh Ebtekar's narrative—and subsequent career—shows why.

The story of this book is almost as convoluted as that of the U.S. Embassy takeover. I was first introduced to Ms. Ebtekar in 1996 by a mutual friend. She was at the time publisher of *Farzaneh*, an Islamic women's journal, and was pursuing a scientific career while rearing two children. Her efforts to interest English-language publishers in her story had been unsuccessful. Some, including reputable houses, had dismissed the project as a fabrication. Others responded with indifference, polite lack of interest and some with overt hostility. Such a book would be "contrary to our interests," they argued.

It was not until I proposed the enterprise to my publisher, the Vancouver-based Canadian independent Talonbooks, that it began to take on life as a book. I met Ms. Ebtekar in Tehran on several occasions, during which she clarified several aspects of her story and answered a long list of questions. Subsequent question and answer sessions took place in her offices at the Department of the Environment on Villa Avenue in the heart of the Iranian capital. This book is also the fruit of those hours of discussion.

Finally, I wish to acknowledge the contribution of Hassan Abdulrahman. Without his deep knowledge of Iranian affairs and his stubborn dedication to see this book through to publication, *Takeover in Tehran* would not exist.

Fred A. Reed
Tehran-Montréal, June, 2000

PREFACE

In the Name of God, the Merciful, the Compassionate.

ON NOVEMBER 4TH, 1979, A GROUP of students from several Tehran universities captured the Embassy of the United States of America in Tehran. They took the diplomats and other personnel present hostage.

In their first communiqué, issued a few hours later, the students explained that they had acted to protest the protection and asylum granted by the American Government to the ousted Shah of Iran. The students considered the seizure of the embassy as their indisputable right of opposition to the American Government's decision to welcome the shah and to its general policy of hostility towards the Iranian revolution. Their act of protest was quickly depicted by the United States Government as barbarous and deserving of punishment.

A majority of Americans displayed little if any sympathy toward the Iranian students during this incident. Most, in fact, condemned the action and supported the American government's punitive actions against Iran. Their countrymen were being held by the students—it seemed only natural for American citizens to support their government.

But the question remains: did the American people (and global public opinion) possess the necessary information to make an informed judgment, to weigh the claims of the Iranian students and those of the American government? Had the Iranian students enjoyed equal access to dialogue with the American people, had they been able to explain the reasons for their initiative, would they have been viewed in the same way as they have been from that time down to the present day?

For decades large numbers of Iranian nationals have been engaged, throughout the United States, in production, commerce and particularly education: living, in other words, side by side with the American people. Has their behavior displayed any sign of barbarous or aggressive temperament? Is not the very fact that millions of Iranians have been living in the United States for the past two decades proof of the respect they hold and the value they attach to that country and its people? Yet a group of these selfsame Iranians, a select group of university students, captured the American Embassy and took its personnel hostage. Is it fair to view their action as a barbarous encroachment on the rights of a number of American citizens without a detailed inquiry into its logical and historical background?

If the action had been undertaken by a group of hooligans or armed robbers, it would have been easy to decry, to consider as deserving of punishment. But considering that it was the work of a group of university students, would not the same verdict be a hasty one?

If today, under present circumstances, the individuals who captured the former American Embassy in Tehran in 1979 would be asked whether they would be prepared to take similar action to secure their rights which had been violated by the United Stated Government, their response would be a definite "no." Still, the circumstances prevailing in the year of the embassy takeover have to be closely examined.

The historical memory of the Iranian nation, and in particular the revolutionaries, of the United States-inspired coup of August, 1953, that resulted in the overthrow of the government of Dr. Mohammad Mossadegh, needs an honest appraisal. That event resulted in the return of Shah Mohammad-Reza Pahlavi to Iran and the continuation of his dictatorial regime. When all the implications of this tragic episode in our history are taken into consideration, an unbiased arbiter would surely judge the students' action has having been the only real avenue for seeking justice from the American government.

Since the victory of the Islamic Revolution in 1979, conditions have never existed for the genuine dialogue that must be a prelude to new relations of mutual understanding between Iran and the United States. Such conditions certainly do not exist at present. The American government continues to deal with Iran from a position of power and authority, granting itself the right to interfere in the affairs of another country. For its part, Iran, given its historical memories and the past actions of the United States, has regarded the American government as an enemy. Obviously, such an atmosphere allows no possibility for dialogue, and hence little possibility of settling outstanding issues.

Twenty-one years have elapsed since the hostage taking. Over these years, the American government has worked assiduously to mask its unjust actions toward the Iranian nation. This has involved an unrelenting and unscrupulous propaganda campaign against the university students and Iran as a whole, in an effort to convince the American people that the "official" version of events is the only and true version. Unfortunately, they have been successful in doing so.

The time has now come for information and firm analysis to be presented to world public opinion and to Americans themselves, to enable them to make a fair and informed judgment of the embassy takeover of 1979, an event which had such a profound impact on regional political development in the Near East, as well as upon the two countries directly involved.

Then, even if with full knowledge of all the facts heretofore hidden, the action of the Iranian students is still condemned by the American people, their view, whether or not it is acceptable to unbiased observers, must be respected.

Do the American people realize that today, the leaders of the reform movement in Iran are the same individuals who captured the former United States Embassy? Have they considered that the supporters of this reform movement see it as the continuation of the revolution that toppled the imperial regime in 1979? Should the implications of this fact not lead to a change in the way these university students have been judged from 1979 through to the present?

The Islamic Revolution of Iran began as a reform movement against a non-democratic imperial regime. It became a movement against a government that strongly suppressed any freedom-seeking voice and did not refrain from liberal use of instruments such as exile, imprisonment, torture and execution in the suppression of legitimate dissent.

During all the years that the shah established and enforced his power through the torture and massacre of Iranians, whether young people, academics, clerics and all other strata of the society, the Iranian people looked on as the American government supported and protected him. Eventually, through exceptional sacrifices and the loss of thousands of martyrs, the Iranian people finally managed to force the shah to abdicate and renounce his dictatorial rule. Yet Iranians soon saw that the United States did not hesitate to continue to support the shah and offer him asylum after he had been driven from Iran.

The Iranian people's bitter memories of the actions of the American government against the interests of their country go much farther back than the period of the Islamic movement. In 1953, our nation was both witness to and victim of the first successful Central Intelligence Agency coup d'état against a sovereign state. That event deposed the popularly elected national and democratic Iranian government of Dr. Mohammad Mossadegh and paved the way for the return of the shah, who had escaped abroad in fear of public anger. So it was that direct American intervention led to the re-imposition of dictatorial rule in Iran for nearly twenty-seven years.

This brief account is sorely inadequate to describe the collective memory of Iranians of the unjust actions of the United States government against them. The bitter legacy and detrimental effects of that 1953 coup are felt to this day in the heart and soul of the Iranian people.

Against the background of American government machinations in Iran, can the action of a group of Iranian students be described as genuinely despicable? They took a limited number of Americans captive for a limited period of time and finally returned them safely to their country and families. Compare that deed to all that the American government has done against the country and people of Iran during the past several decades.

The difficulty that any just arbitration of this incident encounters today is that the university students are still faced with a government that does not remotely practice what it preaches. The actions of the American government are, in fact, entirely contrary to what it claims. This, after all, is a government that prides itself as a supporter of human rights, and as a defender of such rights everywhere. The American government claims to be a supporter of democracy, and is trying to induce any government acting against democratic principles to adhere to these principles. But in practice, does it itself adhere to such principles?

There can be little doubt that the actions of the American government toward Iran during the two eras (the reign of Mohammad-Reza Pahlavi and the Islamic Republic) have produced bitter fruit. It should come as no surprise that the conclusions drawn by the Iranian people concerning the behavior of the American government toward their country and government are sharply at variance with what Washington would like. Iranians believe that they are much closer to human rights and democracy today than they were during the reign of Mohammad-Reza Pahlavi, when the shah clearly enjoyed the complete support of the American government. The Islamic Republic, from its victory and overthrow of the shah to the present day, has been subjected to the continuous animosity, disaffection and injustice of the American government.

If the American people, and public opinion in the West, had access to the information extant amidst the documents of the U.S. State Department and CIA in connection with the actions of that government toward Iran, without doubt their judgment of the hostage crisis would change drastically. Although Americans would surely never come to terms with the capture of their countrymen by the university students, they would nevertheless judge the students' action in a more fair and more equitable manner.

The book you are about to read is a factual report of those events from the moment of entry of the university students into the former United States Embassy in Tehran to the conclusion of the hostage crisis. In it, Ms. Massoumeh Ebtekar, who was present from beginning to end, strives to inform people around the world, and in particular in the

United States and Canada, of all that was said and done during those 444 days, with sincerity and accuracy.

Although her endeavor is a modest one in comparison with the deluge of negative propaganda throughout the world against the Iranian university students and Islamic Iran in general, it is a remarkably substantive account of a hitherto untold story; a story that is still unfolding in ways no one can foresee. Hopefully, this small volume will serve to broaden already open minds (and perhaps even open the eyes of a new generation) of Americans, Westerners, and whoever else might read it, as to what actually took place here twenty-one years ago.

The present work may well help pave the way for dialogue between the two countries. It may well be that the two present antagonists will gain access to new facts that will grant them greater understanding of the realities of yesterday and today. The high wall of mistrust between them could fall.

No one can overlook the pivotal position of Iran in this, the most sensitive region of the world, just as no one can ignore the role of the United States in global affairs. If the two sides can embark upon a genuine joint effort to create a future of peace and sincerity, they can play a remarkable role in the family of nations. May it be so.

Seyyed Mohammad Mousavi Khoeiniha
Tehran, August, 2000

INTRODUCTION

MORE THAN 20 YEARS HAVE PASSED since Iranian students captured the United States Embassy in Tehran on November 4, 1979. At last the time has come to tell the inside story, to relate what really happened during those tumultuous days.

More than a decade was to pass before I could come to grips with the full impact of what we had done. As I looked back, it became clear that time was needed to size up the events that I had experienced first hand, and to put them in perspective. Then too, the political situation in Iran gave me cause for hesitation. It was impossible to forget that our country, for the first eight years of its newly liberated existence, had been locked in deadly combat with the Iraqi forces that invaded shortly after the triumph of the Islamic Revolution. When that war came to an inconclusive end, and Iran embarked on an ambitious reconstruction program, other priorities called.

On a purely personal level, I had married, given birth to two children, begun an academic career, and become the publisher of a journal dealing with women's studies from an Islamic perspective. The capture of the embassy was behind us. True, it had become a cause for public and political commemoration in Iran, and a source of continuing bitterness between our country and the United States. But it belonged to the past, or so I felt. My own life was busy, challenging, full of the problems any working mother faces, and complicated by the constraints of a traditional society such as ours intent on making its own way in the modern world.

As a professional woman, I had experienced a degree of success. But for all the sense of accomplishment, I still had a feeling of dissatisfaction. It was unfocused at first, vague. In my few idle moments, the voices and the faces I had come to know during those 444 days would suddenly surge up into my consciousness, as vivid and alive as they had been so many years before. Perhaps, too, my recollection of these faces and voices was a response to the reawakening, in our own society, to the call for democratization, and to the need for constructive dialogue about the past; and of a realization that, as Iran had changed, the slogans that carried us forward as revolutionary students in 1980 might no longer hold all the answers to the problems of today.

As you, the reader, might expect, telling the tale as we, the students, experienced it has been a story in its own right.

The process that eventually led to this book began in 1992, well before I became involved in any serious political activity. My account, as I imagined it then, would be that of an ordinary Iranian citizen who had been catapulted, as a student, into the midst of extraordinary events. Whatever story I told, I believed, would be not only an account of those events as I experienced them, but an effort to understand them, to put them in the wider context of a country caught up in revolutionary upheaval.

For the sake of those of the students who had gone on to give their lives in the war against Iraq, and for my own sake, I also wanted to give a clear and accurate account of our hopes, our feelings, and of the reasons why we acted as we did—of the beliefs that gave us our courage and sustained us in those tension-filled and difficult days when the hopes and fears of millions of ordinary Iranians were focused on us with such intensity that we often felt we were the very embodiment of those hopes and fears. From this, I hoped, would emerge not only a day-by-day account of a crisis that was to shape the relationship between Iran and the United States, but a portrait of a generation that came to maturity in a time of turmoil, and has gone on to assume the highest civic and political responsibilities, and to face great personal dangers.

Unforeseen pitfalls awaited me. On the one hand, I would try to convey the political and spiritual intensity that made it possible for us to carry through with our audacious plan. On the other hand, I would be writing from a different present, looking back on the thoughts and acts of a student from—I hoped—the vantage point of maturity.

It proved to be a difficult balancing act. I would have to turn a critical yet compassionate eye upon an upheaval that brought down a government, consolidated the revolution, reshaped our country, and set it on course for what it has become today. At the same time, I would have to be lucid enough to put the decisions we made, the words we uttered and the things we did in a wider perspective.

Finally, I decided to take the plunge. When I did, it was as though a burden had been lifted from my shoulders. Fortunately I was not alone. My husband's input was of crucial importance. The opening chapters of the book, relating the prelude to the event and its first days, in which I did not participate directly, are based on his eyewitness account.

Since then, with the support of my family, I have taken on other tasks, the latest one being that of head of Iran's fledgling Department of the Environment. But my commitment to tell the story as I saw and experienced it remains unshaken. My only capital in this endeavor is honesty. And the conviction that my story—our story—has a right to be heard.

In telling this tale, I had another motivation, as strong as the first.

As, over the years, I read the published accounts of the embassy takeover, I had come to feel a growing sense of frustration—and of responsibility. Each of these accounts seemed to be either a distortion or worse, a falsification of the events that I, as a participant, had witnessed close up. At best, they were fragmentary and inconclusive. Some, the memoirs of the hostages themselves, were sincere but their scope—I will be the first to admit—was limited by the circumstances into which our action had thrust them. Those written by journalists and political analysts were another matter altogether. Through them a stereotyped version had emerged in the West, a version seen from an entirely Western viewpoint, presenting what we did as the result of manipulation by political forces in Iran, and depicting us as extremists, fanatics, or as the stooges of dark and ominous powers. The information upon which this version was based was fragmentary, its sources ill-defined, and its bias apparent.

Though it was painful, it certainly came as no surprise to me that this, the officially received version, reflected—with only a few minor exceptions—not a single Iranian viewpoint, not a single Iranian voice. The Iranian participants had never had the opportunity to tell their own side of these events. They were never asked, their opinions never solicited. We found ourselves excluded from our own story, on the outside looking in.

For this we must bear some of the blame. Our silence has lasted too long. We may have created the impression that we had nothing to say. Or worse, that we acquiesced in the "official" version.

This book—which breaks that silence for the first time in print—is intended as a long-needed corrective to the stereotypical account of which I speak, and as an antidote to the distorted images conveyed by the world media not only during and immediately after the capture of the embassy, but right up to this day.

I have yet another incentive to write this memoir. I believe that the cultural gap between the peoples of the developing world and those of the developed world—what we now term the South and the North—has grown wider over the last twenty years. Inequalities, instead of being ameliorated by globalization, are on the increase. Differences in cultural heritage may well account for a part of this deepening chasm, but surely one of its primary sources must be the inaccurate or even biased reporting by Western media of events that have captured the imagination of millions in the developing countries.

Can the misconceptions and misjudgments which have been created by years of conscious disinformation ever be put right, I wondered, as I began the task of sifting through my notes, diaries and memories? Can the American and Iranian peoples ever hope to overcome the barriers of propaganda and fiery rhetoric that now stand between them, and finally come to understand one another? The only way—and this is the ultimate aim of my account of the fateful events of 1979 and 1980 in Tehran—to alleviate tensions between the two nations, is to engage the two diverse and different cultures in a constructive dialogue.

This book is a contribution to the dialogue that must take place, sooner or later.

It is based on my written diary and recollections of the seizure of the American Embassy in Tehran as I experienced it. Even though more than two decades have passed, the memory of those days persists so vividly in my mind that it all seems to have happened only yesterday. The persons and events mentioned here are, of course, all real, although several of us did not use our real names. (Such instances are noted in the text.) When we concealed our identities, we did so not out of fear, but out of our desire to be known as the "youth of the people." We were convinced that our collective spirit and our intentions were much more important than our individual personalities. Such was the temper of the times.

When I was first asked my name, I replied that it was "Mary" or "Maryam," a religious name common to both cultures. In practical terms, it was also easier for non-Iranians to pronounce than my Iranian name. In the event, as "Mary" I became the person who had to bridge the language gap in circumstances fraught with misunderstanding. Little did I dream then that one day, in writing my version of those eventful days, I would once again be throwing myself into a chasm where the same misunderstandings still flourish.

Though we acted in a collective spirit, the opinions expressed in these pages are mine and, in the account of the actual capture of the embassy, those of my husband. They do not represent the feelings, attitudes, or political concerns of any particular group or faction, nor do they necessarily correspond with those held by our group, the Muslim Students Following the Line of the Imam (Imam was the title given to Ayatollah Khomeini during the Islamic Revolution; it signified the esteem and veneration in which millions of Iranians held him.) This version is a personal and interpretive one and makes no pretense of being anything more. It is not a journalistic nor an exhaustive historical account, nor does it paint a complete, all-encompassing picture. Such, eventually, will be the task of scholars: to gather the information at their disposal, and then transform it into history. This book reflects the feelings, the raw emotions and the ideas that we students held and acted on during those days. It should be read and understood in that context, as one of the voices that shape our common story. It speaks in the tones and vocabulary of those heady days and reflects the depth of our convictions. It is not a catalogue of rights and wrongs. Nor is it an apology for what we did.

We, the students who planned and carried out the seizure and occupation of the American Embassy, never anticipated that it would last more than a few hours, a few days at most. Never did we imagine that our act of protest would have such a far-reaching impact on the political history of our country, and of the region.

The event became part of a broader call, shared by many outside of Iran, for a redefinition of international law and of the human rights instruments that had ultimately legitimized the oppression and colonialization of countries like Iran for decades, and that had come to serve only the superpowers when their interests were threatened.

If this sounds like an extreme statement, consider that the embassy occupation clearly influenced the decision of the United States and its allies to back Iraqi dictator Saddam Hussein's invasion of the infant Islamic Republic of Iran. That support was to continue almost without interruption until Iraq invaded Kuwait on August 2, 1990. Even today, as it bombs Baghdad, Washington tolerates the Saddam regime it once reviled as being "worse than Hitler."

Perhaps it still considers Iraq a bulwark against the tide of moral, cultural and political renewal sweeping the Islamic world? Stranger things have happened.

To this day, those of us who carried out the occupation recognize that without the direct support of Imam Khomeini and the encouragement of the huge majority of Iranians we could never have persevered. And yet, questions persist. Fundamental questions to which there are no simple answers.

When we took over the embassy, we were so convinced of the justice of our cause that nothing could stand in our way. Just as millions of unarmed people in the streets had finally driven Mohammad-Reza

Pahlavi, the late shah, from his throne, a handful of students had burst into the inner sanctum of a superpower and humbled it.

When the man whose long rule had brought riches beyond all description to his immediate family and associates, and impoverishment and cultural subjugation to the Iranian people, was welcomed in the United States, we believed that the West was once more determined to subvert our newly won independence. Were the fate and future of our country once again going to be decided in Washington, D.C., which had first brought him to power in its 1953 coup? How could we voice our concern, our indignation? To whom could we protest? From the media establishment and from international bodies, the response was a deafening silence. Iranians, whose immense sacrifices had finally brought down a corrupt dynasty, were once again being ignored.

It was at that crucial moment that our small group of Islamic university students decided to take matters into our own hands. Our revolution had given us a powerful voice. We were determined to make that voice heard, by extreme means if necessary. If that was to be the price of dialogue, we reasoned, so be it.

Few would disagree that the course of action we chose was as drastic as it was dramatic. So were the first weeks, months and years of the Islamic Republic. Today, as our country has entered into a new era of democratic development and as we face a new challenge, to build a society more responsive to the needs of its citizens, circumstances have changed. But the need for dialogue has not.

This book, a first-hand look at a passionate past, is above all a contribution to the exchange among equals that must eventually take place. If we are to judge by today's international climate, the job will not be easy. The gap of misunderstanding and incomprehension that the embassy takeover revealed is still with us today, as wide as ever. Only by speaking frankly and openly about the past can we hope to narrow that gap.

Tehran, Islamic Republic of Iran

Storming the gates. November 4, 1979.

CHAPTER I

IN THE BEGINNING

I CAN NEVER FORGET the date: November 7, 1979. Three days before, several hundred university students had captured the American Embassy in Tehran and taken its staff hostage. I was sitting with a group of my friends—all of us women students—on the Tehran Polytechnic Institute campus. Like just about every other student in Iran, we were caught up in a passionate debate about the takeover, trying to imagine every possible outcome, to predict all probable consequences. Except that for us, it was more than idle speculation. People we knew, including several of our closest friends and fellow students, were directly involved. They had broken through the main gate and disarmed the Marine guards. Now, they were refusing to leave. What had begun as a daring student protest was rapidly mushrooming into an international incident.

* * *

Normally, I would have been in my second year, but in Iran nothing was normal in the aftermath of the revolution that had toppled the shah's regime. I had barely registered as a freshman in chemical engineering the year before when protests and riots broke out throughout the capital, and the country. Classes had to be canceled outright. With the appointment of a Provisional Government by Imam Khomeini, who had returned to Iran from Paris in February, the schools had opened again, but the political atmosphere was so tense and the excitement so high that course content was the last thing on students' minds.

A group that called itself the Islamic Students Association had grown rapidly following the fall and flight of the shah. Others had set up another organization, a committee to support workers. The committee quickly developed into a forum for debating cultural and political issues. I had joined both of them more than willingly—enthusiastically in fact.

Now, as we sat absorbed in our discussion, the embassy takeover and the political upheaval it had touched off eclipsed everything else.

It was at that moment that one of the brothers, as we called the male students from the Islamic Association, hurried up to us, out of breath, and took me aside. He was carrying a message from the students who had occupied the "Den of Spies," as the occupiers had already dubbed the embassy. Would I join them? he blurted out. They would be needing help in interpreting and with public relations.

Just what my "public relations" qualifications might be was a mystery to me, I responded. After all, I was a second-year chemical engineering major.

They might be staying a bit longer than originally planned, he explained. Someone with my command of English would be an asset. What tipped the balance in my favor was my ability to interpret from Farsi to English, a difficult job for someone without a strong command of both languages. I had no professional interpreting experience, of course. But I'd been using both languages for so long that it had almost become second nature. As far as the students were concerned, I was the right person. I was in no mood to argue.

While I was certainly not the only one of the students who could speak English, I had lived for several years outside of Iran, and had attended an international school in Tehran. In 1963, three years after I was born, my father, like many of Iran's most promising university students, had been awarded a scholarship to continue his studies in the United States. Our family first settled in Massachusetts, then relocated to Philadelphia, where my father was to earn his Ph.D. in mechanical engineering from the University of Pennsylvania. During those years I attended nursery school and elementary school, where I learned to speak fluent colloquial English with the American accent I've kept until this day.

When we returned to Iran, although I could still speak fluent Farsi, my verbal skills in English were much better developed. So I enrolled in Iran Zamin Academy, a private school run by Americans who recruited teachers from the city's large international community. Some were European, some Asian, others were from North or South America. Tehran was a much more cosmopolitan city then, and in every class there were students of different nationalities and cultures. For a youngster, it was a marvelous opportunity to get to know people from a wide diversity of backgrounds. Later I understood how instrumental my school years had been in giving me the tools to deal with cultures unlike our own, to understand them and to establish communication and dialogue with them.

Not surprisingly, most of the students in my high school were very much oriented toward Western ideas and values. I remember discussing with a few of them how our generation was being channeled to think in a certain way, to think about certain things and not about others. Ultimately, this profited the people who were trying to promote their own interests by fostering consumerist attitudes in our young generation. As far as many of them were concerned, we young people were not supposed to think about politics, about our future, about our dignity, about a better world. I remember talking about this very subject with two of my friends. One of them had a German mother, the other an Austrian mother—both were bicultural, bilingual kids. They nodded their heads, as if to say, "this is how it is, but what can we do?" We felt that all around us a plan was being put into effect; it was leading us not in the direction of our own interest and benefit, but in the interest of the global power politics that run the world. We could recognize this situation as a form of tyranny. What we lacked were ideas about how to resist it.

Our experience was, I was soon to learn, central to the shah's policy of westernizing Iran, of stripping the country of its religious and cultural heritage. But in the end, the opposite occurred, and many if not most of the younger generation became dedicated opponents of the imperial regime.

Like most Iranians perhaps, we felt that we could tolerate almost anything. But the humiliation we increasingly felt at the hands of the shah and of the Americans became more than we could bear. If you are a practicing Muslim, you believe in the religion as taught by the Prophet, the authentic spirit of Islam: that no human being can submit to anyone other than God. Any submission—in the sense of being subjected to the will or the power of any other human being—is degrading to human dignity, and for that reason is not permitted nor acceptable in Islam. That was one of the spiritual convictions that turned people against the shah and his regime.

I thought back to a day in November the year before, to my mechanical drawing class at Poly. Suddenly, from outside the building had come the sound of students chanting, "Long live Khomeini." It was the first time I had heard the name spoken in public. Up until then, the imperial regime's well-trained riot police had managed to keep all protesters at bay. But not on that day. Suddenly, a shower of stones came crashing through the classroom windows.

Now, as the brother spoke to me and as I thought back to the past, I realized that my own moment of decision had come. I knew and admired this particular group of students, and like everyone else, I could see the extent of popular support for their audacious initiative which had won the unconditional support of Imam Khomeini. "Now is the time to make your service for Islam," said the brother. "There's not a moment to lose." Even at nineteen, I was rarely at a loss for words. But the brother's tone of voice, even more than what he said, transfixed me. I looked at him and nodded.

"Go to the main gate tomorrow morning," he continued, speaking in a low voice, "and ask for Reza" [not his real name], one of my classmates from the Polytechnic Institute.

* * *

When I recall the events of twenty-one years ago, I can appreciate how difficult it must be for non-Iranians to understand not only our motivation, but the particular form our political action took.

In those days of turmoil, uncertainty and crisis, we felt that the fate of our country was on the line, and that we had a role to play in deciding that fate. Talking, thinking and acting politically had become a reflex action, as natural to us as breathing. The fever and the fervor of the revolution had permeated all aspects of the Iranian mentality. They were at their strongest among the young. Perhaps the main component of that fervor was a dedication to the religious beliefs that the shah's regime had tried to strip away from us. Then, too, there was a powerful sense that our national honor had been offended, our culture dismissed and devalued. For nearly a century, after 2,500 years of despotism, our country had been struggling toward a constitutional system of government, one that would be responsive to the needs of the people and not to the whims of a dynasty manipulated by foreign powers.

Politics, in the broadest sense, had long been the main subject of discussion at the family dinner table. Both my parents were familiar with the ideological and philosophical debates that dominated Iranian society. We discussed the relative merits of Marxism, of socialism, of liberal democracy, of imperialism and colonialism, and their impact on our country.

In my final year in high school, I had written a term paper on existentialism, in which I compared the thought of writers like Jean-Paul Sartre and Albert Camus. I concluded that what was going on in the more developed societies of the West, where you erect a glass barrier between yourself and what goes on in the world, does not point the way to a solution to the spiritual dilemma of life. Existentialism had identified the darkness of the world, the sense of nausea. But, I asked, could liberalism, could democracy, could justice itself bring about all that human beings long for?

Both of my parents were academics: open minded people who had no respect for the shah's regime, though, like most Iranians, they had good cause to fear it. Father was an assistant professor in the engineering faculty; Mother held a B.A. in literature, and was involved in volunteer work in the community. As a religious intellectual who had been active in politics during the post-Mossadegh era, my father had often been arrested, though never imprisoned for long periods.

The night I informed my parents of my decision to join the embassy occupiers, no one, including me, imagined how it would influence my future, and shape my marital life. Such involvement would come much later, after the occupation, when I married Mohammad, a student four years older than me whom I had not known when I first joined the group occupying the embassy. Although we met during the long occupation, it had never occurred to either of us at the time that we might marry. Life, in those days, was hard enough to predict from one day to the next.

The young men and women who participated in the embassy takeover did so based on their conviction that their action was in line with the Imam's policy. We believed then that action was essential; we were determined to take a stand against past and possible future humiliation by the United States. Romantic attraction was not, at that moment, a reason for getting involved in political activity. All of everyone's time, attention and thoughts were focused on the task at hand, to make the most of it for Islam, and for the revolution.

Of course, no one could pretend that we students did not feel all the natural urges of youth. But as the shah's policy had been to take away our faith, so too it had tried to undermine our traditional sense of morality by promoting a Western-oriented lifestyle as "modern" and "natural." The more actively that policy was applied, the more stubbornly we rejected it. We wanted not to destroy but to protect our traditions, both cultural and religious. Prominent among those traditions was respect for the family, and for the institution of marriage. We could hardly criticize "America" while practicing its values, which we knew were hostile to our culture. As the revolution crested we, the Islamic students, were moving full speed in the opposite direction to an American way of life.

These views were a reflection of the ideological currents that were sweeping through the society around us. The influence of religious figures like Dr. Ali Shariati, Ayatollah Mottahari and finally Imam Khomeini himself grew gradually stronger and stronger, reaching out to touch people from non-traditional and even from non-religious backgrounds. Dr. Shariati, a deeply religious man who had studied sociology in the West, was a beacon for us. In his lectures and essays, he led thousands of Iranian intellectuals who had become secularized back to Islam, and persuaded them to accept the leadership of Imam Khomeini with courage and devotion.[8]

As a high-school student I had attended his public lectures at the Hosseiniyeh Ershad, a religious institution in northern Tehran. It was impossible for me, as a young person, to understand everything he said, but I could feel that a change in direction was coming. Islam, he taught, could be a viable alternative to the ideologies of fatality and despair that emanated from the West.

I was certainly not alone. Many young people found in Dr. Shariati's message a new meaning and direction in life. I met him shortly before he left for London, where he was to die under suspicious circumstances. We spoke about my views, and he encouraged me to do further reading. That meeting was one of the decisive moments in my life.

Having brought up the matter with my family, considering the risks and dangers involved it was natural that my parents, particularly my mother, would have very real concerns. I could not ignore them, and I did my best to reassure her. Of course, I felt misgivings. 'Where were we heading?' I asked myself. 'Who can predict what may happen?'

But I felt no fear. Something inside me told me I had to go. I felt certain that my parents would understand. They could sense the change; in a way, they had been a part of it. The revolution had come. People had lost their fear. When I left the house early the next morning, it was with their blessing.

An hour later, there I stood, heart beating in anticipation, in front of the main gate of the American Embassy. Around me was a huge crowd that had turned out to support the occupation, straining against the gate and shouting slogans. I was dressed in the long brown coat we call a manteau, and a head-scarf that women in the Islamic revolutionary movement had adopted as their uniform. I asked one of the students standing guard for "Reza." He quickly arrived and gave permission for me to enter. A student opened the black iron gate just wide enough for me to slip through. As the gate clanged shut behind me I took a quick glance around the compound. Everything seemed calm and under control. Students were everywhere; the Americans were nowhere to be seen. "Reza" led me to a large building to the right of the main entrance. This building, I soon learned, was called the Chancellery. We entered and went up to the second floor where I met several classmates—they would be my sisters and brothers from now on—from the Polytechnic Institute. They were all busy at various chores, none of which I could identify. The rooms themselves were in a state of disarray. That was hardly surprising considering the events of the previous three days.

It wasn't long before some of the sisters recognized me. We located a couple of chairs and sat down in one of the rooms for a cram course in the strategy and logistics of embassy capture and occupation. A few hours later my head was swimming with details, right down to the latest developments. "Could I help out in the documents section as well as the public relations unit?" they asked. Dazed and just about overwhelmed, I nodded agreement. At that stage I could never have imagined what kind of responsibility I was shouldering. I could never have imagined how that nod would change my life.

Or how the takeover and occupation would change the life of my country.

* * *

Three days earlier, as Mohammad rushed toward the main gate of the United States Embassy on Taleghani Avenue, chants of "Allah-o Akbar" and "Death to America" filled the air. In a flash, hundreds of students massed in front of the entrance. A few had already scaled the walls of the compound, while others at the main entrance were struggling to cut through the chains that secured the gate. No one, either inside or on the street, had realized what was happening. Everyone, including the Americans, probably assumed it was just another routine demonstration. Demonstrations were commonplace. Tehran in late 1979 was caught up in the ferment and fervor of the Islamic Revolution. The streets belonged to the citizens whose mass uprising had driven the hated shah from power.

Suddenly, the wrought iron gates swung open and the students surged in, chanting at the top of their lungs. Mohammad remembered thinking: at last, the will of our downtrodden nation has emerged into the bright light of day.

* * *

On the morning of November 2, 1979, he had snapped awake, still bleary-eyed from a night of studying. Mid-term exams were only a few weeks away and he was putting in extra hours in an effort to catch up. A glance at the alarm clock told him he had forgotten to set it. The thermodynamics lecture would be starting in less than an hour. He leaped out of bed, washed and dressed, pulling on a sweater as he glanced out the window. The weather had turned chilly, and clouds hung low over the city, hiding the snow-clad mountains to the north. He grabbed his green fatigue jacket and slung it over his shoulders.

As he hurried out of the dorm the concierge waved him over and handed him a note. Someone—it looked like another student, he said— had left it for him earlier that morning. Mohammad stuffed the scrap of paper in his hip pocket and dashed down the stairs. The Polytechnic Institute was only a few minutes away, south on Hafez Avenue in the center of the city, but he had to walk at top speed to make the beginning of the lecture.

Officially, Mohammad was a third year student but because the previous year's classes had been canceled due to the revolution everyone was at least one term behind. Since his family lived in Isfahan, he had moved into the dormitory. The atmosphere made studying easier—the library was nearby, and the students could compare notes day and night. But he had gravitated to the dorm for another reason: it was like an incubator for revolution. Back then, it didn't take much persuasion for young people to get involved in one kind of activity or another. Several of his fellow students had been involved in street fighting in the days before the fall of the shah. In fact, avoiding political involvement in the dorms was an impossibility.

In the years leading up to the overthrow of the shah's regime, Iran's universities had been transformed into hotbeds of revolutionary debate.

All the conflicts that had torn Iranian society apart found an echo on campus: in the class-rooms, laboratories and dormitories.

For a few, political activism was an excellent way to avoid classes, if not to cancel them outright. But for us, at the time, the question was simple: what is more important, academic achievement or the future of the revolution. We had come to see our lectures, study and research as part of the realm of the self. To refuse to serve the nation and the revolution on the pretext that we would miss our classes would be, we believed, an act of selfishness. Today, no one would deny that our dedication to the cause drew much of its strength from the enormous attraction of involvement in revolutionary politics.

It wasn't until he slid into his seat on the wooden bench of the lecture hall that he remembered the note in his pocket. He glanced at it. Written in a nervous script, it seemed to jump off the page. "Contact Mohsen immediately. Urgent." Big deal, he thought. These days, everything was urgent; Mohsen could wait. The class would be over by eleven in any case; plenty of time to get in touch. Just then the lecturer came into the room, and he was quickly caught up in the complexities of thermodynamics. He forgot all about Mohsen and his note.

The subject was tough, tougher than he had anticipated. Better check some reference books in the library, he said to himself as the lecture came to a close. Just then, out of the corner of his eye, he spotted Mohsen in the crowd milling in the corridor. He was a fourth-year honors student in civil engineering, short, dark-haired and energetic, with the short-clipped beard that many students wore to demonstrate their religious convictions. Today as he hurried toward Mohammad, he seemed even more intense—and tense—than usual.

"I told you it was urgent," he said, with a critical edge to his voice.

"Well," Mohammad replied, "I had an important lecture. Couldn't afford to miss it. Besides, I was planning to meet you afterwards."

"Going to class is only one of our responsibilities," he blurted out.

Mohsen never settled for anything less than top marks for himself. Why was he suddenly telling me classes weren't important? God knows there was no lack of distraction during those revolutionary days, Mohammad thought.

"Look," Mohsen went on, his words crackling, "we can't just sit around with our noses in our books and forget what's going on in the world."

Mohammad was about to reply, when something in his friend's voice stopped him in his tracks. He was twenty-three at the time, but already his background had given him a strong sense of commitment.

Back in pre-revolutionary days, most of our reading had been from books that were banned by the shah's regime, particularly those written by Dr. Shariati. A book would be delivered at night, and you had just 48 hours to read 200 pages. Reading a book in such a short span of time gave us the feeling that if we did not learn and digest it, we would lose the opportunity forever to read that book again. It was now or never. If you were caught, the penalty was arrest, not to mention torture or imprisonment. Carrying a book was an act of insurrection, and we knew it.

Mohammad still remembered his first book by Dr. Shariati. It was so tattered and worn that it looked more like a pamphlet. The subject was Hajj, the pilgrimage to Mecca all Muslims are required to make at least once in their lifetime. Shariati preached that behind religious rituals such as the pilgrimage lies a philosophy that has ideological, social and political implications.

The dominant feeling awakening in all of us was the need to decide on our future. This was what Shariati taught us to do. Why are we living, what are we to live for? He got that idea across, powerfully. We became certain that we had to make our decision, then and there; it wasn't something to be left until later. That was our general outlook. We were engaged in a search for the proper way of life; we had to find it and to go after it.

Mohammad knew deep down that Mohsen was right. We couldn't cut ourselves off from the political and social upheavals going on around us, right in front of our eyes. When the revolution broke out, our own concerns seemed petty in comparison with the problems of Iranian society. Still, he had no inkling of what was about to happen.

There was something else about Mohsen: once he got started he was hard to stop. "The U.S. has decided to admit the shah," he said, his voice suddenly falling to a whisper as he looked around. "Look, do we need any more proof about what they think of the Iranian nation. There may even be another plot under way against us."

Mohammad could have been shocked, but he wasn't. The news was no surprise. When the shah had fled Iran earlier that year, most Iranians expected he would attempt a comeback, with help from Washington.[9] "A special meeting has been organized for that afternoon," Mohsen went on. So, that was the urgent part. "Top secret. Think about what could be done. We have some ideas. Be there, but keep it strictly to yourself." Now Mohammad felt a tug of curiosity, mixed with a growing excitement.

The shah had been the symbol of the corrupt dictatorship that had ruled over the country, destroying its culture and undermining its independence. The Iranian people were in chains to the oppressive policies of a regime which enjoyed the unwavering support of the American government. "The regime would not drink water without the permission of the Americans," were the words people used to describe the situation.

The Americans had armed forces, cultural centers and unrivaled political influence in Iran. Their cultural, economic and military attachés had a say—often a determining say—in everything. Iranians felt themselves subjected to humiliating political, economic and social pressures. The government of Iran was committed to safeguarding foreign interests while its people were subjected to kidnapping, torture and even death for speaking about freedom. What few instruments of democracy had existed in our country had been subverted and demolished. The autocratic monarch left no room for the views of the public. SAVAK, the shah's notorious secret police had been organized and trained by the CIA and Israel's Mossad[10] to create an atmosphere of terror and oppression. Directly or indirectly, almost every family in Iran had suffered at the hands of the regime. The revolution had not been a carefully scripted seizure of power; it had been an outburst of anger and frustration.

The meeting was to take place in a classroom in a newly-built wing of the Institute. Very few classes were held there and the smell of fresh paint filled the air. When Mohammad arrived, less than a dozen students were gathered in small groups, talking intently. All of them were people he knew. He went over. As he listened in on their conversation, it didn't take him long to understand that some highly confidential discussions had been held prior to today's meeting. From what he could piece together, a group of eight students, two from each of the four major universities in Tehran, had talked the situation over and concluded that they had to take action. This was the same group that had called today's meeting. Action was on the agenda. But what could it be? What could a handful of university students hope to achieve against the United States, which had just extended its protection to the deposed shah?

All over the country, instability and insecurity were rampant, and much of it—we were convinced—was the work of outside forces. Who could forget the political and religious leaders who had been assassinated since the victory of the revolution less than a year before?[11] Dozens of new political parties had sprung up. Some were determined to test the freedom of expression created by the revolution. Others seemed to be attempting to stir up disunity and distrust. We did not doubt for an instant that the uprisings that were breaking out in the border regions among Iran's various nationalities were fomented or even directly supported by foreign powers.[12] Threats to the revolution seemed to be growing more acute every day.

When Imam Khomeini had returned to Iran in February, 1979, he had appointed a provisional government headed by Mehdi Bazargan, a prominent religious intellectual and leader of the Iran Freedom Movement, the country's foremost secular party. But Bazargan's cabinet, made up primarily of veteran politicians of the Mossadegh era, seemed helpless, paralyzed, unable to act, as though reluctant to stand up to the United States.

Mohammad's musings came to a halt as Mohsen walked briskly into the room. Today, he moved with all the latent energy of a coiled spring. "In the name of God," he said, opening the session with the Islamic salutation that had quickly become second nature for all of us. "By allowing the shah to enter the U.S. the Americans have started a new conspiracy against the revolution. If we don't act rapidly, if we show weakness, then a superpower like the U.S. will be able to meddle in the internal affairs of any nation in the world. We are responsible," he continued, "not only to our country, but to all who love freedom, who honor human dignity and who cannot tolerate the subjugation of any human being to any person or power other than God."

This was not the first time Iran had lived through harrowing times. In August, 1953, a coup d'état engineered by the CIA that overthrew the democratically elected government of Dr. Mossadegh and restored the shah to power had dashed all hopes of establishing an independent democratic system. The price of genuine independence was heavy. A strong sense of devotion and love for the values of the revolution, and for Iran as the homeland of a free people, filled our minds and hearts. Our reading of our own history told us that we had to act quickly. The stubborn and bullying attitude of the American government as it confronted the Islamic Revolution made it clear that we had few alternatives left to consider.

Action was our only choice.

Mohsen had a remarkable capacity for articulating and expressing ideas and feelings, and he could attract and hold the attention of an audience. He came from the provinces, from a middle-class background, and he was as sincere as he was convincing. As he spoke, his listeners could feel a flame welling up in their hearts. "Slavery may have been abolished in the last century, but in reality it has only taken on a new face. People, societies or nations who fear the superpowers, who submit themselves and their resources to them, and who live and think according to the dictates of these powers are not much better than their slaves." Certainly, no one in the room had any problem with the concept. Anyone who had experienced what Iran had been through—and that certainly included us—would have no problem understanding what he was talking about. "We've been under the thumb of the U.S. for more than fifty years. Now, it's our chance to do something about it," he said, then paused. Absolute silence fell over the room.

In the back of everybody's mind hung the suspicion that, with the admission of the shah to the United States, the countdown for another coup d'état had begun. Such was to be our fate once again, we were convinced, and it was to be irreversible. We now had to reverse the irreversible. Whatever action we took would have to break through the thick wall the media had already thrown up around the fledgling revolution in Iran.

We had several alternatives, Mohsen went on, but surely the most appropriate path would be to demonstrate the anguish and despair felt by the people throughout the country—and their determination to resist. It would then become a matter of deciding whether the escalation of demonstrations in front of the embassy, a strike or sit-in right in the street in front of the main gate, or a hunger strike would best serve this objective. One thing was sure, whatever the action, it would have to have enough impact to get the attention of the American administration, and of the international community as a whole. It would have to be explosive.

Then Mohsen dropped the bombshell.

"What we are proposing is a peaceful occupation of the American Embassy—without arms. This will mean taking the embassy personnel hostage not as diplomatic personnel, but as agents of the American government. They are deeply involved in their government's conspiracies in any case. By intervening in our national affairs even now after the revolution, they have undermined international conventions."

The proposal took not just Mohammad's, but everyone's breath away. Mohsen paused again for a few seconds as if to measure the impact of his words, to give the idea time to sink in.

"If you agree with the basic plan of action, we can begin now discussing how to carry it out," he said, looking over the room.

After a long moment of stunned silence, Reza, Abbas, Habib, Rahman, Ali, Hossein, Mahmoud, Ibrahim and Mohammad all started to speak at once. The idea was as exciting as it was audacious, and the responses came fast and furious. They agreed that the people should show their strength. They should prove to the world that God is the ultimate power. They should show the world how deeply committed they were to independence and to their revolution.

Some of those in the room were uncertain where Imam Khomeini stood. After all, a Provisional Government and Revolutionary Council had already been established. "Who are we to take matters into our own hands?" they wondered aloud. Others responded that the country was still in turmoil, the revolution was not yet "institutionalized" and the basic institutions of government such as the Parliament had not yet been formed. But a takeover of the American Embassy would not be likely to offend the Imam, especially considering what was at stake. And the government was a provisional one, after all.

Most were convinced public opinion would be favorable. The first indications had come at a demonstration after Friday prayers the week before. Despite an attempt by the police to divert them from the American Embassy, a group of marchers had simply ignored the new route and made straight for the sprawling compound.

We later learned that another group of left-wing students had come up with a similar strategy, but canceled their plans when the Muslim students captured the embassy. There was a general consensus that something had to be done.

In the end, a strong majority agreed that occupation was the best solution. Though they were far from certain of success, they decided to press on. Finally, after a long and heated debate on what tactics to use, they drew up plans and assigned duties. There would be physical dangers involved and they knew it, but they were so caught up by their plan and so sure that their action was a righteous one that the riskiness of the enterprise never became an issue.

Our plan was to do the preparatory work in teams. One would enter the embassy as visa applicants, scout the grounds and prepare a preliminary map showing the location of the various buildings and units within the compound. The other would piece together a bird's eye diagram from atop the tall buildings overlooking the embassy on Taleghani Avenue and the other surrounding streets. Another, smaller group was to prepare food and supplies for a maximum of three days. At the time, no one ever dreamed the takeover would last longer. The idea was to make a gesture, a bold statement.

Pictures of Imam Khomeini and red headbands with "Allah-o Akbar" written on them were also to be prepared for about two hundred and fifty students. Literally translated, "Allah-o Akbar" means "God is the Greatest that can be conceived." It was the key slogan of the revolution. For us, and for millions of Iranians, it had come to mean the negation of all powers except that of God—particularly the power of the shah and of his American backers.

They all agreed that it was essential to inform Imam Khomeini of the plan, confidentially of course. For this task they nominated Mousavi Khoeiniha,[13] one of the *ulema* (religious scholars) closest to the Imam. Mr. Khoeiniha was the Imam's representative to National Radio and Television. Naturally, they would wait for an official reaction to the proposal before going ahead. The exact schedule for action would be decided at the next meeting, which was set for the following day.

Mohammad volunteered for the team which was to prepare the bird's eye plan of the embassy. As he walked out of the room, he remembered his promise to himself to spend the afternoon in the library, cracking the books. All of a sudden, the thermodynamics exam didn't seem as important as it had that morning. In fact, it already seemed far, far away.

That night Mohammad tossed and turned in his bed, trying to visualize what would happen, what the impact of the action would be. How could he have ever dreamed that a handful of students would capture the imagination of the entire Iranian nation—and set a super-power on its ear in the bargain.

Next morning, after his prayers, he automatically began preparing his notebooks for class when suddenly he remembered the events of the day before. He laughed to himself. As of today, classes were on hold, indefinitely. Instead, he had an appointment with some of his fellow students on Taleghani Avenue, a main Tehran east-west thoroughfare which, before the Islamic Revolution, had been called Takht-e Tavous, meaning "Peacock Throne."[14] They met an hour later, and quickly singled out four tall buildings that overlooked the embassy compound from four directions. For starters, they picked out one on the north side, a residential building. Two of the team distracted the concierge seated behind the desk in the lobby, while Mohammad and another student took the elevator up to the tenth floor. From there they had to climb two additional stories to reach the roof.

Breathing hard, they came out onto the roof and walked over to the parapet. At their feet lay the northern part of the compound. A building which we later learned was the consulate was visible at the western extremity. They could also see three other buildings, one of which was clearly residential, and the northern entrance gate. Although the tall, bushy pine trees that covered most of the compound prevented them from getting a clear view, working quickly they sketched out a map on a piece of note paper and hurried back down to join their friends.

The building they selected on Taleghani Avenue was a Tehran University dormitory. The concierge was adamant: whom did they want to see? Even though he didn't know anyone in this particular dormitory, Mohammad picked a name out of the air. Luckily for them, a student by that name just happened to be a resident, but, according to the concierge, he had gone out. "I want to leave a message in his room," Mohammad insisted. The concierge refused. It was urgent, Mohammad replied. Finally he agreed to let Mohammad slip the message under his "friend's" door.

He found his way up to the roof. Far below he saw the police guards posted at various locations around the outer perimeter of the compound. He also spotted a couple of men walking towards a large structure located near the southern entrance. That, he calculated, was the main embassy building. Later, we called it the central building. The Americans, we were soon to learn, called it the Chancellery. A couple of smaller buildings, storage rooms and a garage were visible on the left.

He completed his sketch, combined the northern and southern views, and rushed back downstairs. The others had gotten views from the western and eastern perspective. They hurried back to the Poly campus to complete the master drawing.

That afternoon, November 3, the planning committee met for the third time in a classroom at Polytechnic. By coincidence, it was also the eve of the first anniversary of the thirteenth of the Iranian month of Aban, when student demonstrators had been shot down in cold blood by the shah's police at Tehran University. Naturally, as their plans took shape, security became a greater concern. The planners posted one of their members outside the classroom door to keep watch. No one appeared.

Ibrahim had developed a detailed overview of the embassy grounds using the information from two of our friends who had succeeded in entering the consulate, as well as from Mohammad's bird's eye sketches. Now he drew an outline with chalk on the blackboard. Later, when they compared that preliminary sketch with what they learned about the inside of the compound and its numerous buildings, they realized just how crude and primitive it was. But considering their circumstances and their knowledge at the time, the map was as accurate as they could expect. Certainly it was good enough to get them started.

Ibrahim, who had a keen analytical mind, had marked down the exact location of the Iranian policemen posted outside the embassy, and noted the possible positions of U.S. Marine guards within the compound. Using this information, they discussed the various buildings and entry points and finally concluded that the students should split up into five groups, one for each of the five main buildings. Their initial entry, they decided, would take place through the main gate on Taleghani Avenue. They would do everything in their power to avoid confrontation with the Iranian police.

Now they faced yet another problem: should weapons be used or not? During the planning sessions, both secret and open, it was unanimously agreed that the takeover must be a peaceful, unarmed action, and that it would rely on the same mass demonstration tactics that had been so successful during the revolution. Then, people had come out into the street with nothing but fists, faith and unity. There had been bloody clashes with police and army, but for the most part, the revolution had been peaceful. The movement had been calm and unstoppable. The victory of the Islamic Revolution was rooted in the people's minds and hearts—not in violence.

The plan was to apply the same tactics to the embassy takeover. This meant that possession and use of weapons could not be permitted. At the same time, especially in the early days of the revolution, it was commonplace for people to carry arms, particularly the members of the many rank-and-file organizations involved in security work in Tehran. It is possible that a handful of students may have entered the embassy premises with arms in violation of our plan of action. But if any arms were present during the takeover they were never used, never even shown. The Americans surrendered for other reasons. They were at first stunned, then overwhelmed by the swift, forceful, disciplined, non-violent action of the students. I'm sure that if they were to be asked today, they would probably admit that our determination, and the sheer weight of our numbers convinced them that resistance would have been an exercise in futility.

Meanwhile, three of the students from the planning committee had met with Mousavi Khoeiniha and asked him to inform the Imam of their plans. He had told them that although he believed the Imam would approve the action in principle, he was reluctant to inform him directly. It might be difficult for the Imam, as leader and supreme revolutionary authority, to announce his consent publicly beforehand, he explained.

The delegation insisted, and Mr. Khoeiniha promised them he would bring up the matter as soon as the proper circumstances arose.

Later that day, they got the go-ahead—or so they thought. The Imam had just issued a message commemorating the thirteenth of Aban. It included a sentence which all but convinced them that they had won his endorsement: "It is incumbent upon students in the secondary schools, the universities and the theology schools to expand their attacks against America and Israel. Thus America will be forced to return the criminal, deposed shah."

It wasn't until after the embassy takeover that we learned that Mr. Khoeiniha had never succeeded in informing the Imam. Still, without realizing it, the Imam had inspired us, his spiritual followers, with a powerful sense of confidence and faith. The statement also made it easier for us to convince other students to join in the occupation. For me, it was certainly a decisive factor

Now the pace of planning and preparation quickened. The core group concluded that between one hundred and one hundred and fifty students, all members of the Muslim Students Association, would be enough for the takeover. The main criterion for participation was that they not belong to any political faction or group.

Then the participants were carefully selected from each of the city's four universities—Sharif, Beheshti, Polytechnic, and Tehran—and invited to a meeting at 7 o'clock on the morning of the thirteenth of Aban at the Polytechnic and Tehran Universities. The subject of the meeting was to be kept secret until the last minute. By now they had become super sensitive about leaks; they knew from past experience that the leftist groups, which were the main opponents of the Islamic students on the university campuses, would do everything in their power to undermine the plans if they were to find them out.

From the beginning, infiltration of the movement by these groups had been one of the students' main concerns. In the wild, wide-open political atmosphere created by the Islamic Revolution, dozens of tiny political parties had sprung up, most of them quite lacking in popular support. Aside from the pro-Soviet Tudeh Party, which had a relatively long history in Iran, there were the Fedayeen, the Maoist Peykar, the MKO, and the Omati. Followers of the West-leaning, liberal Freedom Party and even the Islamic Republic Party which later formed the government, were also excluded from the operation.

These organizations were a grab-bag of political orientations. Many of them were supported by outside powers and espoused pro-Soviet or pro-Chinese policies; others did the same thing without a Soviet or Chinese connection, not to mention the Trotskyites, who seemed to have Western backing. But despite their continual and complex political feuding they all agreed on one thing: any action initiated by the Islamic groups had to be undermined, blocked or destroyed. They considered Islam a backward ideology, a remnant of the past. In the eyes of their foreign backers, an independent Islamic Iran would be impossible to control or influence. They, and not the nationalists or the other religious groups, did all they could to obstruct us. Then, too, they were rapidly losing their supporters as the Islamic movement gained in popularity on university campuses.

The original plan was to occupy the embassy on the fifteenth or sixteenth of Aban. But the group was worried that the Americans might tighten their security measures, so they decided to put the plan into action as quickly as possible.[15] They had to move and they had to move quickly. The students decided to act the following day. From dusk until midnight they drove around the embassy, carefully studying all movements and noting any changes. Suddenly they realized that November 4 was a Sunday. They had no idea if all or most embassy personnel would be in the compound—and no way of finding out. But it was too late. The machinery had been set in motion.

That night Mohammad turned in late. In the darkness, he worried that their action might be taken over by ambitious power seekers. But when he thought of his fellow students, men like Ibrahim and Mohsen, he felt reassured. They were people he knew. He had seen them in tough situations, and he knew he could trust them. Even more important, he was convinced that only good intentions were involved. As he reviewed the feelings and ideas racing through his mind, he became more confident that this was not a blind act of revenge or violence, it was a genuine reaction to save a country's independence and dignity. Slowly, he felt his concern and uncertainty slipping away.

Early the next morning when he awakened, he felt a deep sense of inner spiritual calm and determination. He got up and performed what we Muslims call the "ablution of martyrdom," which means washing oneself not only for the sake of physical cleanliness but for spiritual cleanliness as well. Then came the morning prayers.

Deep down he was convinced, as were all of us, that he was taking part in this event for God's satisfaction. He could well lose his life, and he knew it. Later, during the difficult moments of the operation, it dawned on him that this knowledge had given him a sense of courage and steadfastness he had never experienced before, never even suspected he had. Although they had never discussed the matter before the occupation, all of those who had agreed to join in had performed the very same ritual that morning. They had all prepared themselves for martyrdom. They were willingly prepared to sacrifice their lives for their beliefs.

November 4, 1979. Day was dawning as Mohammad hurried down to Polytechnic for the 7 o'clock meeting. Students from Sharif and Melli universities met on our campus; their schools were too far away from the embassy. Meanwhile, the Tehran University students were meeting on their own campus to the west. Only those who had been invited, and whose names were on a prepared list, were admitted. Once they had entered, they would not be permitted to leave until the session had ended.

As the students filed into the hall they reacted with surprise and excitement as they realized that the chalk diagram on the blackboard represented a fairly detailed map of the American Embassy. At 7:15 the meeting began, with Mohsen and Mohammad presiding. In his eloquent speaking style, Mohsen presented the case with a compelling combination of firmness and conviction. Referring to the Imam's speech, he assured the group that Mr. Khoeiniha had agreed to raise the idea with Imam Khomeini. As for the action itself, so effective had the United States government been in turning Iranians against themselves that everyone was convinced it was high time to strike back, to strike back at least once, and to shatter the fearsome idol.

Most of the Americans who lived in Iran behaved in a way that revealed their sense of self-importance and superiority. They had come to expect extra respect, even deference from all Iranians, from shoe-shine boy to shah. But when a human being feels superior to another, our religion views this as a sin. As we saw it, what matters in God's eyes is sincerity, piety, closeness to Him. In our country, American lifestyles had come to be imposed as an ideal, the ultimate goal. Americanism was the model. American popular culture—books, magazines, film—had swept over our country like a flood. This cultural aggression challenged the self-identity of people like us. This was the idol which had taken shape within Iranian society. We found ourselves wondering, "Is there any room for our own culture?" The idea of idol smashing can be traced far back, to the prophet Abraham, who destroyed the idols with an ax to demonstrate their impotence, then asked his people: "Why then do you worship them?" Perhaps the Americans still believed they were invulnerable. We no longer did.

Mohammad then outlined how the action would take place. A five-member committee representing each university would make the decisions. The committee—which we later named the Central

Committee—was composed of one, and in one case two, student leaders from each university. It was to have full executive and decision-making powers. Ibrahim and Reza represented Sharif University, Mohsen was the Polytechnic representative, Rahim represented Melli University and Habib, Tehran University. Hojjatoleslam Mousavi Khoeiniha, who enjoyed the respect and confidence of the students, and was close to the Imam, would later became the sixth member of the committee at their request.

Even at the planning stage, the students were determined to make it clear they had no support from any political party, group or faction. Mohsen explained that the name "Muslim Students Following the Line of the Imam" had been chosen to underline the fact that they were students and nothing more, and that their convictions were based on Islam alone. The reason for designating themselves as followers of the Imam was to help them rally the many students who were Muslims, and who were intensely sympathetic to the Imam, even though they were not directly involved with the action in its earliest stages. Of course, they were convinced that sooner or later one group or another would try to enhance its prestige by hitching itself to the movement. And they were just as determined not to let them get away with it.

At the meeting, two or three students opposed the operation outright, and threatened to inform the government. But it was too late to turn back. In a matter of less than an hour the preparations would be completed. In the end, nothing came of their protests or their threats.

The students were issued their instructions. Weapons were strictly forbidden. Each of them was given an arm-band bearing the inscription "Allah-o Akbar" and a picture of the Imam. They were to converge on the embassy in twos. There, at 10 o'clock that morning, a banner reading "Allah-o Akbar" would be unfurled behind which the students would begin a peaceful march, ostensibly towards Tehran University. But under their *chadors* some of the women students would be carrying powerful bolt cutters to sever the chains at the entrance gate, as well as a new chain and lock.

The women students followed the Islamic dress code, called *hijab*, which symbolizes both modesty and devotion to God, and showed opposition to the sexualized image of women promoted by the West. Most wore the *chador*, a garment that covers the head and body. Some wore head scarves and long-sleeved, lightweight coats. For decades, the shah had tried to convince women that the only way to liberation was to accept Western movie stars or his wife, Farah Diba, as role models. The Imam gave us an alternative, by inviting us to restore our human dignity and be full participants in society, such that women would value their family roles, as well as their social roles and obligations. At the same time, no one would be permitted to exploit women's bodies and beauty to promote their own interests.

Iranian women had responded. They showed all the courage and daring that had given them a central role in political affairs—which in turn irritated some Islamic traditionalists who hoped to equate Islam with an inferior status for women. There were psychological advantages too. During the first days of the revolution, the presence of women in the front lines of demonstrations and marches encouraged—and in some cases even shamed—their husbands, sons and brothers into active resistance. The front-line presence of women also unnerved the shah's police, who had orders to fire on demonstrators. Often, when the police had to chose between shooting unarmed women in cold blood and loyalty to their commander-in-chief, they had refused to pull the trigger.

Now everything was ready. The meeting ended and they started out in pairs for the destination. The day was cool and cloudy; a gentle breeze was blowing and there was rain in the forecast. The embassy was only about 15 minutes by foot from the Poly campus. Walking quickly, they arrived with ten minutes to spare, at 9:50 a.m. Everything seemed quiet and normal; traffic was light; that section of Taleghani Avenue had only a few shops. Only a handful of policemen were guarding the embassy gates. With a few quick words the students convinced them to stand aside.

10 o'clock. Suddenly the suspense and expectation peaked as a group of students from Sharif University raised the banner. As the chant of "Allah-o Akbar" rang out, students began to converge en masse from the surrounding alleys, stores and street corners. They all hurried forward and joined the main group of demonstrators. There was no turning back.

Students pry open the basement window of the Chancellery.

CHAPTER II

CAPTURING THE IDOL'S DEN

ONCE INSIDE THE COMPOUND the first task of the occupiers was to close and secure the gates. The action could not be allowed to slip into chaos and confusion. Quickly they double-checked that only the students named on their lists had entered. Fortunately, only a handful of curious passers-by had made their way in along with the group. They were asked to leave the premises. Then the students sealed the main gate with a new lock and chain and took up sentry positions at all four entrances.

One group fanned out to search and secure the grounds. In earlier strategy meetings they had determined the points they thought would require extra surveillance. Meanwhile, another group had cut the wires leading to the security cameras mounted around the Chancellery building.

Again following the predetermined plan, each university was assigned to a particular task. The students from Sharif University were responsible for the physical security of the compound and the buildings. Those from Melli were to be in charge of the hostages. Tehran University was to provide services and logistical support and the Polytechnic group was to collect and protect whatever classified documents they found.

As the students made their way through the grounds, they arrested more and more embassy staff, bringing them from the various buildings to two of the small shacks located at the southwestern corner of the compound. In order to avoid any possible conflict, they tied the hands of the captives and blindfolded them. All the while, the Melli University students' representative kept reminding the students that they must treat their captives humanely and avoid violence unless it became absolutely necessary. This was not only our principle throughout the initial phase of the occupation; it was one we respected to the end.

Each member of the staff reacted in a different way. Some were defiant, some stunned, some confident. Some peppered the students with questions and threatened them with trouble. Some were nervous. Others remained calm, but it was clear that they, too, were unnerved. A brief occupation had taken place two months before; they probably suspected this was a repeat of the earlier episode. "The police will come and sort this out," one man said. "You don't know what you're doing," said another.

Less than an hour after the occupation began the students had penetrated and secured all the embassy buildings except the Chancellery. Its two main entrances were barred with steel doors and the windows were equally tightly secured. This part of the job was going to take longer than anticipated.

Since Mohammad and the students from Poly were responsible for locating and securing whatever documents were found, they were anxious to get into the Chancellery building. He took a quick stroll around the compound to size up the situation. It was then that he realized how well they had done so far. The embassy grounds and secondary buildings were already under control and the students were going about their tasks just as planned. Although it was a delicate, high-risk operation they had succeeded in maintaining an exceptional level of coordination and execution.

On his impromptu rounds he noticed that the western gate was not adequately protected, so he asked some students to fill the gap. Then he hurried off to the northern gate. He wanted to remind the group posted there that some Americans might be hiding in the tall apartment building located due north of the embassy. A group from Sharif University rushed to search the building. The Bijan Building, as it was called, turned out to be a residence for several Marines and other embassy staff, just as Mohammad had suspected.

On his way back toward the Chancellery through the embassy grounds, he looked up at the sky. Clouds hung low over the mountains. Fall had come to Tehran. Now, as he hurried from one building to the other, he felt the cool sprinkle of raindrops on his face. When he returned to the Chancellery, friends were calling him to the northwestern side of the building. They had broken the lock on one of the basement windows, pried the iron bars apart, and managed to force an entry.

Being a lean student had its advantages. Without a second thought he joined our sisters and brothers as they wriggled in through the window bars.

It was only as they rushed up the stairs from the basement, chanting "Death to America" at the top of their voices, that the Marine guards realized the students had actually gained entrance to the Chancellery itself. Their first reaction was to attempt to warn the students off by loading and cocking their automatic rifles. When Mohammad saw a rifle trained at his head he flashed back to his preparation for martyrdom earlier that morning. For them, since martyrdom was not a threat, but rather the ultimate salvation, they all marched right on up the stairway, the women alongside them in the front lines as before, disregarding the Marines' shouted threats.

As they pushed by them, his eyes caught those of one of the Marines. Immediately he understood why they had not opened fire. The man was petrified with fear and his hands were trembling in panic. When Mohammad had begun to learn English a few years before, he never dreamed he would be using it in circumstances like these. He couldn't resist whispering in the guard's ear as he elbowed his way past him, "Don't worry, you're safe. We won't hurt anyone."

He did not know if the Marine believed him. Since the Marines were responsible for guarding the embassy, they tried to stop the onrushing students from reaching the first, then the second floor by firing tear gas canisters. But the fumes wafted back up to the top floors, choking the guards themselves. Within a few minutes the students had neutralized the Marines by sheer force of numbers, and disarmed them.

The second floor was sealed off tight behind a steel door. Earlier they had speculated that this was the place where the main intelligence center would be located. It looked as if they were right. The students told the Americans behind the door that it would be best to open it and surrender. "Many of your colleagues and countrymen are already held hostages," they said. "We don't want harm to come to any of them." At first they refused. Mohammad distinctly remembered John Limbert, a political officer who spoke fairly good Farsi, coming out to speak with the students. Was there anyone from the government with them, he wanted to know? We had nothing to do with the government, the students replied.

"Is there anyone from the Revolutionary Council?"

"No, we have nothing to do with the Council," they replied. "Tell them to open this door. We do not want to resort to violence or harm anyone."

A few moments later the door swung open. At last, the Chancellery was theirs, or so they thought. They quickly arrested the Americans and escorted them outside, acting with as few words as possible. In response to questions from their captives, they said, "This is the force of the people, the power of Islam." The students were acting under instructions to keep calm, to keep the hostages calm, and to avoid arguments at all costs. Only a few words were exchanged.

As the students tied the their hands behind their backs, blindfolded them, and pushed them on ahead, the Americans asked, "Who are you?"

"Muslim students following Imam's Line," came the reply.

"What do you want?"

"For America to extradite the criminal shah."

The policy was to stay quiet and not to give the impression that the students were bent on revenge or intent on killing their captives. The Americans, overpowered by numbers, had quickly realized that their captors were deadly serious, that nothing frightened them. They were in a state of shock.

All the while Mohammad kept reminding the students to consider everything as incriminating evidence, and to gather and take care of every single document they found. Then, at the far end of the corridor, they discovered yet another locked steel door. They had finally reached the heart of the Chancellery. Behind that door, they were soon to discover, lay the CIA's intelligence headquarters. The students quickly understood that some people were still hiding there. It soon became clear that they had been working feverishly to destroy the thousands of documents revealing their involvement in Iranian affairs. Even though the intelligence operatives in the room managed to hold out until two o'clock that afternoon, and to destroy a great volume of material, the unopened drawers and safes the students found when they finally broke in reassured them that the Iranian nation would still have access to thousands of untouched files, many of which would turn out to be incriminating.

As his fellow students arrested one of the Americans who filed out of the CIA room, the man turned to him bitterly and asked, "Why are you doing this?" Spontaneously, Mohammad blurted out in the best English he could muster: "To teach the American government and the CIA a lesson, so it will keep its hands off other countries, and particularly Iran!" The words that came out of his mouth and his tone of voice were so firm and decisive they surprised even himself. The American fell silent.

A few hours after the takeover, the Central Committee contacted Hojjatoleslam Khoeiniha and asked him to join them. They also drafted their first media communiqué, explaining why they had taken the action they did. They had prepared the text beforehand but now, in the light of events, it needed some revisions. The final version read as follows:

In the Name of God, the Merciful, the Compassionate.
Communiqué No. 1

It is incumbent upon students (secondary school, university and theology) to forcefully expand their attacks against America and Israel, so that America will be forced to return the criminal, deposed shah. [Excerpt from the Imam's message on the occasion of the thirteenth of Aban.]

The Islamic Revolution of Iran represents a new achievement in the ongoing struggle between the peoples and the oppressive superpowers. It has kindled flames of hope in the hearts of the enchained nations and has set an example and created a legend of self-reliance and ideological steadfastness for a nation contending with imperialism. This was in reality a conquest over the curse of blindness that the superpowers had imposed so that even the intellectuals of the oppressed world could not conceive of any other freedom than under the benediction of another superpower.

Iran's revolution has undermined the political, economic and strategic hegemony of America in the region.

The world-devouring America which has exploited the vital resources of the nations for years, is now indulging in new, spiteful attempts to regain and secure its interests. These include the candidacy of Egypt as a new gendarme for the region, recruitment of military stooges in South Korea or the likes of the criminal Saad Haddad in South Lebanon, the heavy assaults and attacks of Israel and numerous plots against the Iranian Revolution within and outside of the country.

We Muslim students, followers of Imam Khomeini, have occupied the espionage embassy of America in protest against the ploys of the imperialists and the Zionists. We announce our protest to the world; a protest against America for granting asylum and employing the criminal shah while it has its hands in the blood of tens of thousands of women and men in this country.

We protest against America for creating a malignant atmosphere of biased and monopolized propaganda, and for supporting and recruiting counterrevolutionary agents against the Islamic Revolution of Iran; for its inhumane instigation and plotting in various regions of the country and its infiltration of the executive branches of the government.

And, finally, for its undermining and destructive role in the face of the struggle of the peoples for freedom from the chains of imperialism, wherein thousands of revolutionary and faithful humans have been slaughtered.

Muslim Students Following the Line of the Imam

The plan was to hand the news of the embassy takeover, along with this first communiqué, to Radio Tehran in time for the afternoon news at two o'clock, the main news broadcast of the day. It was around noon when Mohammad came upon a group of sisters from the Polytechnic Institute gathered around the telephone in one of the offices on the second floor of the Chancellery. They had been assigned the job of calling the radio station and asking them to dispatch reporters to the embassy.

It was one of these sisters who related the conversation to me later on. She had telephoned the station to tell them she had very important news. When they asked her to identify herself she replied: "I am one of the Muslim Students Following the Line of the Imam."

Where was she phoning from, and what did she want, they asked her.

Calmly she replied: "I am phoning you from the former American Embassy, the present den of espionage."

"What?!" they blurted out. "Repeat what you just said! Is this a joke?"

When she repeated her message the reporter asked her to hold the line for a moment. Before long she heard another voice:

"I'm the news editor; please repeat your message," he told her.

"We have occupied the American Embassy," she repeated.

"You are kidding, this is a joke," came the retort.

"Look in the telephone directory and find the embassy numbers," she told him, "then dial 820095."

He agreed, hung up and called back. He was still astonished to hear her voice at the other end of the line. But he recovered quickly, and said: "This is serious news. Okay, what's your message?"

They were excited, their nerves were on edge, but they couldn't help smiling. It was hard to believe that a group of students could occupy the American stronghold in Iran so easily, without bloodshed and with only negligible resistance.

Throughout the afternoon, as the news spread, various personalities and public figures began contacting the students, mostly by telephone. A strong majority of callers supported the action, largely as a result of their acquaintance with Hojjatoleslam Mousavi Khoeiniha, who had now joined us, and the members of the United Muslim Students Association. Others were curious about the nature of the action and wanted to know what we intended to do. A few had doubts about the consequences. The students were getting involved in a very serious issue, they warned. It might cause a strong reaction by the U.S. "They'll ruin the whole country because of what you did." Supportive or critical, the students who were manning the telephones thanked them all for calling to express their views, and assured them that they were awaiting the Imam's judgment before any further action.

Had the Imam asked them to leave, the students would have done so unquestioningly. They were ready for any eventuality. After all, they had already made their point. But one and one-half days later, when he voiced his support, nothing could hold them back.

The Central Committee issued its second, third, fourth, fifth and sixth communiqués that same afternoon. They provided progress reports on the operation and on the day's developments.

By now the document team, made up of students from Polytechnic, was hard at work. They had located most of the documents and broken them down into broad classifications. By early evening they had packed them into boxes ready for possible transport to a safe location. It was then that Mohammad took a few moments off to visit the safe room at the end of the corridor on the second floor, the place where the Americans had put up the stiffest resistance in order to buy time to destroy documents, computer diskettes and microfiches. Shredded documents were scattered over the floor and piled up in huge barrels. The room's powerful mainframe computers, electronic devices and communication systems left very little room to spare. In one corner he spotted a barrel filled with a colorful powder which, he speculated, consisted of microfiches that had been dusted to prevent access to the information they contained.

As he stood staring at the scene of disorder, he wondered what kind of information these documents contained. Whatever it was, the Americans had done their best to destroy it all, to the very last page. Did the shreds and the dust hold the details of a conspiracy against the revolution, of their contacts and "sources" within various groups? Their future plans, perhaps? As he ran his fingers through the piles of shredded documents he wondered how it would be possible to extract any information from these bits of straw? What an asset it would be for the revolution, he thought, if we could expose their espionage network and pinpoint their intelligence sources.

Later that evening reporters from national television arrived with their camera crews and equipment. The students allowed them in to film and report the preliminary evidence of shredded documents, and showed them the weapons cache which pointed to the Americans' unlawful espionage activity under the cover of a diplomatic mission. It was already dark by then, and as the reporters wanted to film the embassy premises as well, they were asked to return the next day.

The Central Committee was made up of the same students who had planned the event from the beginning. They were looked upon as leaders; each had strong capabilities, and worked together well as a team, although we later heard of differences of opinion. When a serious debate arose, the matter was taken to the students' group as a whole. It sometimes happened that students from each university would form into short-lived "school factions," but this never threatened our ability to function harmoniously.

On that first day the committee met until well after midnight. They tried to analyze what had happened so far and to predict future developments. Then they went on to the logistics of feeding, accommodating and the appropriate treatment of the hostages. It was their conviction that all the Americans' basic human needs must be met. But for security reasons, they had to be kept separated. For the time being, some would have to remain with their hands bound, and in silence.

How to get our message out was also a vital concern for the students. In fact, the capture of the embassy was part of that message. They had observed how the global news networks operated, and they had all seen their pro-American bias. It only made sense for them to expect an expansion and escalation of the anti-Islamic campaign which had accompanied the overthrow of the shah. The students needed a clear, effective public relations strategy and they needed it rapidly.

Meanwhile, Hojjatoleslam Mousavi Khoeiniha had accepted the students' invitation to stand alongside them as long as need be. As an authority in Islamic legal matters he became, in effect, a member of the Central Committee. We students quickly came to regard him as our spiritual guide.

At the end of the long meeting, the first of many that were to follow, no one anticipated any more than a few days of occupation. That night Mohammad never could have imagined that this place would be his home for more than a year; that hundreds of days and nights would pass, full of the tension of unrelenting publicity and constant, intense political maneuvering. But the students were certain of one thing: the people of Iran were behind them. With that knowledge, they were determined to persevere, no matter what.

During the initial days, the students fielded hundreds of phone calls, telegrams and personal visits. Although the majority of the Iranian people were in total support of the action, some criticized it. But the Imam was quick to state his position: "The great Satan is the United States of America. It is making much commotion and fuss...today underground plots are being hatched in these embassies, mostly by the great Satan America. They must realize that in Iran again there is a revolution, this time greater than the first. They [the American government] must sit in their places and return the traitor [shah] soon." The response was overwhelming. Day after day, the people poured through the streets in waves. The students made a habit of coming down to the main gate to greet them and spend some time talking to them, completely astounded at what they had released.

***

The blare of loudspeakers in the street jolted Mohammad awake. For a split second, he did not know where he was. Then, from his sleeping quarters inside the compound, he heard the demonstrators chanting their support. It was not a dream. This was the American Embassy in Tehran, and he was inside. He glanced at his watch. It was time for the morning news.

In one of the drawers in the makeshift dormitory he had found a transistor radio with its batteries intact. But before he could switch it on, Javad burst into the room and snatched the radio from his hands with a laugh. "Late to bed, late to rise. Too late for the news," he teased.

"News? What news?" Mohammad exclaimed, still starved for sleep.

"Just guess. Let's see how good a political forecaster you are."

"The Americans have made a statement?" he guessed.

"Nope. They always talk a lot, but not today," Javad replied.

"Okay, is it something internal then?"

"Could be, could be," Javad drawled, stringing him along.

"Could it be the Provisional Government?" he guessed. "Did they say something?"

"It's more what they did than what they said," Javad answered, laughing.

"Oh God! Don't tell me Bazargan resigned."

"Took you long enough to figure it out. Yes, he handed his official resignation to Imam Khomeini and the Imam accepted."

That was it. One day after the students had taken over the embassy, Iran's first post-revolutionary government had fallen.

Prime Minister Mehdi Bazargan had informed Ayatollah Khomeini he could not accept responsibility under the existing circumstances.[16] The Imam thanked him for his efforts as head of the Provisional Government and appointed the Council of the revolution, which previously had exercised only limited authority, as the governing and executive power.

The Provisional Government had been appointed by Imam Khomeini during the first days of the revolution. Mehdi Bazargan, his choice for prime minister, was a prominent figure in broader Islamic circles. An engineer by training, Bazargan was learned in Islamic sciences and respected by most political figures in the revolutionary movement. After the fall of the shah, the Imam had insisted upon appointing non-clerical personalities to government positions. He believed that the *ulema*—the Shi'ite clergy—should confine themselves to the role of counselors and supervisors.

But many of Bazargan's cabinet appointees were foreign to the Islamic Revolution and its values. Most were not really in tune with popular opinion. They marched to their own drummer, paying little heed to the expectations of the millions of people who had followed the Imam and gone into the streets quite prepared to shed their blood if need be. There was no doubt that Bazargan was facing a difficult predicament. He had inherited crumbling ministries, a deteriorating economy looted by the Pahlavis and their hangers-on, a bumbling, self-preserving bureaucracy, and worst of all, total chaos in the streets.

What he had also inherited, and either misread or neglected throughout his term of office, was the sincere support and backing of the Iranian people. They were mobilized, fully prepared to rebuild the country and sacrifice their dearest possessions for their beliefs. Decisive, efficient administration could have accomplished much had it been able to harness this endless potential.

We students couldn't prove it at the time, of course, but we were sure that foreign elements were actively involved in attempts to weaken and undermine the young republic. Like weeds, thousands of tiny political groups had sprouted during less than six months, each one attempting to convince the people to adopt its views. Every day their newspapers circulated the wildest rumors. It was as if they were determined to create an atmosphere of endless uncertainty. Ethnic and tribal uprisings, which they rushed to support, broke out in all regions of the country. And through it all the Provisional Government dithered and wavered, with the result that security had almost collapsed.

The primary reason for the government's lack of decisiveness was that Bazargan's cabinet, and his whole entourage, had an entirely different perspective on the revolution than the Imam and other leaders of the

Islamic movement. Bazargan was a sincere religious reformist at heart, not a revolutionary. He had mixed feelings about the Imam's tactics, even though they had led to the toppling of the shah. The monarchical system could be modified and improved, he believed. A cautious man by nature, Bazargan lacked revolutionary insight and vigor—precisely the two qualities that were needed at that moment. He had endeavored to solve the nation's problems by step-by-step, conservative measures.

As it turned out, he was the wrong man in the wrong place at the wrong time. Imam Khomeini believed that the shah was a puppet installed and supported by America to secure its regional interests. Once he had been ousted, the revolution would naturally have to confront imperialism face to face if it hoped to hold to its original path. In this context we could understand what the Imam meant when he described the embassy takeover as a "second revolution, greater than the first." The first confronted the despotic dynasty and brought it down. The second took dead aim at the root of all our sufferings, the imperialist system itself.

In retrospect, it was inevitable that the curious blend of conservatives who made up the Provisional Government could not withstand the pressures and fulfill the responsibilities they were facing. Sooner than anyone had anticipated, they had entered into contact with Americans and other foreign elements, in clear violation of the spirit of the revolution. An example had been the earlier meeting of Ibrahim Yazdi, Foreign Minister in the Provisional Government, with American National Security Advisor Zbginiew Brezenski in Algiers on November 1, 1979.[17] The documents we were to discover later in the embassy identified those individuals directly involved in outside contacts and even what appeared to be plots against the revolution and its young institutions.

Instead of relying on the people and their endless resources the Provisional Government was trying to come to terms with an enemy who had the most to lose from the revolution and the most to gain from instability and weakness in the young Republic. The Provisional Government was incapable of keeping pace with a movement that had quickly developed a profound sense of where it was going, and a determination neither to compromise nor to submit.

Moving the Marine guard hostages out of the Chancellery building.

CHAPTER III

SETTLING IN

IMAM KHOMEINI HAD GRASPED substance while others were groping for shadows. He sought to revive the long-forgotten spiritual aspect of human nature, the force that draws human beings toward loftier goals. The Imam, above all else, was a teacher of ethics. Over and over again, in all his classes, he drove the point home: "All humans seek perfection, they seek the best, but they have lost their way, they have gone astray."18

In the Imam's view, all human beings are searching for divine attributes. We students took the message to heart. It gave us a new approach to knowing God in this era, a new way of considering religion, a new way of defining ourselves as human beings.

Intellectually, everybody could agree with the Imam's terms of reference. But not everybody could withstand the pressure and continue with him along his road. Imam Khomeini feared no earthly power or force. He believed seriously and absolutely that there was no power greater than God. And he held fast to the view that no Muslim, no Christian, no human being for that matter, should fear or submit to the military, political or economic dominion of the United States and its allies, to the then-Soviet Union, or to any other worldly power or force. In practice, this doctrine was quite difficult for people to accept. It meant devotion, sacrifice, self-denial and an unwavering faith.

To the extent of our own limited understanding and capacity, we had chosen the Imam's road. Little did we realize where that road was to lead us, and our country.

* * *

On November 8, my first day in the occupied embassy, I was introduced to the members of the Central Committee. We agreed that I would act as their interpreter.

But even before I entered the committee room, one of the students whispered loudly as he saw me walking down the hall: "Surely one of the brothers would be a more appropriate choice."

For all the faith that Imam Khomeini had publicly placed in women, for all the dynamic role they had played in the revolution, caustic or offensive remarks singling us out as women could still be heard, even among the students. During those heady revolutionary days, women had taken such an active role in day-to-day events that we seldom thought it necessary to bring up issues of women's rights, in spite of critical or carping voices.

But we never retreated either, to the dismay and frustration of some who preferred to see us locked up and restricted to the house. It would be inaccurate to pretend that such attitudes did not exist even among the students. The pace of change had been such that some men seemed simply to have been left behind and at a loss.

Most of the ideas I held about women's issues at the time were the result of my own observations. Not only in Iran, but in many parts of the world, women were discriminated against and lacked opportunity. They were not appreciated for their human qualities, but perceived and used as objects for commercial and exploitive purposes. What first fascinated me was the way Dr. Shariati, Ayatollah Mottahari and the Imam himself viewed the question. Imam Khomeini himself was open to women. Islam, he explained, does not want women isolated, sequestered in the home, but rather for them to remain part of the mainstream of social development. Twenty-one years later, when I see how women in Iran have advanced, particularly in education, I can better appreciate how different he was from the traditional religious figures who would rather have seen us pushed aside.

Perhaps one might call this feminism. But in my own case, I never acquired the spirit of feminism from Western authors. My sense of women's rights and responsibilities derived much more from the Iranian context, from Dr. Shariati's book *Fatima Is Fatima*, in which he describes the Muslim woman and her role in the world of today with a mixture of eloquence and penetrating insight.[19]

Within the embassy walls, my policy from the beginning was to ignore the snide remarks and go calmly about the task at hand. I would display the competence and capabilities of Iranian women in the heat of action, I resolved. Looking back, I think I fared just as well or better than any of the brothers on the job, though interpreting was demanding work and I had begun with little more than a strong command of both languages, Farsi and English, and full confidence in my ability to do the job.

Later that day the students held another lengthy meeting. The outcome was a detailed organizational chart and a program for dealing with the documents. Our strategy would hinge on using live television programs to expose the documents we had discovered when we took over the embassy. We would focus on the pro-American elements who had infiltrated the ranks of the revolution, particularly on their friendly conversations criticizing the Imam and their plans to weaken the Islamic Republic. These revelations, we were certain, would clearly show who were the friends of the nation, and who were its foes.

Based on our findings, we would provide the judicial authorities with information on spies and sources within the military or government so they could take appropriate action. And we would translate the political analyzes and reports on various aspects of Iranian culture, society, politics, economy and the military during the shah's reign, and throughout the revolution. These documents would help all Iranians, from intellectuals to the man and woman on the street, realize the true intentions of the Great Satan toward the Islamic Revolution.

It was an ambitious program, but given our almost boundless reserves of energy and single-minded dedication to our cause, we were confident that we would succeed. The dozens of volumes of documents published remain to this day an eloquent testimonial to the inventiveness of the students who pieced the shredded documents together, and a revealing—and incriminating—portrait of the inner workings of a superpower embassy.[20]

The following day I had some unexpected visitors. The students from my literacy class in the shoe factory had somehow managed to locate me. There were thirty of them, workers ranging from twenty to fifty years of age. I had worked with them for only four months, but in that time most of them had learned to read simple texts and mastered the rudiments of handwriting.

Under the shah's regime there had been no serious efforts made to educate the people or to eradicate illiteracy. The palace's infamous "White Revolution"[21] had been nothing but a colossal scheme for enriching the royal family and its cronies, and for creating a westernized middle-class. It succeeded in the first, failed in the second. The welfare of peasants or workers had never been of the slightest concern to the monarch whose family was among the country's largest landowners.

After the revolution Imam Khomeini had appealed to students to launch a literacy campaign for workers and peasants. Like many of my fellow university students, I got caught up in the enthusiasm and agreed to teach classes. This we organized through the workers' committees that were springing up in the factories all across the country as the workers established unions. Of course, there were never any formal or official links between us students and the committees. But our spirit made it easy for us to contact the workers' committees and offer our services.

My job was based in the industrial district of Tehran. It suited me fine; I had never been a member of any group except the Muslim Students, and I didn't want to be tied down ideologically. Here, I could make a direct contribution. I enjoyed teaching; the workers had endured hardships before the revolution and they were eager pupils, even if it meant staying on after their shifts.

I was as delighted to see them that morning at the gates as they were to see me. During our classes their deeply lined faces had brought home to me the hardships they had endured during the shah's reign. I knew, what's more, that I wasn't alone in having such feelings.

The spirit of the revolution and Imam Khomeini's contention that the oppressed workers, farmers and peasants were the "sustainers of our blessings," had encouraged many students and intellectuals to join a campaign in the factories and villages to wipe out illiteracy and poverty. So it was that the *Jihad-e Sazandeghi* (Reconstruction Crusade) was born. It was a spontaneous movement to improve the welfare, education, health care and agricultural needs of Iran's rural people. In later years, the *Jihad* was to bring electricity, drinking water, classrooms, medical clinics and other basic services to thousands of remote villages. It was a feature of the revolution that the foreign mass media reporting on Iran have contrived to ignore to this day.

Now here they were, standing at the main gates with crowds of people behind them, grinning with pride at the sight of their teacher among the conquerors of the embassy! They told me that the news had spread in the factory that their literacy teacher was among the Students Following the Line of the Imam. The workers had decided to pay a visit and express their solidarity with us. "All our sufferings are from America," their banner read. They were sorry our class had been canceled, but they reassured me, "You hold the fort here. We'll ask the literacy campaign to find a substitute teacher for you." They concluded their visit by handing over a packet of letters in support of our action they had penned in their own handwriting.

That same evening, I decided to pay a visit to the hostages' quarters along with several of the sisters. The students responsible for them had divided them up into groups, each of which were housed in different locations within the chargé d'affaires' residence, the warehouse and the Chancellery. The rooms had to be prepared, partitioned where necessary and everything had to be double-checked for security.

As we entered the warehouse, I met some of the students discussing plans for the hostages. We realized that conditions were uncomfortable for them and we wanted to alleviate tension. In the process of learning their identities, we came across several non-Americans. They were promptly released and sent to their respective embassies.

"Do you think we should let them see movies?" the student guards asked.

"Why not?" I replied. "As long as they are to be kept here, it's better that we don't bore them."

I took a look into the partitioned rooms. The hostages were sitting or sleeping on their beds or strolling in the limited space available to them. As I peered into one room, somebody called me.

"Hey, do you speak English?" he said. "Come on, someone tell me the truth. You people are communists, aren't you? The Russians are paying you to do this, right?"

I smiled at him and replied that we were by no means communists but religious-minded people. I told him we were not hired by anyone to do what we were doing, not even by our own government. We were only following the dictates of our conscience.

"Do you really believe all that American propaganda about the Soviet threat?" I asked him. "Don't you think it is a pretext to suppress all movements, even nationalist or religious ones?"

He looked at his feet. "I don't know," he replied. "I can't figure out how a religious person could do such a thing."

"Maybe it's because you don't understand what was at stake for us, and because you have a different idea of what a religious person is. We have new definitions for old terms," I replied. As it was getting late, I asked him if we could continue the discussion another time. He agreed and I returned to the Chancellery. The evening's dialogue, our confrontation and later acquaintance with the hostages led me to believe that many among them were reasonable people who attempted to understand us and our cause and engage in fruitful and constructive discussion. Naturally enough, they had negative feelings about us. But still, many of them did their best to understand our reasons for doing what we did.

On the way back, I met a few of the students from what we called the operations unit. They were discussing their agenda for the next day. Since we suspected that the Americans might have intelligence reports at their residences outside the embassy, we had obtained official judiciary orders to search, seal and lock up these residences. We also accepted the possibility that some Americans might have escaped and would use the residences as hiding places. The brothers had searched some of these buildings and were planning to search more the next day. We had to take everything into consideration. Security, we understood, was the key to our success.

* * *

The pace of developments seemed to accelerate over the next few days—our first full week in the embassy. According to reports we monitored from the major Western news agencies, the American government was attempting to solve the political deadlock through two channels. First, president Jimmy Carter made another miscalculation. He thought that expelling the shah to another country would change the politics of the event, that expulsion could replace extradition as the solution to the crisis. Our Central Committee issued a string of communiqués giving our views on the matter. They reiterated our insistence that the criminal shah be extradited as the sole condition for the release of the hostages. Our messages also included warnings to Muslim and oppressed nations that their governments might be engaged in attempts to grant the shah asylum. This, we argued, should be considered as an insult not only to the Iranian nation but to Muslims everywhere.

Second, the Carter administration initiated mediation efforts in an attempt to soften our position, hoping to reach a compromise. The Americans began by commissioning a Palestinian delegation to begin exploratory talks. In one of our communiqués we informed them that we would not negotiate with any group. Our conditions for the release of the captives were clear.

As our occupation of the Den of Spies took on new dimensions and the support and solidarity of people all across the country transformed the action into a national movement, coverage from the American mass media escalated, and its biases began to show. Since political initiatives and pressure had yielded no results, the American government threw all its energies into torrents of propaganda.

The main-line news media began to churn out strings of lies and damning allegations: we were torturing, starving and maltreating our captives, their lives were in danger, they claimed, without a shred of evidence to back up their wild assertions. Although we had publicly and repeatedly declared that we were bound by our principles to treat our prisoners humanely, the propaganda war being waged against us was intense. We'd suspected the biased nature of world media even before we'd taken over the embassy. We knew that the major radio and TV networks and publishing houses were owned by American media multinationals, often with strong Zionist sympathies.

In order to break their monopoly on interpretation, we sent formal invitations to the ambassadors of several countries which had displayed a degree of neutrality—Syria, Algeria, France and Sweden—to visit and meet the hostages and inform world opinion of the humane and thoughtful treatment they were being given.

Hojjatoleslam Ahmad Khomeini (the Imam's son), Ayatollah Hossein Ali Montazeri, Hojjatoleslam Seyyed Ali Khamene'i (who would later be elected president and is now Iran's Supreme Leader) and Mohammad Ali Raja'i (soon to be elected president) and a long list of other Iranian religious and political leaders visited the students and hostages during that first month.

At the Imam's suggestion we invited Hanibal Borginini, the Vatican ambassador to Iran, to visit the hostages and report on their living conditions to the Pope. By that time, the hostages had settled in. Their living quarters had been arranged and properly equipped with lighting, beds, carpets and other basic necessities. Their conditions had markedly improved in comparison with the early days of their captivity, when due to security reasons, their hands were usually tied. I learned that they had even watched a movie or two over the preceding days.

The ambassadors arrived on November 12. We took them to meet some of the hostages in the chargé d'affaires' residence located in the northern part of the compound. For obvious security reasons, we could not allow them to visit all of the hostages nor learn of their exact place of detention.

As the Vatican ambassador was talking with some of the hostages, lunch arrived. The brothers in charge of catering brought in trays of food. I still remember the meal they were served: meat loaf, mashed potatoes and vegetables. I pointed to the food and told the ambassador,

"The food we eat is much lower quality than this. We usually get rice with a few spoons of minced meat, but we have no complaints. We are responsible for treating our prisoners humanely and one aspect of this treatment means they must eat properly."

On that same day, November 12, Jimmy Carter suspended oil imports from Iran. The Imam responded by cutting off exports to the U.S. Two days later the U.S. froze six billion dollars worth of Iranian assets. The next day, the streets facing the embassy were filled with surging crowds of supportive humanity who simply did not understand fatigue. They were there day in, day out, morning, noon and night. Some even kept an all-night vigil. Those who could not come to Tehran from distant cities and villages would send us their views in letters, telexes and telegrams.

Only when we looked back in retrospect over the years that followed could we truly appreciate the consequences and the full impact of what we had done. We had seen ourselves as part of a spiritual, not a political, movement. A movement with deep spiritual roots cannot be appraised in material terms, nor by normal political standards. Its effects are not proportionate to the number of people who take part in its inception. Its penetrating roots reach across generational boundaries. At the same time, we were determined to apply these spiritual ideas to life in the twentieth century. As events were to show, this was a challenging task.

The day after the U.S. economic sanctions were announced, I was strolling in front of the southern gate with some other sisters when we noticed an unusual group of demonstrators in the street outside. I approached the gate to get a closer look at them. They were three or four hundred men clad in humble village garb. In their hands they carried shovels, sickles and other farming implements. Most of them were barefoot, a symbolic act of dedication. I called one of them to the gate.

"Who are you, brother? Where have you come from?"

"We are peasants and farmers from Varamin (a town 20 km south of Tehran). When we heard about the American economic attack, we decided to walk to this place, barefoot, to express our support and sympathy. We have also brought our weapons," he said pointing to the shovel in his hands, "to show the world that we will struggle to cut off all economic dependence. We can work more to harvest more, but we will not surrender to the U.S." Their wrinkled faces and callused hands testified to the hard life they had endured while the shah and his American masters were busy looting the natural resources that rightfully belonged to these people.

Following the overwhelming displays of support we'd received, we issued a statement asking our fellow students across the country not to close down the schools and universities in support of our action. We also asked them to beware of provocative actions, like the possible occupation of other embassies. We condemned any form of threat or attack on foreign nationals. "We must adhere to our principles…we do not aim for anarchy, chaos and acts of terror and violence," one of our messages warned.

Among the thousands of messages and letters of solidarity that we received, a farmer's cooperative from Torbat-e Jam village in the eastern province of Khorasan wrote in their telegram: "Someone had to stand in the face of those who have imposed so much suffering upon us and you have done it. You have made our hopes come true." And in a letter from several trade unions in Bushehr, a southern port: "Listen to our voices of solidarity from the blue waters of the Persian Gulf. You have spoken our words. You have humiliated our enemy and you have lifted the burden of decades of oppression and enslavement from our backs." "We are prepared to endure all hardships. We stand behind you firmly. Our dignity is in your hands," the workers and employees of the Isfahan steel mill wrote us.

That same day we received a telegram from representatives of government employees in Tehran. In it they announced their plans to fast as a sign of resistance against American economic pressure tactics. We then proposed to fast for five days in support of their action. Considering the poor quality of our food, however, many of us preferred to fast every day, and to eat only enough to keep ourselves going. Fasting, however, was more than just avoiding food. We saw it as an act of worship, a way of exercising control over our actions and our physical desires.

* * *

By the end of the week, we had developed a fairly well-organized filing system containing the biography and job description of each of the hostages. These files were updated by information we obtained in embassy documents or through informal talks and interviews with the hostages themselves. Although some were reluctant to give us information on the capacity in which they served the embassy, others proved willing to cooperate and to clarify matters for us.

When we received a message from the Imam's office asking us to release the women and black (African-American) hostages who were not involved in acts of espionage, we did not have all the information necessary to make a clear-cut decision about many of them.

As I saw it, the Imam had set out to accomplish two things.

First, by symbolically taking the side of the women and of the black population of the United States, he was pointing out that gender and race were still causes for discrimination there. The Imam was saying that the human spirit and its greatest qualities had been sacrificed and degraded in the West. What we understood as human dignity was not fully respected. Women's image had been degraded; they had been reduced to the level of sex objects. Even the women's liberation movement, the shift in family structures and the increased participation of women in the workforce had not resolved these concerns but had, in a way, worsened them.

My sisters and I were certainly aware of the achievements of the feminist cause in the West. But we could also observe that the younger generation was rapidly being taken off course, caught up in a pop culture which seemed to glamorize sex, drug addiction and violence. The last thing young people, particularly young women, were be encouraged to think about was any kind of political outlook that might question the basis of the American system.

The African-American population faced then and still faces a similar burden. In spite of the U.S. government's protestations of non-discrimination, and in spite of the presence of African-Americans at high decision-making levels, the American system was then and is today undermined by racial discrimination that is both insidious and persistent.

My own understanding of racial politics in the United States had been shaped by the life of Malcolm X. Here was a man who had transformed himself, who had left the Nation of Islam, made the pilgrimage to Mecca, and returned with a totally new interpretation of Islam and of anti-racism before he was shot down. From his life and death I had concluded that free speech was not tolerated in the West, especially for African-Americans.

In calling for the release of the women and African-American hostages, the Imam had not only told the world that he understood race and gender discrimination as it existed in the West. He had spoken to Iranians as well. Although racial distinctions of the kind that exist in the United States never existed in Iran, few women in our society could claim that their social rights were equal to those of men. In the Imam's appeal, we saw a strategy for the advancement of women within the framework of an Islamic value system in our own country. That it would be different from the strategies adopted by women's movements in the West was obvious.

The fine points of interpretation aside, however, we had to implement the Imam's decree quickly and efficiently. In a late-night meeting on November 18, we reviewed the biographies and files of the women and black hostages. Altogether, we had to come to a decision about seven women and ten black men. Five or six of the African-Americans were Marines. It was highly unlikely that they'd been involved in espionage.[22] We would determine the status of the others through interviews held during the next few days.

We hoped the black Marines would be more cooperative and sympathetic than the others. Considering their intelligence classification, we could not expect to obtain any useful information from them. I remember two sessions we organized for the Marines. We showed them films of the revolution, the crimes of the shah and told them as much as we could of the story behind the Iranian revolution.

We found out very quickly that, contrary to what we had expected, the lower ranking embassy staff knew nothing of the realities of life under the Pahlavi dynasty. They could not for a moment imagine the extent to which the American government was involved in the sufferings of the Iranian nation. They were completely unaware of the motivations and aspirations behind the Islamic Revolution. But their lack of knowledge was little more than a reflection of the attitude of the American government toward the Islamic movement.

In the course of the interviews which took place in the small buildings behind the Chancellery, a few of the women and African-American men told us that they recognized the right of the Iranian nation to extradite and try the deposed shah. I was involved in interviewing the black Marines. One of them told us, "I would have done it promptly, at least as a gesture of pardon to the Iranians, if I were in his [Carter's] place." Most of the others insisted on non-cooperation and refrained from making any judgments.

The sisters who were doing the interviews with the women hostages had similar impressions.

As we were amateur interviewers playing by ear and gaining experience as we went, unexpected and sometimes amusing incidents would occur. On one occasion, I was talking with some of the brothers in one of the outlying buildings. In the adjacent room two of our women students were interviewing a woman hostage. One was carrying a tape recorder under her *chador* in order to review the conversation later.

Less than an hour later, one of the sisters came out looking flustered and taken aback. What went wrong? I asked her. Shaking her head, she replied, "It shouldn't have happened."

She had pressed the recording button and entered the room with the recorder hidden under her *chador*. They were busy listening to the hostage's statement when suddenly the tape recorder had switched off with a very loud click when the cassette ended.

The sound had startled the hostage and it had taken some time before she could continue. I couldn't help laughing, nor could she or the others present. The hostage had probably mistaken the sound for a gunshot, ventured one of the brothers. The sisters later recalled that it was all they could do to keep from bursting into laughter, which could have given away their tactic of surreptitious taping. No one seemed to worry too much about how the hostage might have felt.

On November 19, we made our final decision. Five women and eight men who had not been involved in acts of espionage (according to our limited information) would be officially handed over to the Foreign Ministry, which would arrange for their immediate deportation. We called Iranian radio and television (*The Voice and Vision of the Islamic Republic*) and invited other foreign and domestic reporters to attend a press conference with the freed hostages. The Central Committee also issued two communiqués, one in the name of American women and the other for African-Americans.

In these statements we identified ourselves with oppressed peoples throughout the world irrespective of race, sex, nationality or religion, and spelled out our reasons (which were those of Imam Khomeini) for releasing the women and the African-Americans. In our statement to American women we wrote, "We are sure that, when you realize the sufferings and afflictions that the shah has brought upon our nation you would, in reminiscence of the sufferings that you, your sons and husbands endured during the Vietnam war, ask your government to extradite the criminal shah."[23]

The *Voice and Vision* reporters arrived at two o'clock. The hostages to be released were brought into one of the buildings that had been prepared for the interview. We had not yet informed the hostages of the decision. It was to be a complete surprise. Hojjatoleslam Mousavi Khoeiniha arrived and the women hostages were taken into the living room where the cameras and lights were prepared. I participated as interviewer and translator. Mr. Khoeiniha read the Imam's message and elaborated on the subject. When they heard the translation, the hostages' reaction was one of delight and astonishment. One of the women leaped to her feet and wept with joy.

Hojjatoleslam Mousavi Khoeiniha with African-American and women hostages prior to their release.

Women hostages react to announcement of their release.

Then we asked the women hostages to express their feelings. They acknowledged the fact that the Imam had been directly responsible for their release and freedom. We gave a similar ceremony for the African-Americans that afternoon.

Later that evening we asked the hostages to participate in a press conference. They all agreed. We saw ourselves, of course, as non-coercive, involved in a process of re-educating our charges. It hardly occurred to us at the time that they would see matters in exactly the opposite way.

We chose the small outdoor area behind the visa building and prepared for the press conference. It would be convened and organized by the public relations unit of which I, along with about a dozen other students, was a part. I was assigned to do the interpreting. That evening reporters asked the hostages about their health and how they were treated during their captivity. They were also asked to express their views on the extradition of the shah. Although they unanimously mentioned the need for a just and peaceful solution, they did not criticize the American government outright as some had done earlier during informal talks with us.

From Iranian friends abroad we learned that the American media, and world media in general, had censored much of this event. It was as if the little the released hostages had said was too much.

Media coverage did not discuss the rationale behind the release of the hostages, even though our action was, we felt, absolutely self-evident. Nor did they focus on the released hostages, as they were to do when the occupation came to an end. The media did everything they could to limit the impact of the release, and to conceal its message. Still, word had gotten through. Among African-Americans, we learned from our supporters in the United States, people appreciated what had happened.

We had scored some points, that much was clear. The Carter administration quickly trotted out Vernon Jordan and Bayard Rustin, two blacks active in the American civil rights movements of the '60s and '70s to denounce Iran's attempt to "divide" black and white America. But our information was that Imam Khomeini enjoyed genuine popularity in those early days in many African-American communities.

Perhaps more important, the event was intended as proof that we had nothing against the American people. Our grievances, our frustration and our anger, all, we proclaimed, were directed against their government.

Twenty-one years later, looking back, I realize how naive we must have seemed, especially to those Americans—surely a majority—who sincerely believe that they democratically elect their government, and that it represents their interests.

I guess in a sense we were. Our intention had been to convince Americans that because of the wrongs Iran had suffered at the hands of the United States government, we were justified in taking hostage and holding American diplomats and embassy personnel. But it may have been an error on our part to presume to awaken Americans to the social ills they presumably had identified themselves, and which were, in any case, their problem. Punishing them for what they had done to Iran would have been reason enough for our actions.

Though we saw ourselves as humane and compassionate in our dealings with the hostages, and took all necessary measures to ensure their safety and welfare, in the final analysis we held the keys to their locked doors. If we had imagined that they would repeat before the television cameras what they might have said to please us in private, we were mistaken. We had established a relationship in which we exercised almost complete power over our involuntary guests, many of whom were career diplomats sworn to serve their country's interests. Yet we somehow expected them to agree with us gladly. Such are the pitfalls of youthful sincerity.

Still, that sincerity ultimately served us well, though in limited ways. Several of the hostages did make an equally sincere attempt to understand our motivations, and to draw general conclusions about U.S.-Iran relations from the incident. Some have remained committed to a different, more healthy relationship between the two countries.[24] But the fact remains that our efforts to instigate a meaningful dialogue came to naught. The United States and Iran were to continue their hostile face-off for two decades. And today, despite the election of a reform-minded government, suspicion and ill-feelings persist and may well take years to overcome.

Shredded documents that were later reconstructed.

CHAPTER IV

SORTING OUT THE DOCUMENTS

ONCE THE CENTRAL COMMITTEE had approved the plan for sorting out the documents, specific responsibilities and roles were assigned. Each group of students would be in charge of a specific function, from classifying and drawing up a complete list of the documents available, to translating or summarizing each one.

The system in use at the embassy classified the documents: Limited Official Use, Confidential, Secret, Eyes Only and Top Secret. During the first few hours of the takeover, the Americans had succeeded in shredding most of the top secret and some of the secret documents. But as we studied the others, we realized that they must contain informative clues about people within the revolution itself. It quickly became clear to us that these people—some of whom held very high positions—may have been attempting to weaken and undermine the revolutionary movement that we felt so strongly a part of.

Every afternoon, I and several other students spent from four to six hours writing summaries of the documents. Once we had completed our work, another group of students would review them and chose the most important ones for immediate, complete translation. The really important ones we would expose publicly, on television.

Those members of the Provisional Government whose names appeared in the documents protested long and loud of their good intentions, and denied any contact with or sympathy for the American system. But the documents indicated quite the opposite. They gave clear evidence of repeated and frequent secret meetings and briefing sessions involving the very people who were now our hostages and influential people in the government, including some of its highest-ranking officials.

The CIA apparently believed that it could manipulate any revolution or political establishment if it could successfully infiltrate its top ranks early on. In Iran, the agency was particularly intent on doing so. After all, it had plenty of past experience.

The documents revealed a formula that was always the same. The two sides would meet for an informal chat over a cup of tea. The Iranian side would display a sense of inferiority in the face of the West and express its eagerness—or the eagerness of its government—to enjoy the blessings of the United States. Then the Iranian spokesmen would criticize the anti-imperialist and religious dimensions of the revolutionary movement in order to win the confidence of the Americans. In the process, they would transmit a surprising amount of high-level confidential and personal information about key political personalities, and even sometimes about the Imam himself. The documents also usually included a psychoanalytical description of the source, including very specific personal traits and details.

One of the documents that struck me was an account of a meeting between a political officer of the embassy and an Iranian Foreign Ministry official. This Secret document was almost entirely devoted to a description by the pro-American official of Imam Khomeini's residence in Qom. Everything was there: the entrances, the windows, the rooms and even the back doors. According to the document, this information was of vital importance to U.S. intelligence.

The CIA was not prepared to let go of such vital and precious holdings. It was no accident that the highest-classified and most sensitive documents had been priority targets for the process of destruction. Two powderizing machines were used, one in the CIA station chief's office in Tehran, and the other in the embassy communication center. Their combined efforts produced two barrels—more than 200 litres—of powdered documents. But one of the machines had malfunctioned and the Americans had to resort to paper shredders to destroy the rest of the material.

Documents we discovered later on revealed that when the revolution broke out, U.S. Ambassador William Sullivan had drawn up a strategy to lighten the paper load in Tehran. Many key items were transmitted to the U.S., and many others were destroyed outright. Still, though only immediately relevant and active files were kept on the premises, their number was immense.

While the Americans had successfully destroyed or shredded a large portion of the secret and top secret documents, many thousands had been left intact in file drawers or safes in the Chancellery. It was easy enough for us to break open the file drawers and gain access to their contents. But the safes, with their large multiple combination locks were another story.

By the end of November, we located a locksmith who specialized in opening combination locks. He spent several hours listening to the clicking sounds of the locks in an effort to break the code. Finally, he was able to open three of the seven safes. Stymied, he apologized and told us he could do nothing about the others.

As the three safes he had opened contained highly sensitive documents, we were more determined than ever to open the remaining four, whatever it took. At first we attempted to open the locks by listening to the clicking of the mechanism just as the locksmith had done. Everybody had lined up to help out, begging for just once chance to crack the combination. We tried pins and whatever else we could think of. Nothing worked. Finally we borrowed a welding machine, a high-power drill and a power saw. The next day some of the students volunteered to work at "mission impossible" using these tools. I remember going constantly back and forth between the Chancellery and the outdoor area where the "safe crackers" were hard at work, asking about their progress.

Nine hours later, they had opened the first safe. I knew they'd succeeded when I heard shouts of "Allah-o Akbar!" We rushed outside to congratulate them. The other safes followed, each one after a full day of hard, tedious work. In less than a week, all the remaining documents were in our hands.

Five days later we happened on a scrap of paper that would have been priceless ten days before. Ahmad, one of the students from Melli, came across it in a drawer in the basement. On it were written long strings of numbers.

"Looks like some kind of code," he said.

"It sure does. But for what?" I replied

"Combinations for the safes," said Ahmad, bursting into laughter.

The most sensitive documents used code words or the term "source" to refer to the people involved. CIA agents or political officers had approached many political figures thought to be "liberal" or pro-West in their thinking in the hope of extracting confidential information on possible weak points or infiltration channels. Some of these people had been identified as potential opposition leaders who would pave the way for the downfall of what they described as "radical, anti-American" parties who would then be replaced by more moderate figures.

Once the most sensitive documents, particularly the ones dealing with current developments and liberal personalities who opposed the anti-American campaign, were organized and summarized in Farsi, some of our brothers took them to the Imam. He had asked us to expose everything we found, no matter who was involved, and he followed each new development attentively.

* * *

Before we exposed or published any document it went through a review process. First we made a summary translation and assigned the document to a classification system we had developed. At the next stage, documents containing sensitive or vital information were sent for immediate translation. The translation would then be carefully edited by someone with a good command of English. Finally, it would be prepared for public release, which we called exposure.

Alongside the Central Committee, we set up an ad-hoc committee to take charge of these operations. It held daily meetings to brief people involved with the documents. The group included people who actually handled the documents, more politically mature students with a capacity for analysis, as well as some members of the Central Committee itself. The committee drew up a general policy and decided on the order in which documents which were certain to have an impact on the course of political development in the country were to be made public.

The process was as labor-intensive as it was painstaking. Everything, from single documents to entire files on a single subject, was classified along with a brief Farsi abstract describing its contents. One of the non-classified documents we found described American cultural policy in our country (see Appendix A). We interpreted the document as a plan for long-term cultural disintegration. It was further supported by a whole series of documents on the U.S. Cultural Center in Tehran. We dispatched it to highest priority level: this was what they had been planning for us.

After the summary and classification were completed, the document was assigned for translation, which was then revised, edited, and sent to the committee which determined whether the original should be exposed on television. If it included sensitive information it was handed to government officials, or at least officials were consulted before we took any further steps.

Sometimes the contents of a particularly explosive document would be issued in the form of a communiqué to be read aloud at the front gate and as a televised announcement. When we did this, media impact throughout the country was powerful and widespread. Less sensitive documents went through a slower process of translation and editing before being made public. Over a period of four years, more than 80 volumes of documents were published.

We determined the order of exposure by the significance of the document, which in turn was closely related to the turbulent political and economic situation in the country. We always held two or three preparatory meetings prior to the weekly televised exposure sessions before going ahead. Two students from the Central Committee participated in the live broadcasts. Their job was to read the most important parts of the documents which had been marked by the committee.

After reading excerpts, they would give a brief explanation of any obscure passages. In our meetings, we decided that the students involved should avoid making any lengthy comments, remain objective and concise, and let the people make up their own minds on the basis of the available information and evidence.

We deleted the names of persons with no direct contacts with the United States. In fact, we simply wanted to expose the names of those involved in the betrayal of their country. It was certainly not our intention to strip people of their dignity and reputation. We were extremely careful not to mention the people whose names may have appeared in various documents unless the evidence against them was, in our eyes, clear and incontrovertible. For all that, in those emotion-charged days, to release a person's name in connection with the United States, especially with the "traitor" label attached, could mean for that person imprisonment or worse. Revolutionary justice was swift, and cared little for the due process that is the foundation of a civil society. But we were single-minded and intent; those considerations weighed lightly indeed.

Once a document had gone through all the steps and a final translated and edited text was prepared, we informed the judiciary authorities prior to the televised exposure. If the evidence warranted it, the suspects were then arrested for further investigation.

Even though we were not professional translators we had managed, through a system of strict control and painstaking editing, to produce extremely accurate translations. How important this was became clear a year later at the trial of Abbas Amir-Entezam, a Foreign Ministry official and diplomat who had done all he could to win the trust of the Americans. He was convinced that the country's prosperity was in the hands of the United States, and that nothing could be done without its consent.[25]

During his trial for espionage, broadcast on national television, Amir-Entezam's lawyer claimed that the translations of the documents were biased, and that their meaning was totally distorted. The court then decided to postpone the trial pending further scrutiny of the documents. Several experts were asked to re-evaluate the translation. It took them a full week to complete their assessment. In the end, they announced that the translations met all applicable standards. For us, it was a crucial test. We all heaved a mighty sigh of relief. Abbas Amir-Entezam, who was fortunate to escape with his life, was sentenced to life imprisonment. He is still being held in Evin prison, in Tehran.

The Chancellery—the "document building" as we called it—was the center of the action. On each floor various groups of students were hard at work on specific subjects. Those dealing with the documents were asked to keep any new information confidential and report only to the person responsible according to our organizational chart.

One evening in early December as I was looking through a newly-opened file, I came upon a box at the bottom of one of the drawers. It contained sheets of standard-size white paper. But since my policy was to consider everything with caution and suspicion I looked the box over closely. On one side were the initials "SWC." It seemed strange to me that ordinary paper would be kept in such a box locked up in a file drawer. I put the box back in its place, but it—and the initials—still lingered in my mind.

A few weeks later I discovered why. One of the sisters who was working on a batch of documents related to the Soviet Union brought me a page of top secret instructions for using special writing paper that contained a kind of invisible ink which could be transferred to ordinary paper under the pressure of a pen or pencil. The ink could later be made to appear by applying water or heat. The student working on the document had no sample of the paper enclosed with the instructions, she said.

"It would be interesting if we could find the paper," she added.

"We have," I exclaimed, remembering the initials on the box of paper in the drawer. Later, we demonstrated the use of the paper along with other secret documents on our weekly television program.

A week later, we came across a similar case. While searching the drawers of an apparently abandoned desk, one of the students from Shiraz University had found a mini-cassette.

We promptly invited students from the other universities with a strong command of English to join us in the documents section. The mini-cassette player was in the military attaché's room on the first floor. Fortunately it was in working order. The tape consisted of about fifteen minutes of talk during which a monotonous male voice droned on about a boiler, its temperature, water capacity, steam valves, as well as troubleshooting and maintenance. Alone, each sentence made sense. But taken together, the succession of sentences was meaningless and unrelated. The voice appeared to be reading a code, perhaps with instructions for a particular operation. We never could decipher it.

As the days passed it became increasingly apparent to us what an incredible collection of intelligence information we had on our hands. There was strategic information on various aspects of Iranian society, particularly its most vulnerable sections. There was material on various political factions and personalities, many of whom had established direct or indirect contact with the embassy.

As we continued our exposures on television, and presented increasing evidence of American intervention in post-revolutionary Iran, the country rallied behind us, encouraging us to make public all the documents we had. Political groups would contact us and ask us to publish documents against their rivals. We politely declined. We were determined to stay objective, and to steer clear of political disputes.

It was only natural that we would come under pressure from all sides. At first, some people thought they could compel us to expose only what they felt was in their interests. But we refused to bend, and kept on exposing documents on the basis of what we saw as their strategic and political content. In fact, the harder they pushed, the more stubborn we became. We resolved to stick to our principles, come what may. Some groups claimed that we were biased and that we only exposed documents against rival groups but the reality was that we were not committed to any group and faction. We played no favorites.

Only a few weeks after the takeover, Abolhassan Bani Sadr, who was then a member of the fifteen-man Revolutionary Council and who was to become president on January 25, 1980, launched a campaign to pressure us to hand all the documents over to the government. He had first brought up the idea at meetings of the council, and spent considerable time and energy lobbying to gain support for his plan. People who were close to him later told us how strange they found it that Bani Sadr was pressing so hard to lay hands on the documents. After all, he had been a strong opponent of our action from the beginning.

Perhaps he thought that the ongoing exposure of the documents would endanger his policies. But perhaps what worried him most of all was that certain personal documents would surface concerning his covert contacts with a certain American businessman.

Finally, we referred the matter to the Imam, the court of last resort for insoluble dilemmas. He ruled that the documents should remain in our hands, and that we should continue to expose them for the whole country to see.

In fact, the Imam instructed us to publish everything, no matter who was involved. "Even if you find something against me, publish it!" he said.

His determination led us to take an unusual step. One day in mid-December, the radio announced that the Muslim Students Following the Line of the Imam were going to expose a document concerning the Imam himself. We had come upon several CIA analyses of his personality. They all concurred in one thing—that he displayed unprecedented self-confidence and decisiveness—and went on to describe him as an individual who would not sell his beliefs at any price, nor compromise his views. Numerous attempts to approach or influence him had all failed. His decisions and strategies were considered unpredictable.

It didn't take us long to realize how far-reaching the social and political implications of our exposure program were going to be. The American strategy of promoting certain pro-West political personalities in the hope of knocking the revolution off course became increasingly plain for all to see. In fact, the exposure of the documents was a short course in international power politics, an awakening for a populace that had been deprived of any form of political expression before the revolution.

One of the first consequences of the exposure of political figures who had betrayed the trust of the country was predictable. Many of the political parties and smaller groups who had supported us at first quickly shifted position and took sides against us when they realized that documents concerning their leaders or advisors might be published.

As we were not members of any party or faction we were free to act independently, and to make decisions unconstrained by outside political considerations. But our independent action had to be based on a painstakingly accurate description of the documents we'd found within the embassy compound. Anything less would have been a serious breach of the trust we felt the population had granted us.

Despite our vigilance, there were instances where students violated these principles. Early in January, we received a tip that the Mujahideen Khalq Organization (MKO), which later proved to be in the service of foreign powers, had obtained a sensitive document from the embassy.[26] We investigated and soon confirmed the reports. It rapidly became clear that they had obtained the document from one of their supporters who had infiltrated our ranks. We quickly identified and expelled the individual. The document itself indicated that the American Embassy had provided information about secret meetings between a member of the MKO, a certain "Saadati," with Soviet diplomats to the Provisional Government through the "Komiteh" forces. They must have believed that the document would strengthen the political stature of their group.

Access to the most sensitive documents was restricted to a small number of well-known students. No one individual had access to all of them; we had developed a system of different levels of access. But the political climate in Tehran at the time was still confused, and political opinions among the occupying students reflected the world beyond the embassy gates. Many of our outside supporters may well have had friends in the MKO, or even been sympathetic to them. Several MKO members had come over to the Muslim Students; when their leadership saw what had happened, they attempted to attach themselves to our movement. But several students had not yet decided to which group they belonged. Back then, the dividing line had not yet been clearly drawn. It soon would be.

Nonetheless, we had completely excluded the MKO and its members from participation in the embassy occupation. Frustrated, they realized how much they could have benefited if only they could have become involved. After the incident, they had no hope of maintaining an intelligence channel within the embassy to protect their interests and further their ambitions.

For us, the episode came as a warning. We tightened our document security regulations and restricted our information links to the outside.

In January, we managed to transform another potentially damaging event into an opportunity by demonstrating our readiness to admit our errors. Early on in the occupation we had decided that two different students would participate in each weekly televised document exposure. Since we were not seeking personal fame or credit, we reasoned that it would be unjustified for the same two students to appear regularly on the air.

Although the two new students chosen that week were at the decision-making level, they lacked the experience of our brothers on the Central Committee. As usual, we briefed them on the documents to be exposed and on the particular persons involved, as well as on the content and procedures to be followed. They were to show no bias in their presentation, we cautioned them.

After the meeting the two left for the television station while we waited for the live broadcast. Our two representatives began by reading the selected excerpts from the documents, and displaying the sections of the English text onto which the cameras would zoom for the audience to read if they could.

Everything started out calmly enough. But as they went along, their emotions began to get the better of them. They began condemning, denouncing, and even sentencing the persons involved—and they kept it up until the end of the program. In a few minutes they had sacrificed their impartiality, and conveyed a sense of reprisal and revenge before the country could make up its own mind, and before the judiciary officials could bring down a verdict.

We were appalled. The "exposure" we had just witnessed was a violation of the standards we had set for ourselves. We felt as though we had abused the confidence the people had expressed in us over the past weeks with their huge demonstrations in front of the embassy, day and night.

As I left the Chancellery for one of the smaller buildings where the Central Committee convened, I was burning with shame and anger. Some sisters who were on guard duty and had missed the program asked me how it was. It took me a few seconds to reply. "Totally unsatisfactory," I blurted out. Then I hurried on before they could ask any more questions.

The Central Committee was in a state of shock. We resolved then and there to take immediate remedial action: an official apology to the country delivered in the form of a communiqué to all the mass media. "The brothers involved failed to respect our standards. They lacked the necessary objectivity. We owe an apology to the nation," we wrote.

"We will not expose any further documents until the nation asks us to do so, as a sign of forgiveness."

It was not long before we were given an answer. The next week, demonstrations were more massive than ever before. People from all walks of life were in the streets asking us to keep up our work.

But the incident had revealed a weakness in our organization, and illustrated the ease with which the moral authority we had won in the eyes of our fellow citizens could be abused and transformed into its opposite. From the beginning, we had felt that the people had given us their confidence. It was up to us to prove that we could safeguard this responsibility without letting our personal interests overshadow theirs.

When the incident happened, we suddenly realized that perhaps our personal motivations had gotten the better of us. Maybe we were getting carried away. After all, we had power. We could ask people to do anything and they would do it. It was a unique position to find ourselves in. We had a curious kind of charisma. The incident had demonstrated that it was no longer enough to just sit there and repeat, "we're good Muslims, we don't have any personal ambition." Danger was always lying in wait. No sooner did we allow our selfish desires to come to the surface than it would pounce. Despite the rapid response of the people, we could not allow ourselves to forget what had happened.

* * *

Among the many illegal activities of the CIA station in Tehran was the fabrication of counterfeit identity cards and passports for its agents. In one of the safes we found forged stamps and seals for airport entry and exit visas for various European, Asian, African and Latin American countries. In another safe, we came upon more than 1,000 false Republic of Ghana passports. We also found several forged passports which carried the photographs of the Americans with false names and nationalities.

Thomas Ahern, one of the top-ranking CIA agents in Tehran, had a German passport with a fake name identifying him as a businessman.[27] The passport was full of forged stamps from various international airports. Since the Frankfurt Airport entry stamp would change in shape and color from time to time, Ahern had been instructed to check with CIA headquarters before using that particular stamp.

The standard American accusation against the students was that by capturing their embassy we were violating international law. But the Americans themselves had indulged in espionage activities in Iran, going far beyond the legal limits set by the Geneva and Vienna conventions of 1961 and 1963. Of course, the right of diplomatic missions to gather information concerning the host country is beyond question. But the limits and nature of such activity are clearly defined in international conventions which consider all acts of espionage and interference in another country's internal affairs as illegal. The Americans had mounted a wide-ranging effort to identify and locate all counterrevolutionary groups in Iran. These groups were then contacted and enlisted as CIA information sources. In many cases, the information exchange was a bilateral matter, with the Americans reciprocating. Wherever they thought that a particular faction might reach the power hierarchy, the organization was carefully monitored and tracked.

In the Chancellery we found dozens of secret and top secret documents dealing with pro-monarchists who were involved in terror killings of simple citizens as well as members of the "Komiteh" (revolutionary organizations set up by local people to organize security in the cities after the collapse of the shah's regime).

The most shocking documents pointed to a political faction called "Forqan," a small group of teenagers who lacked even elementary knowledge of Islam, let alone insight into contemporary political issues. The few leaders they had taught them that the assassination of religious figures would bring about an improvement in their situation. Many people believed that this group, which ultimately succeeded in assassinating Ayatollah Morteza Mottahari and Ayatollah Mofatteh, two eminent religious scholars, was supported and directed by outside elements. Documents found in the embassy bore out their suspicions.

We ultimately found enough evidence to convince us that the Americans had been in contact with the Forqan group via third parties.

The thousands of documents we'd obtained from the file-drawers and safes were more than enough to keep us busy for several months. But we were obsessed by those two barrels of shredded documents in the communications room. The intact documents in our hands were mostly classified as confidential, with a few belonging to the secret category. We knew that the bulk of surviving secret and top secret documents were likely to be found in the barrel of shredded documents. The identity of the hundreds of Iranians who had served the Americans in various strategic areas of the country would be among them.

When our fellow students came to visit the communications room we cautioned them not to touch the shreds. Javad, an engineering student, had warned us. "Don't touch it; the way the paper has fallen into the barrel connects the pieces." He reasoned that the shreds from one document had naturally fallen in the vicinity of one another. Considering how little time the Americans had in the communications room, it was unlikely that they had been able to mix the shreds.

Most of us believed it was impossible to reconstruct the documents. Any attempt to do so would be futile. Finally, Javad made the breakthrough. He was a study in concentration: bearded, thin, nervous and intense. These qualities, combined with his strong command of English, his mathematical mind and his enthusiasm, made him a natural for the job. Working day and night, Javad soon came up with a formula for the probability of reconstructing the shreds of paper.

One afternoon he took a handful of shreds from the barrel, laid them on a sheet of white paper and began grouping them on the basis of their qualities. We helped him for a few hours that day, and we succeeded in putting aside some shreds that belonged to one or two documents.

It was painstaking work: even getting the pieces to lie flat alongside one another was a job in itself. After five hours we had only been able to reconstruct 20-30 percent of the two documents. But Javad was determined. The next day I again visited the document center with a group of sisters.

"Come and see. With God's help, with faith and a bit of effort we can accomplish the impossible," he said, with a smile.

He had completely reconstructed the first document and carefully taped each individual shred together. We could make out the text: it was military information with a source identified as code. We phoned the Central Committee, and they came over along with Hojjatoleslam Mousavi Khoeiniha. He carefully studied the shredded documents and urged us on, stressing how important the documents could be to the defense of the revolution.

Flush with optimism, Javad recruited a team of students to work on the project. By the following day, more than 20 had volunteered. Javad outlined the procedure. Each one would begin with only a handful of shreds to start with, and classify them carefully. Later he prepared flat boards fitted with elastic bands to hold the shreds firmly in place. It was slow, tedious work, and after about a month the first group of students lost patience. We called for a new group of volunteers and the work continued. One sister, Ashraf, an Master's student in mechanical engineering, stuck with the project until the last shred, a total of nearly 20 months. When they hit their stride, the students were reconstructing from five to ten documents per week. Ashraf worked with each group while the hostages were kept in the embassy.

Later, when the hostages were dispersed throughout the country following the failed American rescue attempt, the students were also dispersed, each one attending to his or her studies, or working.

It was then that we arranged for groups of high-school student volunteers, and young people who had been disabled during the revolution, to continue the job. The work continued until 1985. A total of 3,000 pages amounting to 2,300 documents were reconstituted and published in 85 volumes. A vast spectrum of intelligence sources and spies were identified in sensitive positions such as government offices and the military. Several espionage networks, including a full-fledged coup d'état plot, were discovered and foiled.

Meanwhile, we continued to be fascinated by the large barrel of powdered microfilm that stood beside the barrel of shredded documents in the communications room. But it was only two years later, after the hostages had been released, that some of the students from the engineering and medical faculties volunteered to attempt to reconstruct the powder. I had my doubts, but they were determined to press ahead.

The first thing they did was to separate the tiny scraps of microfilm from the powdered paper, using the static properties of the two substances. Then they began studying the shreds of cut microfilm (less than one square millimeter) under a microscope and making enlarged photographs of each. Complex statistical calculations were the next step, to determine the number, size and dimension of each chip in order to evaluate whether this monstrous jigsaw puzzle could ever be put together again.

Initial evaluations were that the job was feasible. But it would be extremely time-consuming and expensive, assuming that we could find sufficient resources to complete it. Unfortunately, we never did, and finally had to abandon the project.

* * *

Some of the reconstituted documents had long-term consequences. Some even shed light upon political events of more than a decade later. One such document pertained to a certain "SD Lure/1," as the CIA referred to him. We obtained seven documents concerning this individual from a safe in what we learned was the CIA station chief's room, in January, 1980. The first document, dated July 27, 1979, dealt with the reports of a meeting between a person called SD Rotter (later identified as Ghashgaie) and CIA officials urging them to contact SD Lure. His telephone number was given in that document, along with the indication that SD Lure first be approached in Paris.

When we checked the number we realized that it belonged to Mr. Bani Sadr himself, the man who was soon to become Iran's president. A later document pinpointed him as a prospective contact and intelligence source. A CIA agent using the code name "Guy Rutherford"[28] (his original identification was "Vernon Cassin") had approached him under the cover of a businessman in Paris. SD Lure had agreed to meet him again in Tehran. The first meeting had taken place a month before the January 1979 revolution, according to the second document.

This document explained that Bani Sadr was told that "Rutherford" was an American "businessman with high-level contacts both in the U.S. business and official world." It continued, "he was apparently sufficiently interested in 'Rutherford' to agree to the latter's request to meet privately." These statements indicated that Bani Sadr knew he was dealing with an influential figure. Considering his political experience, he could not have been naive about the meeting.

"Rutherford" called SD Lure on June 12 1979, and arranged to meet him while ostensibly traveling back from India. He visited Iran under the cover of a company called Carver Associates. The objective of the trip was described as "developing SD Lure and turning him over to an embassy officer."

The remaining documents dealt with the details of arrangements and cover operations for "Rutherford's" arrival in Tehran. Even though Bani Sadr never missed an opportunity to criticize us, we decided that since the evidence did not clearly indicate whether he actually met with the CIA or not, we would not be justified in making them public. Even though we were aware that we could have easily destroyed Bani Sadr, who was a presidential candidate then, the students felt it would be unethical to speak without the necessary evidence. We preferred to stick to our standards rather than attempt to eliminate one of our most spiteful critics, the man who was destined to betray his country.

Early in April the document reconstitution process brought more documents to light. The first was a report on "Rutherford's" meeting with SD Lure at his home on August 29. In it Bani Sadr expressed his hesitations, and criticized the 15-man Revolutionary Council as inefficient. He also expressed reservations about the Imam. The second document was an account of "Rutherford's" meeting with Thomas Ahern. The third, a discussion of his third meeting with Bani Sadr. The final document was Rutherford/Cassin's assessment of his meetings with SD Lure and a summing up of his positive and negative points. "Ambitious and politically astute, he appears to be playing his game cautiously with an eye to the day when Khomeini passes from the scene..." "Being a long-time plotter, he could see his way clear in the future to plot against the regime if either he feels it is drifting away from its revolutionary objectives or that it would be in his own interests to do so…" "He is normally aware that he must be cautious in dealing with those around him…this uncertainty will probably cause him to keep a few doors open" (see Appendix B).

Future events involving Bani Sadr confirmed Rutherford/Cassin's assessment, and demonstrated his capacity for evaluating the personality traits of the other side. The CIA knew they could rely on people who were ambitious, who regarded themselves highly, who displayed no sign of love or devotion to Islam or to the people. They reckoned that people who believed in the Imam would be, like him, uncompromising. The SD Lure case, along with documents pertaining to other political factions or personalities, reflected the analytical capability and strong sense of deduction of the State Department and CIA specialists.

They were well versed in psychology, and were able in their reports to visualize the subject's intentions, aspirations, and views. The only major shortcoming the Americans encountered in their relations with Iran was a congenital inability to admit to a spiritual dimension in human nature.

When the full set of SD Lure documents was complete, we showed them to Thomas Ahern for his comments. Ahern conceded that the American government, and the CIA in particular, planned to contact influential figures in the revolutionary movement. While Imam Khomeini was in Paris, a retired CIA officer was ordered to France to meet Bani Sadr. He had introduced himself as a representative of an American firm, and had expressed a desire to talk with him about the prospects for economic relations with the West. Bani Sadr had agreed.

Ahern added that when he came to Iran "headquarters wanted to follow up on the case and I was assigned to the project. Our final aim was to employ Bani Sadr, but this objective would be realized through various stages. In the first stage he would not be directly informed. He would serve as a financial consultant who would advise on political matters as well. In later stages he would be consulted and advised on more crucial and sensitive affairs."

Ahern also told us that Bani Sadr had agreed to serve as a consultant for a monthly allowance of $1,000. However, he never received any money.

Did Bani Sadr know he was dealing with a CIA agent? we asked Ahern. He replied, "We were not supposed to inform Bani Sadr at this stage that he was dealing with the CIA." However, this account is itself suspect. The unconventional step of offering a $1,000 monthly allowance was not, to our knowledge, a normal business practice. Surely, we reasoned, it would have roused the suspicions of a professional economist familiar with the West with strong political aspirations.

The next area of suspicion was the content of the questions asked. Although they were intended to be economic in nature, they were in reality political and unrelated to economic issues.

The CIA had maintained systematic contact with many influential pro-Western personalities in the administration during the few months before and after the victory of the revolution. But its attempt to influence central policy-makers, and particularly the Imam, were in vain. Had they thought they could change the independent, anti-imperialist nature of the revolution, thus preserving the remainder of their vital interests in Iran? For Washington, the "loss" of Iran was a serious blow, the result of misconceptions and miscalculations by the State Department and the CIA. Now they were trying to correct their policy, in an attempt to compensate for their failure to foresee the overthrow of the shah.

The CIA was faced with a novel dilemma, one it had never encountered before. This time the adversary did not fear the Americans, nor was it intimidated by their threatening gestures. It was as if this adversary was backed up by a novel, unwavering immaterial force, supporting it and urging it on, sweeping aside all worldly powers as it went. The CIA did not succeed in overpowering the will of an extraordinary man, nor could it cause the slightest sense of fear or submission in his heart.

They never were able to understand his perspective, or to predict his strategies. The Americans could defeat a rival in a whole variety of ways. They could use statesmanship, lobbying and compromise, or they could defeat their foe economically, by the use of boycotts, embargoes and pressure tactics, while relying on their immense resources and enormous wealth. And, of course, any military rival could be swept aside by the world's largest, most sophisticated military machine. The one thing they had never expected—a spiritual force—was ultimately to defeat them.

How were they to counter a foe who lacked any of the classical qualities of the enemy? Repeatedly they had miscalculated. Before the embassy occupation ran its course, they were to do so again. Tragically.

Ambassadors of (l. to r.) Algeria, Sweden, Syria and France visit the U.S. Embassy to monitor the welfare of the hostages.

CHAPTER V

NEGOTIATION IMPOSSIBLE

ATTEMPT NUMBER ONE

As THE AMERICAN GOVERNMENT began to grasp the full extent of what had happened, and of its potential impact on the so-called Third World, it moved hastily to broaden and diversify its tactics in an attempt to bring the occupation to an end and release the hostages without making any concession or compromise.

America's allies and Third World clients as well as international organizations were all allied against Iran. That much was clear from the resolutions and declarations of the United Nations (December 4, Resolution 457) and the December 15 ruling of the International Court at The Hague, and the sanctions and political strong-arm tactics that followed. Last but not least was the hostile propaganda of hundreds of radio stations and television channels, periodicals and newspapers. But even the massive campaign against Iran was not enough to compensate for the growing frustration of the Carter administration.

As Gary Sick was later to write:

> The American campaign of persuasion and pressure which was mounted in the days and weeks following the hostage seizure was probably the most extensive and sustained effort of its kind ever to be conducted in peace time. No nation in the world had more resources at its command than the United States. And all of those resources were mobilized to bring the maximum

political, economic, diplomatic, legal, financial and even religious pressure on the revolutionary regime in Tehran.[29]

But these attempts to crush the determination of a country proved ineffective. The Americans were mobilizing their vast material resources in an attempt to eradicate something immaterial. For seekers of fortune or fame, the thought of losing these goals would be enough to cause them to reconsider and seek compromise. However, when the goal is a spiritual one, economic, political and even military threats are not likely to work. Against Iran during the Khomeini era, they were to fail.

The Iranian nation's spiritual motivation was hard, if not impossible, for a secular world to grasp. The American government was astonished, even bewildered, as it faced the unwavering determination of Imam Khomeini, with the whole country fully behind him.

From the first moments of the takeover the Americans were faced with three alternatives: they could submit to the students'—and the people's—demands; they could attempt mediation and persuasion; or they could risk military action.

To extradite the shah to Iran would have had the gravest repercussions for the U.S. imperial system. On the other hand, by admitting the shah, ostensibly for humanitarian reasons, the U.S. had thrown its weight behind the monarchy in opposition to the principles of the Islamic Revolution and democracy in Iran. Extraditing the shah would reverse that position, and be seen as a sign of regret, apology, and perhaps even as weakness.

America's overriding concern was the reaction of its other client states in the region. For heads of state who enjoyed the constant and unwavering support of the United States to become disillusioned was a risk Washington could never tolerate.

Since submission, the first alternative, had never even been considered, the Americans launched a series of high-pressure mediation and persuasion campaigns. From the earliest days of the occupation we ascertained that they were attempting to find influential figures to mediate for them.

Immediately after the takeover we assigned some of the students who had a satisfactory command of English to listen to the foreign radio broadcasts and prepare daily abstracts of news reports on the takeover. BBC Radio, *The Voice of America*, Radio Monte Carlo and Radio Israel were among the stations the students monitored regularly. In addition, we soon began receiving calls from other revolutionary groups sympathetic to our cause, including the Palestine Liberation Organization and several from Latin America.

On Tuesday, November 6, they passed on news of the prospective visit of a two-man American delegation made up of former Attorney General Ramsay Clark and William Miller, a former State Department official, an initiative that revealed haste, carelessness and improvisation.

The Central Committee met to review the matter in detail. We had also learned in the meantime that certain members of the Revolutionary Council—Mr. Bani Sadr and Sadeq Qotbzadeh—had agreed to meet them informally if they came. The committee voted to alert the Imam immediately. He responded with an official statement carried by all Iranian news media the following day:

> In the Name of God, The Merciful, The Compassionate. I have been informed that Carter's special emissaries are on their way to Iran. They plan to come to Qom to meet me. I feel it is necessary to remind all that the American government has hosted the shah and by doing so it has announced its outright opposition to Iran. And on the other hand, as we know, the American Embassy in Iran has been a center of espionage for our enemies. Therefore, the possibility of meeting me is ruled out for the special emissaries, and moreover:
>
> 1) Members of the Revolutionary Council must not meet them under any circumstances; 2) None of the State authorities have the right to meet them; 3) If the U.S. extradites the deposed shah, the top enemy of our dear nation of Iran, and refrains from espionage against our movement, the possibility of negotiation on the subject of certain relations which are in the nation's interest will be open.
>
> Ruhollah Mousavi Khomeini,
> November 7, 1979

The Imam's statement was followed by a communiqué we had issued that same day: "Have we not made it clear that negotiation is impossible and that we demand the extradition of the traitor shah?" Nonetheless, his third condition indicated that he had not closed all doors. For the United States, that one avenue remained open.

The emissaries, who were apparently stuck in Istanbul, had tried in vain to contact us. The students in the communication section who were responsible for handling incoming calls asked me to join them one night in the small phone room in the Chancellery basement. Only a few nights had passed since I joined the occupation, but I was already feeling quite at home. "There's someone on the line. He claims he's Carter's envoy. He wants to speak to someone in charge," one of them said.

"We told him we will not negotiate or even talk, but he insists on talking."

"Then refuse firmly and slam the receiver down," I said. "And don't answer if you hear the same voice. Just hang up." Even an idle exchange with them could have lured one of us into an unwanted situation with unpredictable consequences. We had to be firm and decisive.

Negotiation, of course, was a dirty word in those days. During the revolution the Imam declared that compromisers had undermined their nation. From the beginning, we agreed not to compromise our basic principles. Our country had taken a stand. Not only would we students not back down, we would be the most uncompromising of all. Perhaps what was most astonishing is that, uncompromising as we were, people rallied behind us in their millions.

There were excellent historical reasons for our position, of course. The reign of the Qajar Dynasty, from 1794 to 1925, was tainted with a series of secret agreements to sell off Iran's wealth. Their self-appointed successors, the Pahlavis, sold the integrity of the country through behind-the-scenes deals and concessions. Such, in fact, is the continuing reality in most "underdeveloped" countries where politicians and wealthy elites succumb to the alluring promises of foreign powers to the detriment of the national interest. In Iran the word "negotiation" itself conveys a sense of mistrust and potential betrayal. None of us wanted to replay that tragic theme.

We later learned that Clark and Miller had brought with them a handwritten letter from President Carter. They had also succeeded in talking, though indirectly, with the secretaries of such high-ranking political figures as Bani Sadr and Foreign Minister Sadeq Qotbzadeh. But they never set foot in Iran. On November 15 they left Istanbul in frustration.

The day after Imam Khomeini's declaration messages, telegrams and letters of support poured in. "Negotiation, never! Nothing less than extradition!" chanted the huge crowds of demonstrators that converged on the embassy throughout the day.

Next in line as a mediator was a delegation from the Palestine Liberation Organization. That prospect presented us with a much more serious dilemma.

In the aftermath of the Islamic Revolution, Iran had severed all ties with Israel as a result of its usurpation of Muslim lands and constant oppression of the Palestinian people, not to mention its political and material support, via its supporters in the United States, of the shah's regime.[30] The property belonging to the former Israeli embassy was handed over to the Palestinians, who established a mission there.

From the earliest days of the hostage-taking, the Palestinians in Tehran had contacted Iranian officials in the hope of mediating in the crisis. They then decided to send a senior delegation in an attempt to resolve the issue. However, our position was clear-cut. Even though we appreciated how sincere their efforts were, we were not prepared to make any move without the consent of the Imam himself, and of the country.

We clarified our position in a communiqué broadcast on November 8. There was nothing to negotiate. If there was to be a resolution of the crisis, the shah would have to be returned to Iran. Several senior PLO officers, including Abu Jihad, later visited the embassy. But they came only as visitors, for a friendly exchange of views. Never were they allowed to enter the premises as mediators.

At that time the PLO had a reputable image. Yasser Arafat, the chairman of al-Fatah, was the first foreigner to visit Imam Khomeini after his triumphant return to Tehran. The issue of Palestine and the liberation of al-Qods (Jerusalem) was a vital issue for Iranians, and had become one of the unwavering positions of the Islamic Revolution. We saw the Palestinian cause as a sister revolution to our own. Some people even hoped that the PLO could put pressure on the U.S. They were to be disappointed.

After the failure of the Clark-Miller and the Palestinian missions, the Americans embarked on a desperate campaign to find a channel of dialogue and intelligence, if not negotiation. Henry Precht, the U.S. State Department officer in charge of the Iran desk and a fluent Farsi speaker, phoned the Den of Spies practically every night. His objective was to persuade someone, even one student, to talk to him and come to terms on subjects of mutual interest.

Every night we would spend a few minutes in the telephone room in the Chancellery basement checking the latest news from our informants in Europe and the U.S., and other friends of the revolution throughout the world. One night, I heard a voice speaking Farsi with a foreign accent doing his best to sound persuasive and alluring. As I covered the mouthpiece, one of the other students whispered to me that it was Precht, who soon identified himself.

He had no business phoning the embassy, I told him, returning to the telephone. No one would talk to him; he was wasting his time. It was shortly thereafter that we ascertained that one of the students was spending more time than necessary on the telephone with Precht and other American callers.

It was impossible to guess who it was. Six or more students handled the phone room during each of three eight-hour shifts. The Central Committee decided to monitor all phone contacts carefully, but to do nothing, as the situation still remained uncertain. In an offhand way we let the students working in the phone room know that any display of willingness to talk with the Americans could have grave consequences for our movement. We must act in harmony, speak with one voice, remain determined, and unwilling to succumb. We later shifted one or two of the students in charge of communications. Finally, in March, the uncertainty came to an end.

One morning we found an envelope addressed to one of us on the desk on the second floor of the Chancellery, where we worked on the documents. Inside was an anonymous handwritten letter from one of the students. In it he confessed that he had held regular telephone conversations with American officials. During these conversations he provided information on the students' views, the conditions and the general whereabouts of the hostages, and other information he considered "non-strategic." He felt the deepest regret and repentance, he said. But he revealed nothing of his reasons or his motivation, or the compensation that might have lured him into compromising his principles and his friends.

It didn't take me long to guess the letter-writer's identity. But before making any final judgments I double-checked with his friends and roommates. From them I learned that he'd left the embassy the day before, and did not intend to return. On the basis of the apology, the Central Committee decided to conceal his identity and to take no action against him. There had been an intelligence leak; the Americans—whom we saw as our enemies—might well have obtained crucial information at some of the most critical moments of the embassy occupation. But it never resulted in any tangible benefit for them.

THE HANSEN-ROULEAU DEBACLE

ONE OF THE MOST EXTRAORDINARY mediation attempts was that of the American congressional delegation led by Republican representative from Idaho, George Hansen.[32] This time I was directly involved. During the American Thanksgiving season in late November, 1979, we learned that a delegation of American congressmen was heading for Iran. Its stated aim was to hear the grievances of the Iranian nation, and then try to untangle what had become a case of gridlock for the Carter administration.

The visiting congressmen met with several Iranian officials who'd agreed to the encounter on the understanding that they were representatives of the American people, not the government. Throughout their visit they repeatedly asked to visit the students holding the embassy.

We discussed the matter and the Central Committee gave the go-ahead. Our understanding was that the congressmen had come on their own, and were not using their trip as a pretext to begin negotiations about freeing the hostages. Two members of the Central Committee were appointed to meet with Hansen.

The appointed day arrived. Our public relations section was well-prepared for the meeting, and we had requested that Islamic Republic radio and television record the event. I had been involved with the public relations unit since I joined the students. Considering the huge demand for interviews, the unit was a very busy one; we gave at least five interviews every day. I usually interpreted for the members of the Central Committee and in some cases I was interviewed as the spokesperson for the students.

The delegation arrived on schedule and we guided the congressmen from the southern gate into the public relations section located close to the south-western entrance. The unit was located in the former embassy library. We used the larger rooms for press conferences, meetings and interviews, and the smaller ones for offices.

Mohsen was responsible for the preparations, and led our "welcoming committee" as it accompanied the delegation through the grounds. As we progressed, the Americans looked about them. We could imagine them wondering 'where are they holding the hostages?' In the conference room, which we normally used for larger scale press events, we had set up a longer table and more chairs. Directly behind one row of chairs we hung a large poster made up of hundreds of smaller pictures of martyrs of the revolution. In the center, written in Farsi, was a line from Dr. Ali Shariati. It read: "The Martyr is the Heart of History."

Our choice of this quote was no accident. The martyr who sacrifices his or her life for the sake of a lofty goal becomes an impetus and a source of inspiration for those who follow. He or she, in putting selfish desires aside, strives for the betterment of all.

The martyr is like a heart, pumping the fresh blood of life and vitality into the veins of a moribund and static society, Dr. Shariati had taught us. But how much of this could an American congressional delegation understand? The English translation was posted prominently, but would George Hansen grasp the spiritual dimension of our message? Although we had our doubts, we were prepared to make an attempt at dialogue.

Ibrahim, our chief representative, and Hansen sat on one side of the table and I sat on the other so the cameras could get the proper shots.

It quickly became clear that Hansen had other things on his mind. His initial request was to speak confidentially with the students in charge, then afterwards to talk only about generalities for the cameras. That, he assured us, was standard policy for contemporary politicians and policy makers. But we were neither politicians nor policy makers. What did we have to conceal?

"We see no need for confidential talks. We have nothing to hide from the country or the world. Say anything you want right here," Ibrahim replied, pointing at the television cameras.

Hansen insisted: "Just a few minutes of confidential talks."

The students refused. The showdown continued for several minutes until Hansen realized that we weren't about to back down, and relented.

He was clearly feeling the stress. As he began to speak, with the cameras rolling, his anger began to show in the tone of his voice and the speed of his articulation. First he described the concern felt by Americans for the sufferings of the Iranian people. Then he went on to state that the release of the hostages would enable the Congress to take certain measures for the extradition of the shah.

The students' response could not have been more forthright and direct. Our conditions—in reality, the conditions of the country as a whole as we had interpreted them—would have to be met, explained Ibrahim. We were not prepared to take a single step backward. The American administration had committed innumerable crimes in Iran and must pay for them. However, we were asking only for the extradition of the dictator and the repatriation of our wealth. Was that too much?

As he grew more flustered, Hansen began to talk faster and faster. He had apparently lost control. I was doing the best I could to keep up with his high-speed diction in an attempt to interpret accurately, but it was getting more difficult by the minute. Hansen seemed to be talking at the speed of sound, repeating himself again and again. It was becoming obvious that he had nothing new to say. Neither did we, for that matter.

By now, I was losing patience. The talks—which were more like a monologue—were taking longer than we'd expected. The heat from the floodlights was annoying everyone. Hansen's nervous, impulsive tone had taken on a domineering edge. Even though he was sitting among a group of militant students, he was still determined to have everything his way. After his lengthy outburst, we still didn't know what he was after.

We stated our position for the world to hear: "We have no enmity for the American people. This is not an act of revenge. We only want to restore our natural rights."

Ibrahim's concluding remarks ended the program. As we escorted our guests to the southern gate, Hansen became even more uneasy and visibly frustrated. He mentioned the matter of confidential talks once again as he left. "Impossible," came the answer.

Throngs of people were milling in the street as Hansen and his delegation were leaving. An old woman in the front row was shouting, "Death to America!" Hansen must have realized that his government was up against more than what they dismissively termed "a group of militant students." They had an entire country on their hands. As for the interview, it proved to be what we might call the beginning of the end of his mediation efforts. Later events clarified this for us.

As the session had been broadcast by satellite for the American audience, our friends in the U.S., began calling us to express their views on the encounter. They supported us and admired our resolve. "Hansen was clearly frustrated," one of them said. Some of us were in the communications room all night, and heard most of their views and reports. One of the more attentive listeners mentioned an interesting point which we later followed up on. Hansen had used words which called for a response, but which I had unintentionally overlooked. According to the caller, Hansen had said that just as a government has different departments, here in Iran "you students are also part of the government."

They took up the matter with me. It was well after midnight but I was still awake. At first I was so confident of the accuracy of my translation that I denied hearing any such statement. But then I added, a bit defensively, "Well, you were there, you saw how fast he was talking. I kept asking him to speak slower. I had to interrupt him at shorter intervals to interpret, but yes, I think it could be. We'll have to listen to the tape."

Back we went to the public relations sections where Mohsen was in charge. He handed us the tape. We listened to it carefully. The statement was there, all right. "You students here are part of the government." I was deeply concerned. "How could I have missed that?"

The sisters comforted me. "You did the best you could. Hansen was speaking so fast nobody could keep up with him."

"But that statement has to be answered. It's a lie. We are not part of the government!" I exclaimed, distressed and angry with myself. I assured them I would bring up the matter with the Central Committee.

They were as surprised as I was. The only solution was to raise the point and clarify it in future interviews, which we did. Mr. Khoeiniha brought up the issue in the general meeting of the students after noon prayers. "Hansen made that remark intentionally. He meant that we have done this under orders from the government. We have to respond," he said.

But that was not to be the last of Hansen's mediation attempts. Two days after his stormy visit, the public relations section gave an interview appointment to Eric Rouleau, the prominent French journalist and later diplomat who was then working for *Le Monde*. Since large numbers of reporters were clamoring for interviews, the public relations section would select those whose reporting seemed more honest or balanced. They were then granted interviews in the order in which they applied.

Due to heavy demand, it usually took at least one week from the time the request was made until an interview appointment was arranged.

Eric Rouleau had interviewed the students before. His reports had been relatively fair and objective. When he asked for an interview with Mr. Khoeiniha, the public relations section had, with Mr. Khoeiniha's approval, given Rouleau a second appointment.

Once again, I would be the interpreter. I was waiting when Rouleau arrived, met him and guided him into the conference room. Reza was standing in for Mohsen that day as the person in charge of the public relations section. When Rouleau arrived at 9:45, he phoned the Central Committee and asked Mr. Khoeiniha to come.

Mr. Khoeiniha was always calm, and his gentle manner expressed a deep faith and determination. When he arrived I guided him into the room. Rouleau stood and greeted him as Mr. Khoeiniha took a seat nearby. Three chairs had been arranged in the form of a triangle, with a small table in the middle. Rouleau, as before, had no cameraman or even a tape recorder. He would take notes of what was being said. The Frenchman was then in his early fifties; his hair and beard were already gray.

Rouleau began speaking and I began translating at short intervals.

Initially he thanked Mr. Khoeiniha for granting the interview and commented on his previous interview with the students. Then he spoke a sentence which put my teeth on edge. Reza was standing near the door, close to Rouleau. Mr. Khoeiniha and I were seated. No one else was present in the room. Rouleau said: "I have something confidential to say. May I proceed?" while motioning his head in our direction. He was clearly referring to us, asking whether Mr. Khoeiniha trusted us. Mr. Khoeiniha responded, "No one here is a stranger, go ahead."

Rouleau then launched into a long monologue. The hostage affair had turned into a deadlock to the detriment of our objectives. He was concerned for our revolution, or so he claimed. There was no point in holding the hostages any longer. We had to gain points by freeing them now, he believed. As I interpreted, I was becoming uneasier by the moment. At one point I interrupted the interpretation process and exclaimed in Farsi, "He is trying to say something else. Mr. Khoeiniha. This is not an ordinary interview." Then I resumed interpreting.

After much beating around the bush, Rouleau came to the critical point. "Hansen has a reasonable proposal. I think it is to your benefit. It serves the objectives of the revolution. He guarantees that if you free three, or two or even one hostage and send them back with him, he could convince Congress to pass a resolution for the extradition of the shah, after which he would come back and you would release some more."

'Does he think this is a grocery store?' I thought. I whispered in Farsi, "Just as I suspected. He has come with a deal." I then translated his proposal word for word.

Mr. Khoeiniha was poised, listening attentively until that moment. He cleared his throat and began, "In the name of God, the Merciful, the Compassionate…I ask you Mr. Rouleau: have you come here for an interview or for mediation and negotiation? You have damaged your reputation, Mr. Rouleau, by using the time you were granted for an interview for other spiteful matters. We granted you an interview with the understanding that *Le Monde* has a relatively liberal and objective position among European media, and because we have known you as a comparatively honest reporter. But now you have damaged that reputation. We will not compromise. If we wanted to negotiate, we would have done so in front of the cameras for the world to see, but we have no such intention. Mr. Rouleau, not only will I refrain from speaking with you any longer, but I will ask you to leave the embassy immediately and you will never be granted permission to enter again."

Mr. Khoeiniha made his final statement firmly and before I could finish the translation, he rose and headed for the door at a rapid pace with a stern expression on his face. Rouleau was wide-eyed with shock, as if he could not believe what he had just seen or heard. I stood up as well: "You lost your chance, Mr. Rouleau. Please follow me, I will show you the way out." Reza opened the door as I took the lead. Rouleau followed behind us, shaken. We showed him to the gate.

DOUBLE-DEALING AND DECEIT

IN EARLY FEBRUARY 1979, the Imam was suddenly hospitalized with severe heart complications. His illness deeply affected the students, who by then were coming under increased pressure from certain government authorities to compromise. We believed that in our ongoing campaign we had only the Imam and the people behind us.

We convened meetings in the embassy compound to pray for the Imam's health. Our love and devotion for him flowed from his spiritual power and superior personality. His character was our source of inspiration; his personality and behavior gave us our yardstick for distinguishing right from wrong. Making that distinction may be simple enough in the abstract, but when it comes to the heat of action, you need a model.

Like many Iranians, we were convinced that no human being could overcome his selfishness, his ego-centered attitude, except perhaps a Prophet, a Saint or one of the Twelve Innocent Imams.[33] Imam Khomeini was an ordinary man, but one endowed with an extraordinary determination to rid himself of the lusts and selfish desires that all of us must suffer from throughout our lives.

What could be more natural than for us to feel depressed when the Imam fell ill? It must have been strange for the world to see the devotion of the young generation in Iran to an 85-year-old man whom they considered their role model, instead of some movie star or pop singer.

At the same time that the Imam had fallen ill, we had received several reports from the world-wide network of supporters and informants that we called our "information services" that the Americans had actually contacted Iranian officials, including Foreign Minister Sadeq Qotbzadeh and President Abolhassan Bani Sadr, who had been elected on January 25, 1980, in the hope of devising a scenario for the release of the hostages, with no concessions from the American side.

(We later realized that by transferring Chargé d'affaires Bruce Laingen and another American diplomat to the Iranian foreign ministry, Qotbzadeh had, in fact, established a line of communication with the

U.S. government. The request to move the officials had come from the Revolutionary Council, and was submitted to us by Qotbzadeh himself when he visited the embassy ten days after the takeover. He argued that someone be able to speak on behalf of the hostages, and that the highest official among them be permitted contact with the Americans and allowed to send messages. We were not pleased with this development, but because it came from the Council we agreed. Later we became convinced that Qotbzadeh had been acting on behalf of the Carter government more than on behalf of Iran's revolutionary leadership.)

Because we knew exactly where the Imam stood we were confident that he would not allow such a compromise to take place. In fact, I remembered hearing on the radio his conversation with the representative of Kim Il Sung (December 7, 1979) well before the reports about Qotbzadeh and Bani Sadr were released. In that meeting he spoke about the role of the Majlis that was about to be elected and indirectly ruled that the power of decision for solving the hostage affair should be given to the legitimate representatives of the nation. Others, including Revolutionary Council members, did not take his statement seriously at the time . Either that, or they deliberately neglected it in the hope of advancing their plans for a speedy solution of the matter in their own interests.

On February 20, the Revolutionary Council informed us that a United Nations fact-finding commission would be arriving in Tehran. The aim of the commission, they said, would be to hear the grievances of the Iranian nation which would then be published in the form of a U.N. document. They also told us that the commission had placed one condition on submitting the report. That condition was permission to see all the hostages.

Representatives from the Revolutionary Council came to speak with us about the matter. In one instance, during a meetings at which I was present, we raised the basic question of realism. Had the U.N. launched this initiative on its own or was this another American ploy, this time under a U.N. cover? Qotbzadeh later replied to our inquiry, assuring the brothers and sisters that the mission had been planned by the U.N., not the U.S. Former Assistant Secretary of State for Near Eastern and South

Asian Affairs Harold Saunders' subsequent account of the affair proved Qotbzadeh's claims to be false.[34]

In fact, the United States had actually done the planning and lobbying, drawn up the protocol and, after everything had been decided, asked certain international figures to perform. I never ceased to be astonished how an international and intellectual body of human beings, such as the United Nations, which claims to serve the cause of humanity, could tolerate such tutelage, not to say subjection, from a superpower.

Bani Sadr was now in office.[35] We had not exposed anything relating to his embassy file, since at that time the first four documents we had discovered in which his name appeared were not convincing enough to indicate a tangible relationship with the CIA. We were to realize soon enough that we had been over-optimistic in our estimate of Bani Sadr. Before the elections, he had obliquely referred to the hostage-taking in pessimistic and doubtful tones. He had largely concealed his real convictions, however, until after he was sworn in as head of state. He then began to express open opposition to the views of the Imam, the students and the nation on the hostage question.

Bani Sadr was looking for a rapid solution which would relieve him of the affair and also strengthen Jimmy Carter's position in the upcoming presidential elections. In his memoirs he later suggested that he supported any action which favored Carter's election. The implication, as we saw it, was that he had struck a deal with the Carter entourage. Bearing in mind Bani Sadr's previous CIA contacts and the probability that they were continuing, I would guess, though it cannot be proven, that a deal with Carter had already been done through established contacts. The idea would be for Carter and the Democrats to maintain their control of the White House for another term while Bani Sadr would be freed of the burden of the hostages.

During our many verbal confrontations Bani Sadr and Qotbzadeh denounced us outright, Bani Sadr condemning us for acting like a government within a government.

Tensions grew when they understood how accurate our analysis had been, and how well-founded our consequent suspicion about the U.N.

commission of inquiry. Our network of supporters and informants had informed us, correctly in the event, of the commission's real intentions. The strategy was to unfold as follows: the commission was to refuse to publish any report on Iran's grievances until the hostages had been hospitalized. This would be the result of falsified reports of their failing health by the commission. Then the hostages would be transferred to "safe" hands and freed.

As it turned out, the commission did not care at all about the grievances of the Iranian people. For the commission members, the 50 years of subjugation, oppression, exploitation, torture and subsequent backwardness of thirty million Iranians paled in comparison to the plight of 52 Americans. For six consecutive days Qotbzadeh and Bani Sadr pressured us through all conceivable channels to agree to a compromise.

We had agreed to allow the commission to visit some of the hostages—but not all. The commission insisted on seeing every single hostage. The Imam had by then recovered, and clearly restated that the matter of the hostages would be dealt with by the Majlis. Nevertheless, Qotbzadeh and Bani Sadr ignored his decree in the hope of implementing their own strategy.

I remember one of those nights well. As I was returning to the dormitory at 2:00 a.m. after a session of work on the documents a brother on guard duty stopped me in the dark corridors of the visa building. It was regular practice to stop all passersby and ask for the "night code," a password that changed daily and had to be known by those who moved within the embassy quarters after dark.

To my embarrassment, I had forgotten to ask that particular night's code. Now I was attempting to enter the visa building, where the women's dormitories were located, to get some sleep. In a firm voice, the brother asked me for the password. In the darkness I could make out the outline of the G-3 rifle aimed right at me. "Unfortunately I forgot to ask. I don't know."

He asked me to put my hands on my head. "Identify yourself. Who are you? Where are you coming from?" I gave him my name and university, and told him I was coming from the document center where I had been working. Fortunately for me, he recognized my name, even though he was from another university. "Remember the night code or you'll be caught," he joked.

"Double dealing and deceit" was that night's code—a clear reference to Bani Sadr's scheme.

We resolved to hold fast to our position in the conviction that a national issue, in which the destiny of the people was at stake, had to be resolved on the basis of their own decision and interests and not those of the United States. The so-called U.N. scenario had been written unilaterally by the Americans, with the aim of luring Iran into a deal. Saunders later wrote, "We talked about how each step (of the ploy) could be described in ways and revolutionary language to have maximum appeal in Tehran."[36]

The standoff between us and Bani Sadr and Qotbzadeh soon came to a head. We were determined to take the matter to the Imam and ask his final view on the affair. in the meantime, Mr. Mousavi Khoeiniha had briefed the Imam on the backstage maneuvering. Imam Khomeini had also conferred with members of the Revolutionary Council. We announced that we were prepared to conform to the Imam's instructions.

We knew the Imam very well. He had consistently displayed the same lucidity throughout the years when he led the resistance to the shah from exile, first in Turkey, then in Iraq, and finally at Neuphle-le-Château, near Paris. Imam Khomeini's decisions would not be influenced by personal aspirations or tainted by selfishness, of that we were certain. He would choose what he believed was equitable and correct, and in the higher interests of the country.

Our proposal was that the commission visit some of the hostages whose identities were known and whose illegal activities were in contravention of all the international conventions the Americans speciously claimed to adhere to so strictly. The commission could use these individuals as additional evidence for the crimes of the U.S. in Iran. Our proposal was a tactical one. We knew perfectly well that the commission had no such intention in its mandate. We were also learning quickly that international politics is a rough game. Still, two could play that game, we concluded.

On March 10, Imam Khomeini issued a statement which lifted the pressure from our shoulders.[37] After all, we were students and not professional diplomats, politicians or statesmen. He ruled that the commission could study the relevant documents in the embassy and interview any hostage it deemed necessary in this regard. In the event the commission members agreed to publish their views on the crimes of the U.S. and the shah before leaving Tehran, they would be granted permission to visit all the hostages. In fact, the Imam had approved the initial stages of the U.N. scenario, but added a twist. In a masterful and brilliant stroke, he changed the order of the two stages of the plan. If the commission did not mean to deceive the Iranian nation, its requests would be complied with. The Imam concluded by reiterating that the Majlis alone had responsibility for resolving the issue.

That night it was my turn for guard duty. As usual, the central operations unit informed all students on guard in the embassy over the wireless, "Attention all units, the code for tonight is: 'Imam saved the day.' Repeat: 'Imam saved the day.'" The brothers on the other receivers sarcastically replied in whispers, "And Bani Sadr was about to ruin it!"

The commission left Iran on March 11, empty-handed. But our conflicts with the Bani Sadr-Qotbzadeh cabal continued.

I had one telephone confrontation with Qotbzadeh myself. He had called to try to persuade us of the error of our ways, and specifically to stop releasing the compromising documents we had uncovered. His taste of power had made him even more arrogant than before. He was convinced he alone was correct, and that he could single-handedly bring the occupation to an end.

"You're making the error," I told him. "The Imam has asked us to expose these documents. Only those with something to hide need worry. We intend to go ahead for the benefit of the country."

He accused us of playing into the hands of the "extremists." "We have to solve the matter rapidly, it's not in Iran's interests. I'm just as revolutionary as you are, but you're going too far."

That's when I realized that it was useless. I was wasting my time. In fact, the phone call had come just at the time that Bani Sadr was pressing for release of some hostages as a goodwill gesture. Qotbzadeh claimed to support the students, but he talked against us behind our back. In their view, we were young, emotional radicals.

In one sense, we were. But these were the very qualities that gave us the strength to act as we had. Although we had rapidly acquired a political education in the three months since the embassy takeover, we hadn't yet learned what was foremost in all politicians' concerns: self-preservation. Unlike Bani Sadr and Qotbzadeh, we didn't have a career plan.

At the same time, we knew very well that we had to handle the issue cautiously. After all, there were supporters of Bani Sadr among the students. He was well known as a scholar, an intellectual and as an eloquent orator. He had a strong following. But as the occupation and the struggle over control of the hostages continued, it became increasingly clear that he and Qotbzadeh were playing a double game.

As a result, even the students who had originally supported him began to waver. Bani Sadr's dogged insistence and his intense efforts to transfer the hostages to the custody of the government strengthened our conviction that he was acting on very real commitments he had made secretly to the Carter administration.

Carter was growing desperate, and we knew it. Time was running out. He had lost heavily in many of the primaries, which meant that he was grasping for straws. I later read Harold Saunders' remarks which dovetailed with this idea. "Since none of the few channels to the religious leaders seemed likely to produce results, the administration fell back to the one approach available to it—working with secular figures on the scene."[38]

Carter's only hopes were Bani Sadr and Qotbzadeh; and Bani Sadr in particular. Previous lines of communication had been established with Bani Sadr which could easily be restored. Bani Sadr himself had many reasons to close ranks with Carter against the nation on the hostage issue.

In fact, the idea of the U.N. Commission was also a mask for a deal devised to protect Bani Sadr, who must have sensed what was at stake for him, and for his special relationship with the United States. It was hardly surprising that he intensified his efforts to gain greater American confidence by at least removing the hostages from the students' control. His efforts failed due to stiff opposition from such members of the Revolutionary Council as Dr. Beheshti and finally the Imam himself.

Christmas celebration, December 25, 1979. At the piano, Rev. William Sloan Coffin.

CHAPTER VI

HOSTAGES AND STUDENTS—LIFE ON THE INSIDE

ONE OF THE HOSTAGES waved the book under my nose with a laugh. "Is this really what you think we should be reading?" It was a paperback copy of *The Great Escape*.

During the early weeks of the occupation, before we'd been able to set up a proper library, some of our fellow students had somehow laid hands on a stack of pulp novels and non-fiction books for the hostages to read. It was apparent that they had not been too careful in choosing the titles. I couldn't help laughing.

"Go ahead, read it. You might find some useful suggestions," I replied.

While a deadly serious political struggle was unfolding around us, we also had much more down-to-earth, human concerns. In taking the embassy personnel hostage, we had accepted responsibility for them. Discharging that responsibility became, in itself, a full-time task, one that we had not anticipated when the takeover had been planned. The hostages had begun as our only currency, our bargaining chips. But with the passage of time, they took on a distinctly human dimension.

Over time, the students developed seemingly friendly relationships with many—perhaps most—of the hostages. Some of us spent our watch chatting with them, discussing everything from the quality of the food to international politics. The women students were assigned to the two women hostages who had remained after the release of the first group. We often chatted, particularly when we took them for fresh air and exercise.

The Western media had successfully depicted our relationship with the hostages as one of jailers to inmates. We believed otherwise at the time. Had we not done our best to treat them as human beings? We had to maintain security, of course, but we tried to be as flexible as possible in meeting the needs of the 50 or so Americans. However, I cannot deny today that the hostages were our captives, that we were holding them against their will, and that this fundamental reality was bound to influence the way they responded to us, no matter how much sympathy we expressed for their plight as individuals, no matter how many friendly chats we may have had.

Considering the strong anti-U.S. government feelings which we experienced during those years, even that could prove difficult at times. As days passed and we pieced the shredded documents together, we found more and more stark evidence that the embassy had transgressed diplomatic norms and had quite consciously involved itself in attempts to undermine the Islamic Revolution. As it became clear that many of the hostages—particularly those at the higher levels—had been deeply implicated in these maneuvers, we experienced the greatest difficulty in maintaining a civil attitude. We had to keep reminding ourselves that we had captured the embassy and taken the hostages out of principled opposition to a grievous offense to our country, motivated by our religious convictions and with a view to restoring our rights. We had not acted out of revenge against a handful of spies and guards.[39]

As for the hostages, if they ever tried to "turn" us they certainly were not very good at it. They must have realized we had enormous popular support, and we had the feeling they knew that their government had been involved in wrong-doing. I recall an argument with one of the hostages. I was trying to explain that the monarchy's oil policy was designed for the benefit of the United States, and that Iran had been the loser. The hostage reacted by saying that it was Iran's fault for raising the price of oil. "You Iranians are always blaming others for your failure to take responsibility," he said.

For security reasons the hostages were held in different places at different times. Their windows were barred, but could be opened for fresh air and natural light. They were given regular outdoor exercise. But if they were caught stealing, hiding, or passing notes, these exercise privileges were denied. One hostage who stole a radio from a sleeping student was deprived of exercise for a week. There were a few instances where hostages turned violent, but never directly toward the students. Any violent outbursts would also lead to probation, or loss of library and movie privileges.

For me, the two hour night guard duty was a good chance to catch up on my reading. During my shift, the women were asleep and only rarely would the hostages need to use the washroom. Then they would have to be blindfolded in the corridors for security reasons. However, my favorite shift was sentry duty in the woods on the embassy grounds, where I could breathe in the fresh air during the cool hours before sunrise.

The daytime security shifts were much busier. In the morning, we prepared and served breakfast, which we delivered to each of the hostage's rooms where, as a rule, they ate, either alone or with their roommates. When they were dispersed to the provinces following the failed rescue operation, the routine was modified, of course. But we always attempted to keep life as predictable as possible for our involuntary guests.

The morning routine also involved taking them for a bath. We had access to a limited number of bathrooms in the other sections of the embassy and the walk between them was a long one. We preferred to take them two by two, by car, to the ambassador's or the chargé's residence and back. Most days, when the weather was fine, we arranged for the hostages to exercise outdoors for half an hour. We had cordoned off a large space behind the ambassador's residence for this purpose. There, either singly or with their roommate, they could jog or do calisthenics. We kept the hostages separated to minimize the possibility of contact and communication among them.

Then at one o'clock lunch was served. The food was of excellent quality, thanks to the embassy's Pakistani cook, Muhammad Yusuf,[40] whom we paid $2,000 a month. He knew how to cook for his former employers, and most important, he knew where things were. Prepare the food they like, we told him. It was typical American fare, of course, especially in the early days. Meals would consist of fried chicken, meat-loaf with green beans and mashed potatoes, soup, spaghetti, steaks with vegetables, hamburgers and French-fries.

As we had never planned to detain the Americans for such a long time, our supplies had been planned to last for two or three days. As soon as it became clear that we were going to be holding the embassy for an undetermined period, we were forced to do some serious budgetary and logistical planning.

Within the embassy's walls we had come, soon after the takeover, upon a large supermarket with a seemingly endless variety of foodstuffs, clothing, household appliances and anything else you could care to think of. Termed "the commissary" by the Americans themselves, the market was reserved exclusively for diplomatic personnel. Nothing like it in terms of scale or variety existed in Tehran. Gigantic freezers packed with meat and vegetables were to provide food for the hostages throughout their stay in the compound.

We ourselves never touched that food. One reason was that the meat was not "halal," meaning it was unfit for consumption according to Islamic dietary laws. So the Sepah, Islamic Revolutionary Guard Corps (IRGC), volunteered to provide us three meals a day. But their generosity created another problem: the food was terrible, usually consisting of that Iranian staple, rice, with microscopic lumps of meat, just enough to keep our stomachs full. For the evening meal, traditionally the main one in Iran, they usually prepared what we called "cutlet," a kind of fried meat that had the taste and texture of shoe leather. Small wonder we preferred to fast.

But we couldn't complain. The hostages were well fed, and, although our food was close to inedible, we never starved. All we had to do was serve ourselves and clean our dishes and utensils. Every once in a while, relief came in the form of food offered to us by people who were giving thanks for prayers answered. This food was home-cooked and delicious. The combination of mass-produced military food and offerings left us with almost no expenses for feeding ourselves.

After the needs of the hostages had been met, most of the clothing and other durable goods in the commissary were distributed to needy families. A group of students was appointed to oversee planning and distribution with the assistance of local charitable organizations. The great majority of the students had no access to the embassy supplies, and little knowledge of their existence.

As one of the few with access, I still remember the large quantities of cake mixes. The remaining women hostages would spend hours in the kitchen transforming the mixes into cakes with frostings and icings, which were then shared with the other hostages. On more than one occasion they offered the students a slice of cake, but many of us politely declined.

Inside the embassy we also discovered a cache of dollars. This we spent on the Americans, and on various items related to them throughout the 444 days, as well as paying current operating expenses at the Den of Spies. The embassy's vehicle pool we used for transportation within and outside the compound.

When the hostages were finally removed from the embassy grounds, the system of allocating and distributing food and budgeting expenditures became much more complex. But no matter what arose, we knew we could count on the people. The links we had built up over the weeks and months proved to be solid and long-lasting.

* * *

Early on in the occupation, officials from the Red Cross asked to visit the hostages. We granted their request, but restricted it to one area where no more than 20 were being held. As the Red Cross inspectors arrived dinner was being served. To this day I remember the menu exactly: soup, rice, minced beef, carrots and green peas. While the officials were visiting the hostages' rooms and checking their conditions, I suddenly heard shouting from down the hall. I hurried off in the direction of the voice.

One of the older hostages, Mr. Keough, was complaining loudly and bitterly. In front of him was a tray of hot food. He was waving a spoon in the air.

"This is uncivilized!" he shouted.

The Red Cross officials rushed into the room.

"What exactly are you complaining about?" I asked him.

"I cannot eat without a fork. It's uncivilized."

"But how can you eat rice with a fork? And forks create a security problem for us," I answered.

I was wasting my breath. He was determined to get his fork, right then and there, in front of the Red Cross delegation which was quickly taking note of the event as a denial of human rights.

The hostages spent their afternoons watching films, or visiting the library. Other days they would spend in their rooms, reading, writing letters or playing games. Dinner was served early, American style. I later read the memoirs of several of the hostages, particularly those of Rocky Sickman. To his credit, he paints a fair picture of those days. He even comments that, "the service was great, like a hotel, if only we'd been free." In another day's entry he comments on the friendly relations that developed between many of the hostages and the students, which gave the lie to the propaganda then circling the globe. Of that label used to malign Swedish humanitarianism, the "Stockholm Syndrome," not a trace was to be found.

Letters from friends and relatives were allowed on condition that they contained only family news and expressions of love and emotion. We could not run the risk of allowing intelligence information to leak through to the hostages, or news that might make them nervous or desperate. In that sense, no news was the best news. Many of the hostages would admit later on that hearing the news—particularly as it involved the ups and downs of the embassy crisis and the Tabas attack— would have made them increasingly nervous and impatient.

Still, there can be no doubt that the hostages experienced trying times. During the first days, due to a shortage of space and for security reasons, we were forced to move about ten of them, including the military attachés, out of the embassy premises to a deserted residence belonging to a former member of the royal family. Only a handful of students was involved; no one else was informed.

This group was held at the palace for a month. By that time, security at the embassy had improved and the situation was stabilized. In the meantime, we opened up a large area that had not been previously used. Then the group was transferred back to the compound.

At one point, three or four of the hostages developed severe dental problems. We arranged with a local dentist and took them to his office to have their teeth filled. In addition, we saw to it that the entire group had monthly medical and random dental check-ups. Robert Ode, one of the hostages, insisted on suntan lotion when he was allowed out of doors. There was plenty of it in the commissary, so we kept him well supplied.

But despite our best efforts to meet the daily needs and feasible requests of the hostages, it would not be fair to say that we were totally successful. Our response was to set up a special committee to manage hostage affairs. Students were assigned responsibilities for coordinating and overseeing food preparation and service, daily programs, interviews and overall security. One of its jobs was to prepare a file on each individual hostage. The files included notes on their jobs, their behavior and their problems.

One evening in late January, as I was working on the documents, one of the students on the hostage committee came to see me. He asked me if I could spare some time to solve a serious problem that had come up. One of the hostages had gone on a hunger strike. I agreed immediately, knowing that since most of my fellow-students did not have a strong command of English, they might have some difficulty communicating with the Americans.

We made our way quickly to the Chancellery building. There, in a room on the first floor, I came upon Don Hohman, the mission's health officer. He was sitting on a sofa, his head hanging on his chest. He had been without food for three days. I began by saying, "Mr. Hohman, I have come to see you and hear your requests. If they are within our power, we will fulfill them."

At first he kept silent. I told him that his hunger strike would make things more difficult not only for him, but for everyone, and it would solve nothing. He replied that he cared about nothing, not even his own life. Life was a God-given blessing to be preserved, I answered. We must make the best of it by struggling against obstacles and patiently enduring difficulties.

He was no longer important to anyone, Hohman repeated. He no longer had any incentive for living.

"You're wrong," I told him. "Your life is important for two groups of people."

First, his family was eagerly awaiting his return. His children were longing for the day that their father would come home. And second, his life was important to Iran, as a symbol of a country's legitimate demands.

I told him that if we had not seized the embassy, the world would never have realized how much suffering and oppression the American government had inflicted on our people. But today the media have been forced to depict, even though in a distorted manner, the discontent of the Iranian people as a consequence of fifty years of American domination.

Hohman was listening. It was as if he wanted to hear our reasons for taking them hostage. In dealing with him, I had to walk a fine line between the human and the political aspects of the case. I had to explain that the hostages were taken to uphold and safeguard human values, while somehow admitting that holding people prisoner was not, in itself, a human value. We had to strike a delicate balance. We wanted to make hostages' lives as bearable as possible; this was dictated by our religious beliefs. But we had to stick to our principles, to the reasons that had driven us to action in the first place. I went to talk to Hohman with the goal of understanding his motivations, and of encouraging him to understand ours. Other students may have been harsh with him, I admitted. It was obvious from our acts that we were not happy. But, I reassured him, we were not looking for revenge.

In normal circumstances, I explained, no one would have cared a whit for our grievances, as the whole world system is subjugated to America's imperatives. The international judiciary and legislative system, the

United Nations and the International Court at The Hague, and even the international bodies that claim to defend human rights—all are under American influence.[41] Where would we take our case? Who would listen to us?

The decisions of the powerful have never benefited the oppressed. If the downtrodden want their case to be considered and their sufferings made known, they must find a new strategy, one capable of paralyzing the existing institutions and mechanisms of domination.

Our discussion continued until well after midnight. Finally, Hohman had begun to talk about his feelings for his family. "They are the only thing I care about, and I don't even have their picture." One of the students went off to search Hohman's belongings. He quickly returned with a picture of his wife and children. "I'm a vegetarian," he added. "I can't eat most of the food you serve me."

"I'll speak with the food distribution unit and try to remedy that," I said.

In spite of his gloomy claims that he did not care for or believe in anything, Hohman was a genuinely committed, caring individual. Gradually, he began to relax, his voice became warmer. Finally, I asked him, "Would you like to eat something?" He nodded. I spoke to some of the students in the room. It was now 3:30 in the morning. Where could we find food at this hour? Somehow they did: a large can of fruit cocktail, which they served on a tray with a spoon. I was exhausted. I said goodnight to Hohman and stumbled through the darkness back to the women's sleeping quarters in the visa building.

* * *

In mid-December, 1979, we began to make plans to celebrate Christmas for the hostages, at the suggestion of Imam Khomeini. The Central Committee drew up a plan to invite American clergymen who believed in "liberation theology" and were open-minded in their social, and political outlook. Since Christmas is a season for renewing or strengthening ties with the Creator, we reasoned that such a celebration would lift up the morale of the hostages.

Our friends in the United States agreed to find suitable persons and to invite them to travel to Iran. As people on the receiving end of United States foreign policy, we knew that Americans knew little of what its government did in their name. This was no accident, but the direct consequence of the covert nature of those policies. We also knew, via our "sources," that parts of the American population were not particularly content with the prevailing political trend, nor with the socio-economic path the nation was following. This mentality was noticeable among many clergymen, we soon learned. Reverend William Sloan Coffin, Reverend Thomas Gobbleto, and Father William Howard of the Council of Christian Churches were among them. Archbishop Hilarion Capucci had also made known his desire to attend the ceremonies. In recognition of his life-long struggle against Zionist oppression, we extended our warmest invitation to the prelate of Palestine.

We decorated two of the largest rooms in the Chancellery with a Christmas tree and other ornaments in keeping with the American holiday season tradition. Our creative Pakistani chef prepared cakes, cookies and other traditional sweets. Some of the hostages, the women included, also volunteered to help bake the cakes and cookies. One of the rooms had a piano. We asked Iranian Radio-Television to tape the ceremony. We would then broadcast it by satellite as a good-will gesture to the American people.

Early on Christmas Eve, 1979, the American clergymen arrived. We spent some time with them discussing plans. Initially, they asked for a program to include all the hostages. We could not accept the request for two reasons. The first was that we had already prepared and decorated two separate rooms, in which no more than fifteen people could gather. Secondly, we had security considerations.

The clergymen argued that the spirit of communion is the spirit of being together. We accepted the concept, for in our faith we have the same idea. According to the sayings of the Prophet Mohammad, the benefits of congregational prayers are seventy times greater than those of individuals: the larger the group, the greater the chance that someone with pure intentions and clean heart would be present. We finally agreed that the hostages could participate in the ceremonies in groups of four to five, though even this caused us a considerable security headache.

Then the festivities began. Later in the evening Archbishop Capucci arrived. The students greeted him warmly and led him into one of the rooms where prayers were being offered.

I was helping out in the larger of the two rooms when I learned that the ambassador of the Vatican had arrived as representative of the Pope. Apparently he spoke very little English, but was fluent in French. Our brothers knew I had a fairly good command of French. Then we went into the public relations unit where the ambassador was waiting.

The ambassador was a short, plump man of middle age, wearing a clerical collar. He also seemed to be in a hurry.

We students respected the hostages' religious practices, I told him. Then I asked him why religion is becoming less and less important in human affairs. Why has it been reduced to a few moments of personal prayer? Why have humanistic philosophy and scientific advancement gained more respect and a larger following than religion in the Christian world? Could it be that the Vatican is presenting a version of religion that people today cannot relate to, and making it marginal in people's lives? Perhaps religion had lost its force because figures such as the Pope did not have the courage to confront oppressors and speak for the oppressed? (see Appendix C).

It soon became clear to me that the ambassador was growing uncomfortable with this particular line of questioning. He wanted to see the hostages, he said, rather curtly.

A pair of students came to guide him to the ceremonies. They asked him to cover his eyes with the blindfold they provided. He seemed offended at first, but when we explained that this was standard procedure for all visitors, he acquiesced. Then he was led to the room where Capucci was waiting.

Other students led in the hostages in small groups. They sang Christmas carols and said prayers. Then the hostages had an opportunity to chat with Capucci and the Papal representative over tea and cakes.

Capucci was relaxed, joking and laughing, and making everyone feel at home. The Pope's representative looked on. The ceremonies continued until practically all the hostages had taken part. The last service was given at 3:30 am. As the hour was late, Capucci stayed overnight in the embassy.

The following morning after breakfast, Capucci made a point of commenting on the food and care given to the hostages. He recalled that during his illegal detention by the Israeli regime in Nasseriyeh Prison the inmates were treated worse than animals. He and his fellow prisoners were kept for months in dark, damp dungeons and were actually fed food for dogs.

"They would open the cans of dog food in front of our eyes. I became terribly sick and thin during those years. However, that is good for the spirit. The lighter you become, the higher you can fly."

Capucci had a lively sense of humor, and quickly established strong connections with all the students who met him. Not only his thoughts but his actions strengthened our belief that divine religions, Islam and Christianity in particular, have much more in common than most of us had imagined.

Another remark of his that stuck in my mind was his praise of Iranian women. "In Arabic, if you wish to describe a brave woman, you say she is like a man. But now in Iran," he said pointing to us, "you have turned this definition on its head."

A MOTHER'S COURAGE

AS THE HOSTAGE CRISIS INTENSIFIED, the Carter administration increased its opposition to attempts by American citizens to visit Iran and hear the views of the Iranian side first hand. Finally, travel to Iran was banned altogether. But family ties and maternal affection soon broke those fetters.

I was hard at work in the "bee hive," as we called the public relations section, when one of the students guarding the main gate came looking for me. Since I had appeared on television newscasts around the world it was routine for reporters and other interested people to arrive at the gate and ask to see "Maryam" or "Mary." But this time something unexpected awaited me.

The two of us walked down to the gate. There, to our astonishment, we found not a reporter but an American couple. The woman's name was Mrs. Barbara Timm, from Oak Creek, Wisconsin. She explained to us that she was the mother of Marine Sgt. Kevin Hermening, one of the U.S. military men held hostage. Despite Carter's orders, she had come to visit her son. There was a man accompanying her, the Marine's step-father.

"You are asking for something that is very difficult," I said. "Nobody has been granted such permission."

"I have come all this way only to see my son," the woman answered. "If possible, let me meet him just once."

"I will refer the matter to the Central Committee. I doubt they will accept, but you can come back tomorrow and get the answer," I told her.

That afternoon we discussed the matter. Most of the members believed that a mother who had traveled such a great distance under such difficult circumstances driven by her love for her son should not be turned down. The two were middle-class Americans; their outlook was simple, down-to-earth, sincere, and uncomplicated by political considerations. Others raised the possibility that she or her husband might be used as an intelligence source by the CIA, or that they might convey certain messages to him that would cause us security problems later on.

The committee weighed the risks against the humanitarian considerations. The human factor won out, and we decided to allow Mrs. Timm and her husband to visit Sgt. Hermening.

The committee also felt that we should explain to the couple why we had taken their countrymen hostage. To do this we quickly organized a one-day program for the mother and her husband. She had earlier asked that a third man, whom she identified as a lawyer but whom we suspected of being a CIA agent, could join them. That request we turned down.

The following day, when Mrs. Timm and her husband came to the gate, we told them that the committee had agreed to respect her wishes on humanitarian grounds. We described the program we had planned, and asked them to be ready at 8 o'clock Wednesday morning. We asked them not to tell anyone, especially reporters.

On the appointed morning three of us from the public relations section left the compound on schedule in a late-model Cadillac belonging to the embassy. We headed west toward the Intercontinental Hotel, now re-named "Laleh," the Farsi word for tulip (after the revolution, the tulip had come to symbolize the martyrs who had sacrificed their lives in the fight against the shah's regime.)

In arranging a program for the Timms we were not seeking publicity. In fact, we did everything we could to avoid it. Our intention was to give them a chance to get the feel of Iran, and to understand why we thought and acted as we did. All the reporters we had encountered were only interested in the immediate story, the more exciting the better. They rarely cared about the content or the impact of the reports they filed. For them, a mother's visit was nothing more than a pretext. But, despite what we had seen of the Western press until then, we never dreamed they would go to the lengths we were soon to witness.

As we had feared, a crowd of reporters armed with cameras was milling around in front of the hotel. We drove around to the rear entrance and went directly upstairs. One of the students knocked on their door and Mrs. Timm and her husband opened. The third man was with them in the room. Once again they asked if he could join us. We answered "no."

As we turned the corner into the hotel lobby, we saw another swarm of reporters inside the main entrance. They spotted us before we could clear the rear door.

"Where are you taking them?" one American newsman shouted. Before I could answer Mrs. Timm replied, "It's absolutely none of your business!"

By the time we got into the car and back onto the street, four cars jammed with reporters were waiting for us. Some were perched on the roofs of the cars, filming as they followed along behind us, others were hanging out of the windows. Mrs. Timm was becoming more and more annoyed.

"What a nuisance these reporters are. Why don't they get lost?"

Those were our sentiments exactly.

Instead, we tried to lose them. It was a chase scene straight out of a Hollywood thriller—or an absurd comedy. Majid, one of the leading students, was behind the wheel. He was one of those people who simply won't change their mind once it's made up. He was also one very skilled driver. Suddenly he swerved the huge car down a narrow alleyway, then doubled back down another alley in an effort to shake our pursuers.

So there we were, zigzagging at high speed through the southern sections of Tehran in an embassy Cadillac, heading for Behesht-e Zahra, the cemetery where thousands of martyrs mowed down by American weapons lay buried, with a squadron of cars crammed with reporters in hot pursuit. In the back seat we were trying to carry on a conversation about the history of Iran's revolution, and to explain why people felt anger toward America—but not toward Americans. We kept on glancing behind us. Our pursuers were still hot on our tail. It is to the Timms' lasting credit that they ignored the strangeness of our situation and listened to what we were trying to say.

Mrs. Timm and her husband were unpretentious Americans from a small town in Wisconsin. Like many Americans, who know very little of their country's foreign policy, they were innocents in the true sense of the word. They began asking questions about Islam, and about the causes of the revolution. We explained that, as we understood it, the concept of separation of church and state had arisen from centuries of corruption of the church in Europe; ambitious clergymen had exploited people's religious beliefs which eventually brought about the rise of humanism, which teaches that man has no need for either the teachings of the divine prophets or of their moral code.

As the Cadillac sped south, weaving through the narrow streets of Tehran's slums, we argued that while science and technology have advanced certain aspects of human life, its social and spiritual side was being shoved aside, to be replaced by moral decadence. It was at this precise moment, in Iran, that Imam Khomeini had begun to present religion in a totally new light. He taught us to find and know God in new ways, and opened for us an undiscovered path towards the Creator.

The Imam had defined religion, God, love, life and death in such clear and understandable terms that he seemed not only to be speaking a profound truth, but pointing the way toward salvation. So it was that he had carried with him the younger generations, those whose instincts led them to search for the truth. Many Iranian young people, especially those who had been educated in the United States, were quite familiar with the dazzling attractions of Western life. But they had chosen instead to extend their human horizons, and step into the realm of the undiscovered.

Mrs. Timm and her husband spoke in a soft mid-Western accent. They actually showed a lively interest in what we were saying. At last they were hearing the other side of the story, at first hand, uncensored and direct. They had also realized that we were not, as the American media and government constantly portrayed us, a mob of militants or wild-eyed terrorists. Behind our actions there was a deeply committed and idealistic rationale. If they were given a fair chance, we had always believed, the American people would be able to understand this rationale.

To this day, I still believe that if Americans had accurate information about the operations of the United States government in many parts of the world, where entire countries were under U.S. political, economic or even military domination, they would make a different judgment. If they had known what really happened in our country, about the national movement in Iran, about the shah's repressive regime, they would have understood better why we acted as we did. But they did not have—and do not have—that information.

Although Majid had successfully lost two of the cars that were tailing us, two others managed to follow us all the way to Behesht-e Zahra. We asked the guards to prevent them from entering, but they claimed they were not authorized to do so. In the end, we had to put up with them.

The idea of martyrdom, however, had been harder for Mrs. Timm to grasp. "Does it mean that a mother does not care for her son when she allows him to go and protest against the shah?" she asked. Her question was quite natural. How could she understand the depth and beauty of martyrdom when the media that were her only source of information, and the only source for most of the American people, had never even bothered to discuss it? How could they?

"This is not the first time in human history that people have been prepared to die for their beliefs," was our reply.

As we got out of the car to visit the last resting place of the thousands of men, women and children who had given their lives in the struggle to overthrow a despotic ruler supported by the United States, I could see that Mrs. Timm was deeply moved. We explained that for human beings who seek perfection and hope to make the most of their lives, God is the supreme manifestation of knowledge, power, mercy and love. The absolute. He has sent his messengers to guide humanity toward Him, by encouraging us to adopt those very qualities.

While this can be done through a conscious and disciplined effort throughout a lifetime, it might also require a confrontation that could result in the loss of life. The quest for justice which alone can free humanity from its shackles sometimes means struggle. Such struggle is justified and beneficial whether it brings success or death. If we continue to move in the direction of truth with pure intentions we have succeeded, no matter what the final outcome.

The martyr sees death as a success, as a sacrifice for society, as a step toward the sublime. He or she loves life just like any other person but he or she sees a more advanced state of achievement in struggle and choosing to give up his or her life. The mothers of these young people cherished their sons and daughters just like any other mother. They loved them with all their heart. But when their children chose to struggle, to serve as a model for others, these same mothers saw it as a supreme blessing. A gift given only to the pure.

We visited the graves of the martyrs of Black Friday, when the shah, in desperation, had ordered his special guards to open fire on thousands of demonstrators protesting against the monarchy. Thousands of women, children and men fell in their blood in that incident.[42] A State

Department spokesman declared the next day that while the United States did not underestimate the importance of events in Iran, they were confident that the shah had full control over the situation. They were assured that proper military action has been taken in Tehran and other cities, he added. The unwavering support of the American government for a criminal monarch had resulted in the massacre of thousands of Iranian freedom seekers. In visiting the graves, the Timms got only a small glimpse of the powerful feelings and of the reasons behind our requests for the extradition of the shah.

It was probably as hard for the Timms to understand as it was for us to explain the philosophy behind the revolution in words our American guests could understand. Our difficulties were magnified by the reporters who continued to dog our footsteps, taping our voices and filming our actions. When finally we decided to leave Behesht-e Zahra, the chase began again.

Once again Majid displayed his breathtaking, and hair-raising, driving skills in losing the "bad guys" who, it seemed, were deliberately trying to torment us. We had planned to visit some of the impoverished areas of the southern areas of the city, but the thought of being hounded by the reporters convinced us to simply drive through. As we did, we discussed the huge gap between the richest and the poorest in society. The shah had claimed to be leading the country to the "doorway of the Great Civilization," but here in the southern slums of Tehran, we told our guests, is what that civilization looked like to us. Even today, though the face of Tehran has changed almost beyond recognition, I still think back to that day whenever I visit the southern part of the city.

After another series of heart-stopping maneuvers, we managed to lose the reporters. It was past lunch time, so we stopped off at a local fried-chicken restaurant to eat. By the time we returned to the embassy, it was well after 4 o'clock. A huge crowd of reporters and television crews were lying in wait for us at the main entrance on Taleghani Avenue. We took the back entrance. One of the apartments in the northern section of the compound had been prepared for the family reunion. Its small living room was furnished with couches and a table. We led the Timms to one of the adjacent rooms where they could rest until arrangements were completed and we were ready.

Sgt. Hermening was brought to the apartment and we showed him into the room to meet his mother and stepfather. The reunion of the family was an emotional scene and Mrs. Timm was genuinely grateful. The mother and son held hands throughout the meeting. Fruits and sweets were served, in Iranian fashion, followed by an American-style dinner including stuffed turkey and cranberry sauce. No reporters were allowed entry except a crew from Iranian Radio and Television. The Marine was free to speak about family matters and ordinary issues, but we had asked him not to mention anything that could be considered intelligence information regarding his location or living conditions.

Nevertheless a leak occurred. Sgt. Hermening used the word "here" to describe his location, and this gave the Americans confirmation that the hostages were being held in the embassy. Mrs. Timm couldn't have been less interested in that kind of information. The same could not be said about her husband.

That evening Sgt. Hermening spent several hours with his family. After dinner and a tearful farewell, it came time for us to take our guests back to the hotel. Since the reporters were keeping all the main entrances under surveillance we decided to exit through one of the smaller gates on the southeast side of the compound. We told the Timms that if they wanted to avoid the prying eyes of the journalists they could lie down on the back seat and cover their heads with a blanket. That was exactly what they did.

On the way back to the Laleh, Mrs. Timm told us how thankful she was for allowing us to see her son. She also expressed her sympathy for all that the Iranian nation had suffered. She certainly regretted that her country's government had supported the crimes of the shah, but she had reservations about directly condemning American foreign policy. Still, it was clear to us that both she and her husband now had a much better understanding of the Revolution, and of why we had taken the hostages.

All of us admired her courage and determination in setting out on such a costly and risky journey. She had succeeded in reaching her goal, and perhaps much more. Such is the nature of a mother's love and a woman's determination to accomplish the impossible.

From the very first days of the embassy takeover the safety and security of the hostages was one of our primary concerns. Not only did we have no intention of harming the Americans, we were determined that no one else would. Our belief was that as prisoners or hostages, they should receive the most humane treatment possible. This was why we decided to hold most of them within the embassy proper, especially in the early stages of the occupation.

As we saw it, there were three sources of danger for the hostages. First of all, there were the students themselves. Several had suffered, as victims of or witnesses to persecution, repression and intimidation, from the crimes and injustices of the shah, or tasted America's bitter support for his tyrannical reign. Feelings ran deep. Although most of our fellow students were well educated about Islamic beliefs and displayed self-discipline and patience, there were some among us who would have liked to take personal revenge against a select few of the Americans for what we or our friends and families had suffered.

During our congregational Friday prayers, Hojjatoleslam Mousavi Khoeiniha spoke repeatedly to us about our responsibilities: "The well-being and humane treatment of our prisoners must always be uppermost in our minds. We should be considerate of their problems and needs." Still, a few of the students felt he was being soft on the hostages.

We heard reports of some students muttering that the hostages were being treated too well. I remember one of the disgruntled ones telling me one day: "People are dying of hunger in this country. These Americans are agents of their government. They share the responsibility for our sufferings but you feed them steaks and vegetables. We students don't get this kind of food. We sleep on the ground, but they have soft beds to sleep in."

"Do you remember Capucci?" he said, referring to the Archbishop who had visited the hostages at Christmas. Capucci had expressed his wonder and approval at the high quality of food served them. Then he had added that in the Nasseriyeh prison, the Israelis had served him bone soup for breakfast and dog-food for lunch. "They would spit in our food before handing it to us," he had added.

"But we're not the Israelis," I replied.

By then the student was smoldering with anger. I listened patiently and reminded him that one of our revolution's goals was to revive the forgotten dimensions of humanity. If we hoped to restore human dignity, how could we mistreat prisoners today? To back up my point, I reminded him of the death of Imam Ali. The assassin who had fatally wounded the Imam with a poisoned sword was imprisoned by Ali's sons. But even in his dying moments, Imam Ali was concerned about his murderer, and instructed his sons: "Give him the food you eat, treat him kindly. If I live, I know what to do. If I die, you may not torture him. You may execute him but with only one blow, or you may forgive him if you wish."

By now he had apparently cooled down. He was still argumentative but the fire was gone. "Some of them are criminals," he contended. "We have all the proof we need." I answered that if Imam Khomeini deemed it necessary, hostages directly involved in acts of espionage would be handed over to the judicial authorities who would bring them to trial before a legally constituted tribunal.

Finally I told him, "we have not come here to eat well and sleep comfortably or to take personal revenge. We're here for a superior goal." For the time being he was mollified, but we decided to bring up the matter with the Central Committee. We were concerned that the outside political factions that were looking for ways to exploit the occupation might gain a toehold and cause serious trouble. We agreed to expel anyone we considered a serious threat, and to keep a close watch on anyone else with similar views. In the end, no more than six students in all were asked to leave.

Our next source of concern, paradoxically, was the people themselves, our strongest allies and supporters. At critical moments in the occupation they would flow by in their tens of thousands, like waves, shouting their support for us. Sometimes the physical pressure on the front gates on Taleghani Avenue was more than the locks and chains were meant to bear. But despite the enormous crowds, their demonstrations were always orderly and controlled.

Our greatest worry was beyond our reach: the incompetence of the Carter administration. On November 20, 1979 an American naval task force led by the aircraft carrier *Kitty Hawk* was transferred from the Philippines to the Persian Gulf. This move prompted us to relocate fifteen of the hostages to safe houses in the northern section of Tehran. With them went some twenty students to act as guards and provide the necessary services.

By early December they were all returned to the compound where security could be maintained and all services provided efficiently.

But the American attack on Iranian territory on April 24, 1980—the Tabas incident (see Chapter IX)—changed all that, dramatically so. We were compelled to move the hostages from Tehran, to divide and dispatch them with groups of students to provincial cities, including Qom, Isfahan, Tabriz, Mashhad, Jahrom, Yazd, Mahallat, Shiraz and Khorramabad. The women and a handful of the men hostages remained in the embassy premises. The women students, myself included, stayed in Tehran along with about a third of the brothers.

Most Iranians felt even more strongly than ever that the American government was intent on destroying their revolution and their country. Their concerns seemed fully justified, as five months later Iraq staged a massive attack on Iranian territory to start a war that would continue for eight years. Some of the hostages, we knew by then, had been accomplices of the American government in its acts against Iran. These feelings became particularly heated after the debacle at Tabas: in many cities we got wind of serious threats to harm the hostages. We made a point of concealing their real places of detention. Since massive demonstrations were held in front of the American consular offices in Tabriz, Mashhad and Shiraz, we arranged to keep the hostages in other locations in those cities.

At the same time, we encountered a powerful sense of willingness to cooperate. People offered us their homes, their services and their cars to help us maintain the hostages' securely in their cities. Time and time again people would serve food to those who had come to demonstrate their solidarity with the Imam and with us. Sometimes between 4,000 and 5,000 people were fed in front of the consulates in Isfahan and Tabriz. The food was given in the name of "nazr," a vow made to perform a positive deed if one's wish has been fulfilled, and offered in memory of Imam Hossein, the son of Ali and fourth Imam, who was martyred by the Umayyad caliph in the Islamic calendar year 61 A.H. (682 A.D.)

Just as Hossein had died a martyr's death on the battlefield at Karbala in an unequal battle against the forces of power and arrogance, people in Iran had come to feel that the American government represented an arrogant power that cared little for human dignity. Imam Khomeini had labeled the United States the Great Satan, and indeed the Iranian Islamic revolutionaries, ourselves included, felt that they were facing a symbol of Satan in the world.

Despite the difficulties we experienced, including the logistical problems of guaranteeing proper food, comfort and health care, exceptionally hot weather, two failed escape attempts in Isfahan, an automobile accident on the way from Khorramabad to Tehran and many lesser incidents, the hostages were all brought back safely in August 1980. Once in the capital, they were taken under our direct supervision to a new location in the southwestern suburbs of Tehran which had been prepared for them by the students.

Although their living conditions were not as good as in the embassy, we could be completely certain of their security. Most were kept together in groups of four or five. By then, some had developed conflicts and preferred to be alone or change roommates. One of them, Bill Belk, had apparently even threatened to kill his roommate if we did not change his room.

We provided them with games, particularly chess, as well as books and a VCR along with cassettes of American films from the embassy. Once or twice a week each room could watch a film, accompanied by popcorn and potato chips.

Later, I read Tim Wells' book *444 Days*,[43] in which Belk, Bruce German, Rodney Sickman and others describe how well they were treated by the students. In the same volume Barry Rosen expresses wonder that he was not discriminated against by the students in spite of his being Jewish.

I recall very well one lengthy discussion some brothers had with John Limbert, a political officer with a strong command of Farsi. He was usually willing to talk over a whole range of issues with the students.

One of those subjects was Iran-U.S. relationships. Why had our two countries come to this? Who was to blame? In discussing the political forces behind these issues we quickly realized that we were dealing with experienced diplomats who possessed a high degree of technical skill in the art of deal-making, not to say subterfuge and concealment. We were simple, direct and transparent in our aspirations and actions, as most students are. It took us some time to understand that their world, the world of diplomacy and espionage, was one where skills such as deal-making were esteemed and cultivated.

Limbert however, was a bit different. He had an Iranian wife; his manner was calm, he was sympathetic to the students. His policy was to talk with us, understand us and to try and bring us to understand American policy. If, like Limbert, you are coming to another country, you have to have an understanding of that country to interpret it successfully. Was he responding to Iran, or was it a case of manipulation? Probably both.

I heard this story from one of the brothers who had visited him at the safe house where he was being held, in Isfahan. They noticed several slogans written on a wall, including "Down with U.S.A., U.S.S.R., Israel and South Africa." When he saw them staring at the wall he said, "why don't you just say 'Down with everyone. Down with the world.' Wouldn't it be easier?"

"That's not exactly what we mean, Mr. Limbert," they said. "Is it our fault if certain governments violate the basic rights of other human beings."

Limbert smiled and replied, "you have a rationale for everything. But why have you locked yourselves up like us? Why don't you go after the good things in life and enjoy yourselves? Why are you wasting your youth this way?"

The answer wasn't as simple as the question, they told Limbert. First, they explained, no one had forced us into our present condition. "Most of us have a good, prosperous life waiting out there for us. As university graduates with advanced degrees we could make good money in private enterprise. We could marry equally well-situated women, buy a house, a car, start a family. In fact, some of us already have these circumstances but we've chosen this way, because we feel the revolution is at stake and requires personal sacrifice at this stage. We would rather dedicate our lives to the satisfaction of God, to the freedom and independence of Iran and to the well-being of our compatriots. There are times in the history of every nation when sacrifices have to be made to restore its integrity and dignity. It's true, some of us are tired of being imprisoned along with you. We would much rather go out into the poor villages or to the battlefront and serve our country. But we have a strong sense of responsibility; that's what keeps us going."

* * *

For all our seemingly friendly relations and long chats with the hostages, covert contacts, secret messages and escape plans were never far from the their minds, whether in the embassy, in remote cities or in any location. In retrospect, it was foolish of us to imagine that they would act in any other way. After all, we were dealing with a select group of specialists: espionage agents and diplomats.

We had to admit that they showed a high degree of inventiveness. Some would tap out codes on the walls, or leave messages in the toilet or bath. Many of these contacts must have gone undetected. In the embassy, the hostages were on their home ground, so to speak. But when we did come across a secret message we read it and left it in its place. In one instance, some of us developed a disinformation campaign using toilet paper, and managed to confuse the CIA agents for quite a while.

Other times we could only marvel at the ingenuity and resourcefulness of the hostages in gathering an unbelievable collection of useful items.

We found most of these objects during routine security checks and searches. Limbert and his roommates had managed to steal a radio from a student who fell asleep on guard duty. Malcolm Kalp had on his person a twenty toman bank note along with an iron-cutter the night he attempted to escape in Isfahan, where we used guard dogs for security. Kalp had collected bedsheets and tied them together, soaked a chunk of meat in dissolved tranquilizers and thrown it to the dogs, then cut through the bars over his window and begun to lower himself to the ground. But the dogs had not fallen asleep, and caught him halfway down. Although I was not present, I believe he was put into solitary confinement.

Other hostages spent their time differently. Thomas Ahern, the CIA station chief in Tehran, decorated the walls of his room with portraits, including those of Imam Khomeini and Dr. Mossadegh, whom the CIA had helped to overthrow in 1953. Mike Metrinko, the other CIA officer whom we thought to be deranged, hated everyone and was hated in return. He preferred to stay alone and bounce a ball against the wall of his room from morning until night.

In October 1980, fifteen of the hostages were relocated to the northwestern part of Tehran, for security reasons. They were directly supervised by students.

Meanwhile, the women hostages Elizabeth Swift and Katherine Koob, along with Robert Ode, the eldest hostage, and Don Hohman, were kept within the embassy. On the whole, I believe they fared better than the others. The women were allowed regular access to the kitchen and were free to cook whatever meals they wished. They also enjoyed fresh air, exercise and showers more frequently than the others.

Of all the hostages, Richard Queen was the calmest. But Queen had serious health problems which flared up in December, 1979, when he reported to us that his left hand was not functioning properly. We placed him under regular medical supervision and Hohman was kept close to him. When his condition deteriorated in late June, we took him to a hospital. The examining physicians diagnosed him as suffering from a central nervous system disorder, probably multiple sclerosis. Immediately we asked the Imam's permission to free him. Imam Khomeini decreed that he should be set free immediately and returned to his family. Procedures to release him were completed quickly and Queen was on his way home on July 11, 1980.

Among the escape attempts, Bill Belk's misadventure stands out. One night in mid-December, 1979, I was sitting in one of the second-floor rooms of the Chancellery. It must have been around midnight when I heard shots from the compound. I went over to the northern windows for a look, but it was dark. All I could see were several students running towards the northern sector. I opened a small window and called out to one of the guards below, "what's all the commotion?"

"Looks like one of them's gotten away," came the reply.

"Who is it?" I asked.

"Bill Belk was in the residence. His guard fell asleep."

I was fuming. How could some of these brothers be so irresponsible?

Along with two of the sisters I hurried to the residence. The students were already searching inside and outside the building. "He couldn't have escaped the compound; we will catch him," Hossein, the head of the operations unit assured me. We were looking around us in growing desperation when we heard a shout: "I've got him!"

He'd discovered Belk shivering miserably in a barrel of cold water.

The student who had spotted him first was a woman from Melli University. As she told me the following day, she was on guard duty near the warehouse when she noticed someone hurrying through an opening in the barbed wire.

"'Stop!' I told him, and recognized that he was a hostage. But before I could do anything he grabbed my feet and tried to pull the machine gun out of my hands. I managed to call for help, and before he could remove the magazine I pulled the trigger with the gun pointed in the air. He tried to grab the barrel of the gun but I pulled the trigger again to fire the second shot. When I spotted him running toward the parking lot I switched on my walkie-talkie and screamed: 'Hurry, one of the Americans is out! Hurry!' By that time two of the brothers were after him."

She had displayed considerable courage and responsibility, particularly in comparison to her companion who had fallen asleep at the switch, allowing Belk to escape in the first place.

I felt so upset that I went straight back to our quarters to rest. It could have been a disaster, with at least one person killed or seriously wounded. A gun had been fired. What if he had escaped? It would have been very hard for the students, and probably worse for the hostages. It might have been impossible to control the few hotheads among us. But eventually, everything turned out for the best.

We had no intention of harming Belk, but our punitive instincts got the better of us. We kept him in solitary confinement for several weeks. On Christmas the students brought him a peace offering, a branch from the decorated Christmas tree and some cakes and tea. We did not want him to feel completely forgotten on that holy night.

CHAPTER VII

MEDIA WARS

IN LATE DECEMBER, 1979, we received from an American reporter a copy of an anonymous letter that had been originally sent to the *San Jose Mercury*: "Thank you for this opportunity to provide confidential background for your newspaper staff on the current situation in Iran…I am communicating with you now because of the circus atmosphere of current news stories. A copy of this letter is also being sent to Professor Noam Chomsky of MIT because he has been objecting to the superficiality of media coverage of the Iranian situation. The stand of the U.S. on principle, that we cannot extradite the ex-shah to be tried for his alleged crimes and that we will not negotiate to free the captives in the American Embassy in Tehran but that our government cares deeply for the fate of these hostages is a preposterous stand. It reflects badly on our news media that you accept it at face value. The American public is being driven into a xenophobic hysteria by what amounts to a fairy tale, with the full cooperation of the press and television, when what you should be doing is analyzing and reporting on the techniques by which this xenophobia is being manufactured. It seems hardly enough improvement to have made since the Spanish-American war that now we wait until the U.S. State Department supplies us with yellow paper, before we conduct yellow journalism…"

Since we could not determine the identity of the item's author, we could not vouch for its authenticity. But like several other anonymous messages we were to receive in the course of the occupation, it seemed—and seems today—like a perfectly accurate description of the situation.

We may have been center-stage newsmakers for a six-month period from November 1979 to April 1980 on a national as well as global level, but it didn't take us long to realize that our message was not getting through to world public opinion intact. Reporters, whom we imagined as entrusted with the moral obligation of serving as the eyes and ears of the particular media or country they served, failed to maintain their impartiality and objectivity. The Americans were the worst offenders by far. They sought to extract from almost every report or interview conclusions that would serve their interests. In fact, they contributed to widening the gap that already existed, to deepening misunderstandings and increasing the enmity and antagonism between Iran and the U.S.

We believed, perhaps naively, that viewers should hear both sides of an argument and judge for themselves. But the mainstream media never even gave the American public that chance. Instead they created a skewed picture of us as "militants" and "terrorists." Iranians in general were depicted as backward "religious fanatics." They never missed an opportunity to arouse the patriotic feelings of the American public, the better to make the crimes of their government fit for human consumption. There were, however, among the reporters decent individuals who did their best to change the prevailing picture. One of them, whose name I cannot recall, sent us this message: "I am enclosing for your information, a statement that I tried to give to the newspapers here. They refused it saying I couldn't prove it. I told them there was a precedent for extradition of the ex-shah, because they were publishing an allegation that there was no precedent in American law for such an action. I told them that, on the contrary, when Marcos Perez Jimenez fled from Venezuela in 1958, the new government charged him with embezzling over thirteen million dollars and that in 1963 we yanked him right out of his mansion in Miami, Florida, and sent him back to Venezuela to stand trial for his crimes. He was convicted and served five years in prison, after which he was allowed to go to Spain. When I offered this to our newspapermen, thoroughly researched with references to prove it, they didn't even bother to write it down. They just weren't interested in correcting the untruths they were printing..."

When it came to relations with the press, we were amateurs with no previous experience. We had to improvise as we went, although we learned rapidly. Soon after the embassy takeover, we converted the library into our public relations unit headquarters. It consisted of a large room that we used for press conferences or for meetings with prominent personalities, and a smaller room for individual interviews. The corridor outside did double duty as the office and telephone room where we answered incoming calls.

At first our interviews were all open, in the form of press conferences, with domestic and international reporters invited to attend. One reporter at a time would question the students, whose answers would be translated. Gradually, we began to get more requests for one-on-one interviews. We had also begun to realize that press conferences on the international level were counterproductive. They were difficult to organize, and even more difficult to manage, not to mention being time consuming. Worse yet, most of the information conveyed was distorted, and what little did get through appeared as bits and fragments of statements made.

As a result, we decided to allow private interviews for those reporters and media we felt were less hostile, less reliant on their government's interpretation of events.

A loose network of Iranian students living abroad—mostly in the United States—were our eyes and ears. They were in daily, direct contact with us, and kept us abreast not only of new developments in the countries where they lived, but also of reactions to the events in Tehran. We asked them to analyze and evaluate each journalist's work. What they told us helped us decide whether or not to grant an interview when a particular reporter showed up at the embassy gates.

It was not long before a staggering number of requests for interviews began to pour in from television and radio stations, newspapers and magazines around the world. After consultation with our support team abroad, we weighed each request, rejected or approved it, then planned and scheduled the interview. Usually two or three groups or individual reporters were given appointments every morning from 9 to 12 o'clock.

The interviewees were members of the Central Committee who had been granted full authority to speak for us.

The reports we received on the impact of those interviews, particularly the ones given to American reporters, were extremely discouraging. In some cases we were sent videotape recordings of what had been broadcast in the U.S. or Europe. Lengthy interviews amounting sometimes to 45 minutes were reduced to two or three minutes. Certain specially selected shots were shown with voice-over by another reporter. Hardly one word of what we said, hardly a single word of our message about the extradition of the criminal monarch, that we considered the American government as our enemy, and not the American people, got through. Our words were either censored or badly distorted. We could surely have been pardoned for thinking that the networks and the media were seriously afraid of letting the American people hear our side of the story.

Such was our first-hand experience of press freedom and freedom of expression, Western style.

It was not long before the inflow of information from our interviews, and the nature of the coverage we were receiving, convinced us to reconsider our public relations policies. We announced that no interview would be given to any American television or radio reporter unless it was to be broadcast live and uncensored. This was the only solution.

Not surprisingly, American reporters, not to mention those from other countries, were obsessed with the possibility of interviewing the hostages. In early December, after a lengthy discussion, we came up with a set of guidelines. The interview would have to be taped and broadcast direct immediately after the interview, but we would reserve the right to edit out any material we considered inappropriate, or compromising for the security of the hostages and the students.

Before the interview the students would deliver a message to the American people. If the message was not broadcast, the interview would not be either. Questions had to be submitted for prior review and we had the prerogative of suspending the program at any point. We presented our conditions to the three American networks, ABC, CBS and NBC. As we had anticipated, the competition was fierce in spite of the restrictions we'd imposed. The first network to broadcast an interview with a hostage would reap huge rewards in the ratings. As for us, we asked nothing and were paid nothing.

The first proposal came from NBC, which attempted to bargain over some of the conditions. We remained steadfast, and the network eventually agreed. A tentative date was set and the hostage affairs unit was asked to select a hostage for the interview. Then the public relations unit was given the task of preparing a five to six minute message for the American public. It would explain the reasons for our action, our beliefs and thoughts, and our religious convictions. The message was to be written in simple language; it was to be clear and concise.

The hostage affairs unit proposed William Gallegos, one of the embassy's Marine guards, as the interviewee. Everyone had agreed that the Marines would be the best choice, given their honesty and simplicity. Gallegos was a calm, collected young man who had always behaved well. He was from a Latin background, which won our sympathy. We approached him and asked if he wanted to speak about his conditions and feelings. At first he was reluctant, but quickly the possibility of speaking to his family overcame his fears and he agreed. He promised to avoid all reference to his whereabouts, his living quarters, and any other question that might compromise security.

On the appointed day we ushered the NBC crew into the compound after a routine check of their equipment. Then we reviewed the conditions with them one more time; they reiterated their agreement. I was to read the message but, anticipating the publicity that was sure to follow, I was reluctant to appear on screen. "Couldn't someone else do the job?" I asked. But the Central Committee was convinced that, as a woman student "Mary"—I, in other words—would be the best person. Meanwhile, we had arranged the library for the interview. Behind me was a picture of Imam Khomeini; beside it was a large photograph depicting the worst and most despotic nature of the shah's regime.

The NBC interviewer, whose name I do not recall, sat facing me and Gallegos. The interviewer began by introducing the hostage and explaining that the student wished to read a message to the American people.

I began, "In the Name of God, the Merciful, the Compassionate." The message took exactly six minutes and 40 seconds. It summed up the reasons behind our actions, and our religious convictions, and emphasized how close Islam and Christianity were to one another. It included references to Jesus, and underlined that the Imam, the leader of the revolution, had pointed to oppression as a common burden in many parts of the world,

I stated that we had no ill feelings toward Americans; they, like us, were victims of the policies of their government. That government had supported the tyrannical and despotic regime of the shah, which the people of Iran had overthrown. If the Carter administration was sincerely interested in the welfare of the hostages, it could have returned the shah, or apologized for American support for his regime.

I tried to speak calmly, with determination. I think I was reasonably successful.

Then the interview began. Gallegos introduced himself, then the interviewer asked him about his living conditions and his daily activities, and about his thoughts on the embassy capture. His answers were very cautious. Finally, the interviewer asked him to send a message to his friends and family.

Once the questions were finished the interviewer suddenly broke our agreement. Turning back to me he asked, "Now may I ask you a question?" For an instant I was taken aback. But I quickly recovered.

"No you may not," I replied.

The interview was over.

As we had agreed, we took the tape to the Iranian TV studios to check it over carefully and make sure that it would be properly broadcast on NBC's morning show. We reviewed the footage, particularly Gallegos's answers. At one point he referred to "the mushroom" which we assumed was a reference to the location where they were being held. We decided to overlook it, since we regularly moved the hostages.

Then the NBC group started bargaining again. Our message was too long, they told us; we would have to cut it. They were particularly worried about a section in which we had directly and explicitly mentioned Carter's incompetence. We stuck fast to our position. It was all or nothing, we said. A few moments later they came back with another proposal. Their last question to me and my negative reply would damage our prestige, they claimed. If we would delete parts of our message they would delete the question. By that time it was quite late, and teams from CBS and ABC were waiting behind the closed doors of the satellite room. They had assured us several times that if NBC did not comply with our terms, they were prepared to do so.

Exasperated, we told NBC that we would hand the tape to their rivals if they did not respect our original agreement. Finally NBC gave in. The tape was broadcast intact, as promised, although we soon learned that reaction shots of the Marine's parents in the studio had been edited in to arouse the emotions of the viewers.

NBC was to pay a heavy price for that interview, according to a *Newsweek* report published a week later. U.S. regulations apparently prohibited broadcast of any anti-government declaration lasting longer than five minutes. Our message ran one minute and 40 seconds over the limit. Still, considering the wide gap between our cultures and the numerous existing points of difference and misunderstanding, the message was short.

Nonetheless, telephone calls, letters, and even telegrams, poured in by the hundreds from a wide cross-section of Americans, including university professors, political activists and even prisoners. Many were written by women. These messages showed that something, however fragmentary, had gotten through.

As a result of appearing regularly on television, Mary, as I was now known, received dozens of letters every week. Many letters were full of sympathy, but some of them were antagonistic. Some of the letter writers felt that by wearing a scarf and Islamic dress, I was accepting oppression. Others believed that by translating or speaking on behalf of a group of men, I was proving the subordination of women in Iran.

Meanwhile, in the aftermath of the Gallegos interview on NBC, our routine of four to five interviews per day with newspapers, television and radio stations from all corners of the world not only continued unabated, it became more hectic. Not all our encounters were adversarial. I can still recall an interview with a British Muslim organization. They had requested an open discussion-interview which they taped, and later aired several times at their cultural center in London. Another memorable event was the visit of a group of Panamanian students opposed to the political asylum granted the shah in their country. They had raised money to pay their way to Iran and stayed in the country for ten days. We welcomed them to the public relations unit where we held a meeting and exchanged views on the Islamic Revolution and the fight against imperialism. Our thinking was alike in many ways.

Hundreds of reporters, not to mention representatives of political groups and factions applied for interviews or meetings with the students. Among them were several high-profile Iranian and international political personalities. In particular I remember appeals for a meeting with the students on behalf of Nureddin Kianouri, head of the pro-Soviet Tudeh Party.[44] They reasoned that as they claimed to be anti-imperialists, they shared common ground with us. But we never believed for a moment that we and the communists had anything in common. They phoned us constantly and came to the gates repeatedly. Each time, they went away empty-handed. "We have nothing to do with communists," we told them.

Another, even more controversial figure who attempted to ingratiate himself with us was Massoud Rajavi, head of the MKO. Initially his followers phoned on his behalf asking for an appointment, which we immediately rejected. Then he made a personal appearance at the main gate with a handful of his militia supporters as a publicity stunt, ostensibly to proclaim his solidarity with our movement and, if possible, to gain the prestige of entering the embassy grounds.

The Central Committee examined his request and voted unanimously to reject it. The decision was a blow to his campaign of self-promotion. At the same time it reassured the country that we were not giving in to political pressure, nor seeking support from political factions. As subsequent events were to show, the name Massoud Rajavi was soon to become synonymous with treason of the worst kind, when the organization he led attempted an armed overthrow of the fledgling Islamic government and touched off a bitter civil conflict that was to claim thousands of lives.

The next live interview was given to the Canadian Broadcasting Corporation. A student named Reza and I were chosen for the task. During the interview we presented prima facie evidence of the illegal acts of passport forgery and espionage originating in the American Embassy.

The evidence consisted of two passports, one identifying Thomas Ahern, whom we had discovered was Tehran CIA station chief. The other was a German passport with a different picture of Ahern, under a total different identity with a German name, nationality and birthplace. Ostensibly Ahern traveled as a German businessman; in reality, he was on assignment for the CIA.

The Canadian interviewers had hardly expected this kind of revelation, and were taken aback. We ended with a pointed question: "How much longer will Europe allow the United States to push it around, interfere in its affairs and act as its godfather in international relations? When will Europe adopt an independent identity?"

The interview was broadcast live in Canada and many viewers in the U.S. and Europe later saw all or portions of it. Though we were unaware of it at the time, we had touched on one of the major questions of the coming decades: to what extent would an economically and politically unified Europe be able to operate independently of the United States?

In January, the American networks approached us with another proposal for a live interview. We concluded that since these same networks had not broadcast reports on the Christmas ceremonies given for the hostages, it would be a suitable opportunity to speak with the American people face to face. The flow of letters and contacts after the Gallegos interview also encouraged us to try again.

We scheduled the interview in the satellite broadcasting section of Islamic Republic Television at 6 o'clock in the morning. Habib and I were selected to represent the students. Habib was one of our leaders; he had a firm, calm and self-contained manner. Mohsen was assigned the job of accompanying us to the TV station and looking after all arrangements. On the way we discussed what we would say.

We arrived on time; the Americans were waiting for us. The interviewer was a tall, heavy-set man named Barry Serafin. Habib and I took our seats in the small room where the taping would take place.

Serafin handed me an ear piece through which I could hear the voices in the New York studio. He wore a matching earpiece. At the signal Serafin began, speaking in an authoritarian tone. There was very little time, he said. He wanted short, clear answers to his questions, and nothing else. He went on to say that the most important question for the American people was the exact number of hostages we were holding, since different accounts had confused them.

Habib began with our standard invocation, "In the Name of God, the Merciful, the Compassionate," followed by a tribute to the American people. He went on to say that he did not believe their main concern was the exact number of hostages, but why the event had taken place; what had the U.S. government done in support of the shah; what were the grievances that had driven the Iranian students to take such drastic action. Habib had not finished his statement when Serafin interrupted, saying, "I want the answer to my question and nothing else."

I began interpreting Habib's statement, pointedly neglecting Serafin's aggressive interruption. Serafin jumped in again, "You are not answering our questions."

"You don't even allow us to greet the audience," Habib said, his voice calm yet firm. "Are you afraid our words might change some people's minds?" I translated. Serafin repeated his question: "How many hostages are you holding?"

"About 50 Americans are being held," Habib replied. "They are in good health and living under suitable conditions, but they are now only a diversion which the American government is exploiting to channel public opinion away from the main issue, which is the mistakes, incompetence and oppressive nature of American foreign policy in Iran and in other parts of the world."

After the translation, Serafin asked, "What are the conditions in which you are keeping the hostages?"

"We have prepared the best possible living arrangements for them," Habib said. "Our recent Christmas celebration was taped for the American people, but the American government did not allow it to be broadcast."

Again Serafin broke in during my interpretation, complaining that his questions were being evaded.

This time Habib, who had been quite calm until then, replied sharply, "I don't understand why you are so rude and impolite. Is this an interview or is it a trial? Are we in court or on television? What we must tell the American people is that your media and government do not want them to hear our message. They are afraid that if people learn of the realities they would change their outlook toward many things."

I translated the statement quickly and accurately. Serafin announced that the interview would continue after a short commercial break.

As I listened over the earphone I heard the commentators in the New York studio quickly attempting to neutralize the possible impact of our words on the viewing audience.

Things cooled off somewhat in the second half of the interview. But Serafin was still almost as aggressive. He asked about the possibility of an Iraqi attack on Iran. Habib responded that since the United States was caught in a stalemate, they might resort to any form of retaliation, including encouraging Iraqi forces to attack Iran. This would only endanger the lives of the American hostages and cause greater instability in the region. Finally the interview came to an end. The most obvious impression conveyed, as opinion polls we saw later indicated, was that the interviewer had been rude and the students treated unfairly.

Some of the reporters who visited the embassy were more inquisitive about the deeper motivations for our action. In contrast to those who asked the usual superficial questions in an attempt to stir up world opinion, a small handful were attempting to get a more accurate picture of us and our movement. One of these was not actually a reporter, but a

Canadian author, Robin Woodsworth Carlsen.[45] He was a slender, middle-aged man, of medium height who dressed simply in casual clothing. His manner and approach were much different from the reporters we normally encountered. Carlsen was looking behind the scenes, searching for the students' inner motivation. His manner of questioning reflected a certain faith and awareness of spiritual matters and beliefs. He was one of the few who tried to grasp the essence of the Imam's charisma and the spiritual dimension of the revolution. He appreciated the level of esteem and veneration that the people had for Islam and for Imam Khomeini. Carlsen was also able to understand some parts of this enigma: the strength of Islamic belief in the midst of an era characterized by the hegemony of the most materialistic civilization the world has ever seen.

* * *

One small room in the public relations section was reserved for answering calls from people who wanted to express their views or share their problems and difficulties with us. The phones would begin ringing before 8 o'clock in the morning and continue until late at night, non-stop. Two shifts of two or three students each would respond and record the callers' views or questions.

The people of Iran had immense expectations of us. They were convinced that we wielded unlimited executive power and had the ability to solve all their problems and give them advice and counsel. This was by no means the case; whatever power we had we drew from the massive popular support that had rallied behind us, and from the documents we had seized and painstakingly pieced together. Only later did I begin to understand how much power we appeared to wield.

Our telephone log books also served as straw polls. Particularly after we had exposed documents or staged press conferences or public interviews, people would phone in and speak their minds about what they had just seen. These reactions gave us a grasp of how the country saw us at every step of the way.

One of the callers was a mother who insisted that one of the students speak with her son. The boy, she said, was discouraged and was paying no attention to his studies. I happened to be in the phone room the fourth or fifth time she called. The sisters handling the phones waved me over to talk with her. It wasn't entirely clear to me why I should do this, but I took the receiver anyway. A young voice asked me excitedly, "Are you really one of the students speaking from the Den of Spies?"

I was, I answered. How he wished he could have been in my place, to have done something, something important and exceptional, he said, speaking excitedly. I replied that we were ordinary people just like him and that there was nothing special about us. But he could become exceptional if he worked hard at being good in all the qualities a human being should have, things like character, spirit, diligence in studies and in work. Then he would be capable of things he could not even dream of. Human beings have enormous resources, but only if they aim for the ultimate will they truly succeed, I told him.

The conversation ended with the hope that we speak another time. I never heard from him again, but his mother phoned several days later to thank us for the conversation. It had made a positive impact on her son's attitude.

Another story I'll never forget was that of an elderly woman who had lost her only piece of land during the shah's rule, and who called us every day begging us to do something to help her. All we could do was suggest that she follow the established procedures to restore her rights, but it was hopeless. Her expectations were beyond our ability to fulfill.

A LIBERATION CONFERENCE

DURING THE FIRST two or three months of the occupation, several liberation movements from other countries approached us. They proclaimed their solidarity with our action and expressed a desire to meet. We believed not only that our own goals and objectives made us part of a broader anti-imperialist movement, but that our action had made us one of the leaders. It was not long before we came up with the idea of convening the first worldwide gathering of liberation movements. The Central Committee approved the idea and set up a three-person sub-committee to organize and manage the program. One of its members was a woman law student from Melli University.

The sub-committee located and contacted dozens of such movements, and closely examined their programs and profiles. At the time, Algeria was host to many of the liberation movements we wanted to contact. A delegation of three students flew to Algiers to extend personal invitations to the movements we felt were closest to us, most sympathetic to our achievement, and that we could help the most.

From among them, 23 were invited to participate in a gathering to be held from January 3-9, 1980. The organizations invited included the Algerian National Liberation Front; the Palestine Liberation Organization; the National Liberation Organization of Palestine; the African National Congress; the Southwestern African Peoples Organization of Namibia (SWAPO); the African National Unity Organization; the Oman Liberation Movement; the Polisario Saharan Liberation Organization; the Eritrean Liberation Front; the Chilean Resistance Front; the Chad Liberation Organization; the Fatani Liberation Organization; the Muslim Liberation Movement of the Philippines (MORO); the Lebanese Movement of the Oppressed; the American Indian Movement; the Uruguay Liberation Front; the Arabian Peninsula Liberation Front; the Canary Islands Movement; the Afghan Muslims' Liberation Movement; the Dawa and Peykar Parties of Iraq; the Argentine Liberation Front; and the El Salvador Liberation Organization. Of these, sixteen groups finally came to Tehran. The others regretfully informed us they would not be able to attend.[46]

We proposed that the gathering set itself three objectives: first, to recognize the inhuman nature of American imperialism and expose its criminal behavior; second, to familiarize our guests with the Islamic Revolution; third, to exchange views and information on questions of mutual interest to all such movements.

Imam Khomeini greeted the guests in a special message to be read at the opening ceremony. In it he said, "Liberation movements must realize that succumbing to oppression is worse than oppressing. O, oppressed peoples of the world, rise. Rise and free yourselves from the claws of the enemies of humanity. Do not surrender to oppression for God is with the oppressed."

The gathering was staged in the Qods (Jerusalem) Hotel in the center of Tehran. Two floors of the hotel were reserved for our guests, and the group of students who were in charge of organizing the event moved onto another floor a few days before the program began. The workload during those early days of January was back-breaking. Planning and organizing for an international conference was something for which none of us had the slightest experience. It required a vast array of skills. But somehow we not only survived, but thrived. We financed the conference with the cash we had discovered in the embassy. But we also received support from the hotel, and from several local Islamic organizations.

During their stay the delegates met with high-ranking officials of the Islamic Republic, including Imam Khomeini, Ayatollah Montazeri and members of the Revolutionary Council.

German supporter giving students a gift. Mohammad-Reza Khatami on left.

They were flown to Qom by helicopter to visit the Imam, who made a speech in which he emphasized the necessity for unification and integrity in the fight against imperialist domination. He elaborated on the spirit of religious struggle toward a divine goal. Then he went on to discuss and define the strategy for a successful revolution, such as the one he had led in Iran.

Revolutionary movements, he explained, could never succeed unless their goals and strategies were in tune with the problems and sufferings of the people. No revolutionary movement could hope to achieve victory unless it sank deep roots in the hearts of the people. As long as revolutionary thought was confined to intellectual circles victory could never be won. Only a truly grass-roots mobilization could resist any form of compromise.

To give our guests a greater insight into post-revolutionary Iran, we took them to visit the martyrs' cemetery at Behest-e Zahra, to the slums of southern Tehran and finally, to the former monarch's luxurious palaces in the northern suburbs of the capital.

The conference format consisted of an official statement from each representative describing their movement, their objectives and their position on U.S. imperialism. We had delegated Hojjatoleslam Mousavi Khoeiniha to speak on our behalf. In his presentation, he sketched out the basic motivations behind the Islamic Revolution. After the structured sessions, informal talks continued every day until the wee hours. We were eager to learn about the principles and the strategies of the different liberation movements, and they were anxious to see at first hand the changes that were occurring in Iran, and to feel the pulse of the revolution.

We witnessed the dedication of the native peoples of North America, and for the first time we began to understand how cruelly they had suffered in their own homelands. Their tragedy reminded us of the Palestinians.

The conference also gave us an exceptional opportunity to learn about liberation movements in Latin America. I remember in particular the eagerness of a woman from Uruguay to learn about Islam and our revolution. We spent several hours with her discussing and exchanging experiences. Several of these movements were, at that time, operating clandestinely, and even in Tehran their members kept their faces covered for fear of having their identity revealed. We attributed their problems in attracting wider popular support to a lack of understanding of the cultural dynamics of their own societies.

But we, too, had much to learn from these guests. We found out from first hand sources the real nature of foreign domination, and the best tactics in the fight against colonialism in all its disguises. Throughout, we found a common thread, a sense of commitment to human values, truth, and sacrifice. I am sure that they also learned much from us, as participants in a revolution that had actually taken place.

The final resolution of the conference condemned American policy throughout the world, and all forms of military, economic, cultural and media aggression against oppressed people, particularly Iranians. It singled out the U.S. as the main enemy of the oppressed, expressed solidarity with the Palestinians and condemned the Camp David agreement. It called on liberation movements to form a united front against their oppressors. And finally, it expressed solidarity with the Islamic Revolution in Iran and with its leader, Imam Khomeini, and demanded the extradition of the criminal shah and the repatriation of the wealth of the Iranian nation.

The gathering was unique in several respects. First, it was organized and hosted by a student organization and not by a government. Because of its non-governmental status, it was free to act independently of conventional diplomatic considerations. Secondly, it brought together a broad spectrum of revolutionary groups from the four corners of the world.

Ultimately, we found that the participants shared a common goal: to fight against imperialism within a common framework. They believed that religious belief would act as the ultimate motivating force to relieve the plight of the oppressed. Even though most of the groups were Muslim many, including those from the Americas, were Christians committed to liberation theology.

The consensus among the participants was that the downtrodden would be able to mobilize their resources on the basis of their common interests, and that liberation theology would be the touchstone. Indeed, this universal doctrine was to become a powerful influence throughout the world in the decade to come. Throughout the world, Islamic movements found a fresh vitality and emerged as a critical new factor in the quest for a just world order.

FIFTY AMERICAN GUESTS

OUR SUCCESS IN CONVENING the conference of liberation movements set us wondering what else we could do in a similar vein. A few of us had an idea: we would invite representatives from grass-roots organizations in the United States to visit Iran so they could witness for themselves the oppression and injustice of the shah's regime and our motives for seizing the embassy and taking the hostages. We felt that through a constructive dialogue with the students and the people of Iran we would be able to influence their attitude toward us and toward Iran. We also wanted to tell the people of the United States that, contrary to the claims of the media, we did not consider them as our enemies although we believed their government was responsible for much of what our country had suffered.

The idea was submitted in the form of a proposal to the Central Committee. Then, after discussing it in general meetings of each university group, we decided to go ahead. We let our friends and supporters in the U.S. and Canada know about our plans, and asked them to chose likely candidates from among teachers, politicians, journalists, community activists and academics—people with an open-minded, critical attitude who, we hoped, would be able to judge our actions fairly and objectively.

The program was an ambitious one and we set ourselves strict deadlines. We would be responsible for organizing a complex and demanding program, and for making sure that our invited guests were properly looked after. At the same time, we had to maintain proper care of our uninvited guests, the hostages. So we shared the work, and those of us who would be in contact with the visitors delegated their responsibilities to other students. For the duration of the conference, we cut back on our "normal" tasks such as document processing and organizing interviews.

By late January we had received word that the invitees had been approached and that they had agreed to participate in the program. Members of the delegation came from all over North America and from all walks of life, from farmers to clergy. They included representatives from all major racial, religious and ethnic groups. In Iran, we had to plan for and organize an intensive program of activities. Our first step was to approach top ranking officials, including the Imam, about our intentions. Imam Khomeini gave us his blessing. But considering the particularly bureaucratic mentality of the Foreign Ministry, and our previous experience with them during the Conference of Liberation Movements, we decided to advise the guests not to apply for visas in the United States. We conferred with Sadeq Qotbzadeh, who had by then become foreign minister. He agreed that our tight schedule made this approach imperative.

The Americans who had accepted our invitation were prominent personalities from different regions of the United States. They came from various backgrounds but they had one thing in common: despite the intensity of the propaganda against us, they wanted to hear our side of the story.

But when the Americans arrived, Qotbzadeh and his officials denied ever having made such a commitment, and refused to issue visas. Fuming, we immediately contacted members of the Revolutionary Council and informed them of the situation. They instructed him to issue the visas. So it was that our guests, who arrived almost all together, were able to enter Iran with only a short delay at the airport.

It was late in the evening when they arrived at the hotel. After they had settled into their rooms we invited them to dinner in the restaurant, where we gave them a warm message of welcome. We had decorated the hotel lobby with pictures of the revolution and quotations from the Imam. From the moment they arrived, we felt an atmosphere of warmth and understanding. We were certain then that we had done the right thing.

The following day began with a visit by bus to Behesht-e Zahra. There we had prepared one of the mourning rooms with scenes from the revolution. When Imam Khomeini had returned victorious to Tehran in February, 1979, his first stop had been here, where he announced the establishment of an Islamic government. Since then, it had became the first place foreign visitors to Iran would visit.

We also showed them a film. I was in the audience that day; I still remember vividly how deeply touched the guests were by the images of the revolution. They saw how the monarchy had attacked and massacred the people with the total support of the American government. Some were even in tears.

Next came the visit to the slum areas around Tehran, inhabited by former peasants who had migrated from their poverty-stricken villages to the capital seeking a better life—a replay of a tragic scenario common to all developing countries. These slums could not really be described as a residential area; the dwellings could not be considered as real shelter. But people lived in these shacks built from scraps of wood, cardboard, plastic, tin and aluminum. Our American guests had a chance to peek into those grim hovels that people called home and chat with their inhabitants.

The people they met expressed their solidarity with the revolution. They had been its strongest supporters, and their hopes and expectations were enormous. Even then, these hopes were a source of concern for us. We felt apprehensive that the revolution might not be able to fulfill them and satisfy the most oppressed people in our country.

These first two visits gave our guests a dramatic picture of what they could expect to encounter in Iran.

Later, when we visited the luxurious palace of the shah's younger sister Shams in Karaj, a suburb of Tehran, they could measure the immense distance between the wealthy regime the United States had supported so stubbornly and the poor.

Their next visit was with Ayatollah Montazeri, then the designated successor to Imam Khomeini.[47] They presented him with a bouquet of red tulips to symbolize the sympathy of the American people for the hardships of the Iranian people. The Ayatollah in turn handed one of the tulips back to them, as a symbol of the power of martyrdom as a unifying force, to take back to the American people.

The delegates also met with Hojjatoleslam Ali Khamene'i[48] and exchanged views with him on American policy and the revolution. We had also arranged a meeting with the residents of a rehabilitation facility for the disabled of the revolution. There our guests were able to meet the young men and women who had sacrificed their health for the cause of the Islamic Revolution. They had been shot and injured during the street demonstrations. Their sense of conviction and high spirits were a cause of wonder for the visitors. The chance to sacrifice themselves for Islam was still a blessing, they told us.

We then took the group to visit the embassy itself. There they met with one of the members of the Central Committee who explained the reasons for the takeover and Imam Khomeini's thoughts on imperialism, oppression and the responsibility of the oppressed.

Since they had expressed a desire to meet the hostages, we arranged for an encounter with two of the people—I cannot remember their names— who held relatively sensitive positions in the embassy hierarchy. Our guests spent more than an hour asking them questions about the embassy's role following the revolution and about the conditions of the hostages since the takeover.

As the visit of the group to Iran coincided with the ceremonies commemorating the anniversary of the Islamic Revolution, our American guests were able to witness the huge demonstrations that filled the streets during the week of 22 Bahman on the Iranian calendar (February 12). An incident occurred that week that could have turned tragic. A temporary grandstand from which a large number of foreign guests were viewing the ceremonies collapsed from overcrowding. At first we were terrified that some of our charges might have been injured. However all were safe and sound.

They later told us how impressed they were at the speed and efficiency of the first-aid workers and marshals who helped them reach their hotel safely. We knew that it was a reflection of the unity and spirit of collaboration that had been at work throughout the revolution. Whatever the emergency, people would drop everything to help one another.

One of the things that had the strongest impact on the group was a meeting with five members of a family who had been imprisoned and tortured for political reasons during the shah's reign. The family described their tragic experience in graphic detail. The methods of torture and inhumane treatment by the shah's agents were hard to reconcile with Jimmy Carter's professed commitment to human rights. To further round out the picture, the delegates were taken to Evin Prison, where most political prisoners had been detained and tormented by SAVAK, the shah's secret police. They even met some imprisoned SAVAK members who explained how they had been trained in Israel by Mossad specialists in torture methods while in close "professional" cooperation with the CIA.

Throughout their stay in Iran we held several informal gatherings during which we traded views on everything from Iranian customs to women's rights.

Women's rights proved as sensitive an issue to discuss then as now. *Hijab*, the Islamic term for modest dress, usually including some form of head covering, is usually described in the West as a way of depriving women of their rights. It then followed that Islam in general, and Iran in particular, practiced discrimination. However, our first encounters helped undercut these stereotypes. At the embassy, women students served side by side with men and held positions of equal authority. As women, we were clearly not deprived of our freedom to think, speak and act. As Muslims, however, we abided by a set of norms which we felt were intended to uphold the dignity of women and men alike.

These norms are cultural as well as religious. We explained to our guests that in the Islamic world, a different mentality prevails. The role of women, their social position and family responsibilities derive from the principles of our religion. *Hijab*, in our society, draws a line between private and public space, between the family and the street or workplace. The concept, we soon realized, was a difficult one to understand in a society that is notorious for its commodification of human beings, particularly women.

We also argued that, from our perspective, and contrary to Western claims, exploitation of women was more widespread in North American and European society, though masked by a dazzling superficiality.

We also spent hours talking about lighter matters, such as Iranian customs and food. Everyday dishes like *khoresht*, a kind of meat and vegetable stew, were mysterious to our guests, as was the saffron which we use to season almost everything we eat. We took the curious to markets where they could buy it, and showed them how to use it, getting yellow fingertips in the process.

In the evenings the students' choir, which was organized by a talented member of our group, would sing revolutionary songs, and afterward the Americans would respond with pieces like "We Shall Overcome." We talked with the delegation's leaders about the possibility of continued contacts, better organization, and plans for the future.

But the group was far from as cohesive as we had hoped it would be. As individuals they were sympathetic, compassionate and caring, but they had no networking system in the United States, no organizational ties to speak of. When we asked them about issuing a statement of views on the plight of Iran, their reactions were mixed. Some agreed, others objected, fearing that such an act might cause problems for them when they returned home. Most had no particular affinity with organizations or groups, and had divergent views about the possible repercussions of their visit to Iran.

We bade farewell to our guests with the hope that as members of American society, these 50 men and women would sow the seeds of understanding toward Iran in their country.

It no longer came as a surprise to us that the American media which waited, hawk-eyed, to pounce on the slightest hint of news about the hostages, were uninterested in the visit of the 50 Americans. In fact, they all but boycotted the entire event. Of this dramatic and cordial encounter between two different cultures at a moment of high antagonism, almost nothing was reported. Anything that might convey the impression that Iranians were logical or reasonable, that the people occupying the embassy were students and not "militants" or "terrorists" appeared to have been reflexively censored and judged unmentionable by the major American media outlets. The fact that Americans, in defiance of their government's wishes, and Iranians had come together at the most difficult of times, and had spent several days in dialogue and exchange of views on the most controversial issues, seemed to have escaped them altogether. For the mainstream media, it was as if the whole event had never even happened.

As a forum for establishing human relationships among people of widely varying views and backgrounds, the visit accomplished much of what it set out to do. But we may have expected too much of our American guests, and overestimated their capacity to challenge the dominant "official version" of events. We had hoped that they would somehow be able to convey to the general public the message of what they had seen in Iran, and their understanding of our position. As it turned out, we were victims of our own idealism. We had not realized how totally the mass media had come to dominate all Western public debate.

Even today, I still do not have a comprehensive grasp of what these people were able to achieve. We had not organized a systematic follow-up system. Maintaining contact became difficult, especially as the atmosphere of crisis deepened after the ill-fated rescue mission. I do know that many of them organized speeches, seminars and interviews once they returned, but little more. A Committee for American Iranian Crisis Resolution was established after the conference, and for several months was active in trying to reduce tensions between the two countries. It published books and pamphlets on Iran. But for all the sincere efforts, its impact was limited.

Among the guests, one name stands out in my memory: that of Randy Goodman, a vivacious sociologist, photographer and journalist from Boston. She wrote several feature articles portraying Iran in an objective light, and edited a book entitled *Tell the American People*, an anthology of essays and photographs that were intended to improve American understanding of the Islamic Revolution in our country. But for all the efforts of individuals like Randy Goodman, it had been unrealistic on our part to imagine that 50 people could bring about a rapid, general change in attitudes in a country like the United States. Today, more than 20 years later, are those old attitudes slowly changing? If they are, it will be in part thanks to the seeds planted two decades ago by the Americans who braved official disapproval to witness events in Iran for themselves.

Iranian peasants demonstrate in support of the students.

CHAPTER VIII

WITHIN THE WALLS

LIFE INSIDE THE AMERICAN EMBASSY COMPOUND during the months of November 1979 to April 1980 unfolded in two distinct and paradoxical ways. On the one hand there was the understandable uncertainty of the American hostages who spent their days in relatively comfortable captivity.

On the other hand, there were the thoughts, hopes and aspirations of 300 university students during those turbulent 444 days.

Who were these young revolutionaries? What force had pulled them away from their calm and comfortable family life? What had moved them to deprive themselves of the carefree life and pleasures of youth and to plunge deeply into political action that would later complicate— and even cost some of them—their lives?

It was widely assumed at the time that the students who occupied the embassy had been hurt by American policies, that their action was little more than personal retaliation or revenge. But, with a few exceptions, this was not the case. Although, as Iranians, all of us had directly or indirectly experienced American interference in and domination of our nation's affairs, almost all of us became involved in this extraordinary movement on the basis of a wider concern—and on faith.

Accounts published in the Western media invariably portrayed us as fanatics and narrow-minded zealots. Since the term "student" contradicted such categorizations, the media used terms like "militants" or "captors" instead. We students were not, however, an intrinsically violent faction or group. That there were such groups in Iranian society I would never deny. But one of the cornerstones of our policy was to keep those groups far removed from any involvement in the embassy capture, and later, in the long-running drama of the hostages.

We did believe that the peaceful occupation and arrest of U.S. embassy personnel was the only way in which we could express our concern, and our anger at the American decision to grant the shah asylum, to the world. We were convinced that American domination represented a serious threat to our country's values and dignity.

The hundreds of letters that we received as students and those that were directly addressed to Mary, the name I used during the occupation, did confirm to us that a part of our message was getting through despite the high walls of misinformation and often virulent propaganda. Many of them came from individual Americans who had seen our live televised interviews and had listened to our message broadcast prior to the first hostage interview.

A letter addressed to the Imam reads as follows: "I am a carpenter, living and working in the city of Seattle in the United States of America. I and many of my countrymen feel that our government's support of the former shah was an error and contributed to the suffering of many Iranians. I have made a letter of apology and am having fellow citizens sign and send copies of the letter to you and other leaders of Iran. I hope to provide the leaders of Iran with sufficient letters of apology to influence yourself and them of the sincerity of our feelings. My prayer is that the many letters will be a major factor in solving the crisis between our peoples. Please forgive our transgressions…"

Another letter addressed to Mary from an American college professor reads as follows: "First let me introduce myself. I am an old man who had taught French for many years and who is now teaching English as a second language at Tacoma Community College in the state of Washington. I have had many Iranian students in my classes so I have been following the revolution with great interest and hope that it would succeed, that the ex-shah would be deposed and that Iran would gain a free government…You have succeeded in getting the attention of the American people and a certain amount of education concerning the ex-shah and the U.S. government has taken place…in all of this I am glad that you have been careful to distinguish between the U.S. government and the American people…"

I, as Mary, also came in for criticism by some Americans in their letters as "a woman who has accepted subjection to male dominion because of the scarf she was forced to wear."

A Mrs. Nancy M. wrote Mary dozens of letters explaining the political system in the U.S., and day to day developments. She was skeptical of both Democrats and Republicans. Neither, in her opinion, could change the face of America. She would send me newspaper clippings on important articles. After the aborted mission at Tabas she wrote: "It upsets me to hear your leaders talk about Carter and the American people and blame the raid on him and on us. Do you understand Maryam that the American people have nothing to say about these sort of things…We the American people have no voice in this sort of action…I pray that God will help your country and mine to make the right decision in this world shaking matter…" She always closed her letters with "someone who cares about you, Nancy." Nancy was but one example of the many sincere Americans who were uncomfortable with what they understood about their government's involvement in Iranian affairs.

A professor of religion at Fairfield University in Connecticut expressed his mixed feelings in a letter to Mary: "You have appeared twice on American TV and I have been impressed with your dedication…If I were your professor in Tehran and I observed a deprivation of human rights under the shah you would have heard about it in my class. It may have cost me my freedom or my life…As a standard bearer for a new government proclaiming a refreshing liberation you should shout to the world about freedom and the dignity of the human person. Yet you have chosen as your symbol of justice, hostages…"

Another letter read: "I'm a 22-year-old co-ed at San Diego State University in California. I am studying art history. I'd like very much to visit you and your captives and hear your side of the tale. We (other students and I) don't really know why you're holding our citizens as captives. I'd like very much to visit you and hear what you have to say.

This is no government plot. I am no one important, just a student who wants to find the truth…" Another letter from San Diego, dated January 10, 1980, read: "You have a beautiful name, Mary. The name of the mother of the Prophet Jesus. Jesus was a revolutionary person in his time too. In your statements on TV you speak about justice and the innocent. Jesus did not accomplish his plan with violence…"

The lives of the students, for the most obvious reasons, could not have been more different than those of their charges. One of the few things we did share was confinement in a particular location in particularly trying circumstances. I am not, of course, attempting to depict us as victims. The hostages had been given no other choice but confinement. We, on the other hand, chose confinement in those premises and under those circumstances, in absolute freedom. We remained free to stay with the group, or to leave it whenever we wished. As long as we remained, we had to follow the rules and abide by our own internal regulations. The hostages did not have this option. They could only wait.

* * *

The northern door of the embassy opened onto Bijan Alley. It was the main entrance and exit for the students. A student guard (usually one of the sisters) sat in a small room by the door, recording all entries and exits. We were allowed one day off each week, which could be extended to 48 hours if necessary. The date and hour of our exit was noted in a large log book.

I usually took Fridays off to see my family, but not until the end of the first month. I had managed to phone my mother several times. Finally, at the end of November, she came to see me at the gate. She brought a large bag of chocolates and toffees, and asked me to divide them among the students. I promised her I would visit home the following week. She went away contented, relieved that I was healthy, safe, and in good spirits. Not all the students' families were as supportive as mine. Though most were proud of their children's' involvement, some were concerned about the possible outcome, and a few were dismayed.

Even when I took Fridays off to visit my family I could not look forward to any rest. Friends or other family members would drop by, bringing with them dozens of questions about the embassy, the hostages, the documents and everything else. I had to spend hours discussing matters with them, apologizing when confidential questions came up that I could not answer.

In January, 1980, a strange thing happened. It was at the time when Carter was attempting, through various channels, to negotiate a way out of the imbroglio. A friend of mine had asked me several times to visit her at her apartment in north Tehran. I had declined until she called me one night at the embassy and almost pleaded with me to come and see her. It was important, she added. I was under the impression that she was talking about a family matter, so I agreed to stop off for a few moments that night.

This friend had been educated in the U.S. and returned to Iran after completing her studies. We chatted about this and that until I asked her to get to the point. I had to be back on guard duty in an hour. It was then that she began telling me about a certain Iranian friend of hers in the U.S. who was in regular contact with her. The friend believed that, due to strong contacts in the U.S. Congress and elsewhere, he could influence thinking over there if only we would soften our position here.

I quickly realized how wrong I had been in supposing that my friend wanted to discuss family business. I explained to her that I had no authority to speak with anyone and that I would certainly not have come to her house had I known her intentions. Then the phone rang. My friend answered, and after speaking with the other party, exclaimed, "It's him, it's Mr.—!" just the man I was telling you about. What a coincidence! My friend is very anxious to speak to you personally."

For a moment, I was stunned. The name was disturbingly familiar. Rapidly I rummaged through my mind attempting to remember where I'd seen or heard it before. My friend was holding the receiver, "It's a long-distance call. Don't waste any more time."

I could not move a muscle; my eyes were closed tight in concentration. Then I had it! "His first name is Fereydoun, right?"

"Yes, it's Fereydoun. Do you know him? Good. Come on, he's on the line."

"I know him very well," I said, and told her to tell her friend to hang up and call back later. My friend did so reluctantly; she seemed surprised and hurt that I had slighted her.

Quickly I explained that I had seen the name in two or three documents at the embassy. The man, Fereydoun, had led a small counter-revolutionary militia group. In the first months after the fall of the shah he had been in close contact with the CIA station in Tehran. My friend was taken aback. "Are you sure it's the same person?"

"His surname and first name are the same. Drop him. Don't get involved with that kind of person," I advised her before leaving for the embassy. She never spoke to Fereydoun again.

* * *

Under the organizational system we had developed, all major decisions were made by the Central Committee.

Beneath the Central Committee were six sub-committees. The Operations Committee handled security within the compound; the Documents Committee was responsible for the translation, exposure and publication of the seized and reconstituted documents; the Public Relations Committee arranged media interviews, contacts with the public and meetings with officials; the Services Committee provided food and other basic necessities; the Information Committee was in charge of intelligence and security; and the Hostage Affairs Committee dealt with everything related to our charges.

Each member of the Central Committee was responsible for learning the views of his or her university through regular meetings held every two weeks in the quarters inside the compound assigned to each. In the course of these meetings questions involving internal or external affairs were taken up and decided upon. The Polytechnic students' meetings were usually held on the ground floor of the consulate building, where the brothers and sisters would sit in two groups on the floor to exchange views and discuss current problems.

Sessions began with a brief report to the assembled students from their Central Committee member, followed by a round of questions, answers and proposals. Matters discussed ranged from simple questions of accommodation to complex issues of world politics. Every student was free to express his or her approval or discontent, and to make proposals on any matter they chose. Each proposal was put to discussion and when a consensus was reached, or few opposed, it would be forwarded to the Central Committee.

As with any group of people, especially young people, living under tense and crowded conditions, sharp differences of opinion and even personality conflicts did arise. But they were remarkably rare, and when they did occur, were related almost exclusively to political disagreements. There were cases where individual students opposed Central Committee decisions. I remember in particular four students from Tehran University who voiced opposition on even the most minor issues and tried to cause discord among the students. In a general meeting, more than 300 students voted to ask the four to leave the premises.

Life inside the Den of Spies began early in the morning. By 6:00 a.m. the hostage units were busy preparing breakfast for their charges, while the logistics unit was distributing bread, milk and cheese for us. The operations unit changed shift at 7:00 a.m., the document unit began work one hour later. The public relations unit was already hard at work preparing for interviews which usually began before 9 o'clock.

I usually slept until 8:30 because of late night guard duty. By that time most of the sisters in the visa dormitory were awake and preparing to begin work. We all performed morning prayers on an individual basis before sunrise. A phone call from a fellow student in charge of the public relations unit was a sign that reporters had arrived and I was expected to be there.

On Mondays and Thursdays we fasted, so breakfast was out of the question on those days. Fasting, for us, was an act of worship, and a form of spiritual and physical discipline. We believed that by controlling our powerful physical drives, we could educate ourselves to behave as our logic and wisdom guided us, and not be the slaves of our desires. When we fasted, it was as if we were departing from selfishness, and moving toward perfection and toward God. It gave us a feeling of lightness, of spiritual buoyancy.

On the other days, when we were not fasting, we took a simple breakfast, then headed off to our units for a busy day of work. We shared the housekeeping chores equally; each student, male or female, had to clean the rooms twice a month.

As noon approached the sound of the *azan*, the Muslims' call to prayer, filled the air, beginning with "Allah-o Akbar," and ending with, "Hasten to perform the best of all deeds, the worship of God." We usually dropped everything we were doing to make our ablutions, then to pray. Congregational prayers were held on Friday in the compound, in front of the southern gate or on the sports field. Of course, those of us who had sensitive responsibilities or were on guard duty could not join in.

In Islam, congregational prayers have an additional dimension. The unity and oneness of a society is guaranteed when it abides by common principles and a common goal. The best way to achieve the goal is by praying together.

Between our noon and afternoon prayers, Mr. Mousavi Khoeiniha would speak to us for about 20 minutes. His subjects were usually spiritual and ethical concerns, sometimes organizational or political issues. "If we want to overcome the external enemy, we must strive to develop strong personalities while we cleanse ourselves of selfishness. We must not think in terms of what is good for me, but what is good for society, for humanity, what brings God satisfaction."

Many may pay lip service to such goals. The difficulty arises when we try to apply a set of values in our own lives. An old Persian proverb which the Imam liked very much says, "It's easy to become knowledgeable, but how difficult it is to become 'human.'" What I mean is that during the revolution, the embassy occupation and the war with Iraq I encountered ordinary people who had succeeded in dominating their particularities, their pride, their selfish desires. Willingly they brought comfort and joy to others, often at the cost of deprivation for themselves.

After midday prayers we had lunch in the embassy cafeteria, except on days when most of us were fasting. Revolving teams of students served the food and washed the dishes afterward. Our team was assigned to dish washing duty twice a month. Each time took four hours of strenuous work. There were always plenty of plates.

At mealtimes, as in most other activities, the sexes were segregated. The women students sat in the upper tier of the cafeteria, the men below.

Adjacent to the cafeteria entrance we had put up a bulletin board where the latest communiqués or interesting newspaper articles were posted. After a month had gone by, something new caught our eye. Every day at noon we found a hand-drawn caricature posted on the notice board. At first no one knew who had drawn or posted the cartoons. The subjects included satirical glimpses at our own internal affairs, as well as humorous looks at national and international issues.

The ink drawings never exceeded more than a single sheet of paper, but the message was always concise and clear. I still remember one cartoon showing a hostage awakening his sleeping guard to be escorted to the bathroom. Or another one in which a well groomed hostage eating a delicious meal was asking a student: "Who is whose hostage?" In addition to the aesthetic value of the drawings, their content reflected a personality that could analyze events with a critical, yet humorous eye.

The artist's identity did not remain concealed for long. We soon found out that she was one of the students from Melli University. Her cartoons were a constant source of good cheer for us during a time of intense political struggle and high tension. Her artwork even created a market. I learned later that some of her works had been taken without her consent. In fact, high spirits and good humor could flourish everywhere, if only we could take off our political spectacles and see things in a more human light.

Sometimes the humor inherent in situations expressed itself in strange ways. Take guard duty, one of our most serious responsibilities.

Every two hours, day and night, a contingent of 60 students took up sentry positions in the compound or with the hostages. Each of them carried a walkie-talkie and one of the G-3 rifles we had been given by the military. Though we had entered the embassy without arms, the need to provide tight security within the compound had early on made it necessary for us to establish armed patrols. Meanwhile, men from the Sepah—Iran's newly formed Revolutionary Guard corps—stood guard outside the walls.

While standing guard, which soon proved to be a boring and monotonous activity, some of the students used the wireless for communicating amusing and humorous statements, and even short plays, in addition to our routine security checks and messages.

One of the students who usually stood guard in the early hours of the morning had a particular talent for impromptu radio drama. The operations unit would ask him to stop fooling around but it wasn't long before his sense of humor would get the better of him. On cold winter nights he would introduce his sketches with howling wind and chattering teeth. Then, in a shivering voice, he would describe the plight of a student sentry trapped by a snowstorm in the small forest in the center of the compound that we called the "jungle." One actor simulated the roaring of hungry animals which were about to pounce on our freezing hero. Finally, at the end, he would admit that the poor sentry was freezing because his socks and coat were full of holes.

We had memorable times in the "jungle," which was little more than a pine grove. One afternoon in early spring I was on sentry duty, standing in for a friend, when a group of sisters from the Polytechnic Institute turned up unexpectedly. They pointed to a black mulberry tree and asked me to help them pluck some of the plumpest, sweetest berries, the kind that seem to grow only on the higher branches. They wanted the berries to decorate a dish of fruit for the brothers from the Sepah who were standing guard outside. I begged off, explaining that I was on sentry duty. It would only take a few minutes, they pleaded. I found it impossible to refuse.

Though I had never been much of a tree climber I did my best. By the time I had half-filled the small basket they'd given me, I spied Hossein, one of the students from the documents unit, on his way from the residence. I tried to hide among the leaves but it was useless. "What are you doing up in that tree?" he asked. "I didn't think you were that big a slave to your stomach."

I attempted to explain that I was doing a favor for a group of sisters, but now they were nowhere to be seen. He walked off, laughing at the sight of having spotted one of the most serious sisters in a mulberry tree.

Only moments after he turned the corner I noticed the operations unit car which would occasionally check security throughout the compound. Bad luck always comes in batches. The car was heading right in my direction, and I was still in the upper branches of the tree.

Abbas Varamini, a top student in the Melli University sociology department who had received extensive military training, was our operations commander. He was one of the most popular students; honest, generous and totally dedicated. He was also a volunteer social worker who helped orphan children in his spare time, educating and training them. Everyone loved him. His humble yet firm personality was always an example for us.

Varamini stepped out of the car.

"Who's on guard here?" he said, then inquired by wireless to check the list. I heard the crackling response: my friend's name, with mine as substitute. I did everything I could to stifle my laughter. Varamini turned his head from side to side with a puzzled look on his face. He picked up my G-3 rifle from where I had dropped it and drove off in the car. I remained silent. The sisters were nowhere to be seen. I finished picking the berries and climbed down. Then, as if on cue, they reappeared.

Where were they to defend me when I needed them? I asked. Now everybody in the embassy would find out that I was climbing trees when I was supposed to be on guard duty. They went off with grins on their faces to deliver the berries to the Sepah guards outside the main gate. I headed for the operations unit to get my rifle back. Halfway there, Varamini spotted me. "Where on earth were you?" he said.

Trying to look surprised, I asked, "Why, what's wrong?"

He grinned and handed me my rifle. That was the end of the episode.

* * *

Wherever students go, courses and books are sure to follow. At least that's how it seemed to us when, in the space of a few weeks, we transformed the Den of Spies into a series of impromptu lecture halls. There, over and above our routine tasks, was where we held classes every afternoon, given by lecturers we ourselves selected and invited. Although most of us were from the engineering and law faculties, with medicine also well represented, our improvised courses focused on much broader, and deeper, questions.

Hojjatoleslam Mousavi Khoeiniha conducted a lecture series on the Imam's methodology in applying Islam to contemporary life. It was an opportunity for us to admire our teacher's keen intelligence and his grasp of the multitude of ways that religion can satisfy the natural human thirst for betterment and progress while at the same time presenting a solution for the problems of the age.

Part of the course consisted of lively discussions among students who were familiar with most of the existing theoretical alternatives. Most were conversant with Marxism and the history of communism. Many had lived in the West and experienced at first hand the prevailing attitude there, which encourages young people to choose a carefree life motivated only by the consumption of surplus value as a powerful sedative to pacify their turbulent spirit and conscience.

In fact, to us, Western capitalism and what was presented as its antithesis, Marxism, seemed to focus exclusively on the idea of surplus value. They differed only in their assessment of who should be the rightful beneficiary of this surplus: the people who financed the commercial enterprises and the factories, the capitalists; or the people who worked in these enterprises and factories, the workers. Both systems seemed incapable of imagining a life in which things had primarily an inherent value, rather than a surplus value

Another scholar, Hojjatoleslam Haeri Shirazi, who later became Friday prayer leader in the city of Shiraz, taught a course in ethics. His lectures focused on the dimensions of human nature, and how each individual must educate their "self" in emancipation from the chains of our self-centered desires and wishes.

Political analysis and international relations was the topic of another series of courses given by a team of specialists from the universities.

Perhaps the most popular of the lectures, aside from those given by Hojjatoleslam Khoeiniha, were by a fellow student, Sa'id Hajjarian.[49] Even as a student, Hajjarian had developed an uncanny ability to analyze and foresee events. His lectures were very popular, and were one of the high points of our impromptu study program.

When it finally became clear that the occupation might continue indefinitely, most of us had applied for and obtained a one-year leave of absence from our respective universities. Iran's Cultural Revolution, which took place in 1981, would soon result in the closure of all the country's universities for an additional year.

The shah's regime had set up a purely colonial education system. Iran's young people were neither prepared nor taught to meet the needs of their country. In fact, the psychology of education under the Pahlavi dictatorship was designed to create a passive, dependent attitude in students. Ideally, when technology and science are introduced into a country, they should not necessarily bring along with them the Western culture which which first learned to exploit them. Individual countries should have enough self-esteem to appropriate and utilize technology and science as tools to build on and develop their own intellectual and cultural capacities. The shah was intent on absorbing everything the West thrust upon him, blindly and uncritically. The Cultural Revolution was an attempt to reverse that trend, to restore self-esteem and to liberate students and faculty to pursue science in the interest of the nation.

The movement had another, more down-to-earth motive. After the fall of the Pahlavis and the disappearance of SAVAK, an atmosphere of total freedom prevailed: political groups of every description, from Marxists to pro-Americans, used the universities not only as an ideological headquarters, but even as military barracks and arms depots. In one incident, a leftist group managed to smuggle two truckloads of ammunition into Tehran University.

The convergence of these issues sparked a resistance movement among students and faculty who wanted to see the universities serve the country, not foreign interests. During the year they remained closed, teams of university faculty and students worked together to redesign the curriculum and to draw up the basic principles of a cultural transformation.

As new educational objectives were set, most curricula were modified. New courses in ethics and ideology were introduced. Those faculty members or student groups and parties who felt out of tune with the changes either left the universities on their own, or were asked to leave. Still other students left voluntarily to serve in remote villages, helping to educate the people and to build schools and health centers.

A year later, the universities reopened. The undertaking had been an ambitious one. Its success depended on the extent to which the people involved were truly convinced of its necessity. Did Iran's Cultural Revolution do what it set out to do? It may still be too soon to say, though their behavior during the first two decades of the Islamic Revolution would certainly indicate that students themselves have lost none of their questioning spirit and energy. Cultural transformations of the kind we hoped to bring about cannot but take generations, and they must meet the challenge of changing times.

* * *

After the Tabas incident, when the hostages were dispersed across the country, living conditions at the embassy changed substantially. Far fewer students were needed as there was no longer a security threat within the compound itself.

Later, when the war began, all the students, men and women alike, were given intensive three-day military training sessions at a nearby Armed Forces camp. Naturally enough, Abbas Varamini was our commanding officer. For him, military training was a serious matter. Those three-day training sessions bordered on hellish, but we learned to put up with it. The women followed exactly the same program as the men; neither shorter nor easier.

On the first day of training I showed up late and was punished accordingly. The penalty was an extra hour of guard duty that night, for a total of three hours. We had set up our tents in the compound and wore full battle dress. That night it began to rain. There I was, standing guard in the cold.

Once my three hours were over, I slipped into my tent, pulled off my boots and greatcoat and fell sound asleep. But in doing so I had disobeyed our commander's orders always to be alert, and to sleep with our boots on and our rifle close to our head.

I had been asleep for less than an hour when I heard staccato bursts of automatic weapons fire. "We're under attack!" someone shouted, and before I knew what was happening I heard Varamini call us into formation. Suddenly a tear-gas canister rolled into the tent, filling it with choking smoke. It was a full-scale attack drill, at 4:30 in the morning. Everyone had grabbed their rifles and was dashing towards the muster ground. Everyone except me, that is. I was still searching desperately for my boots in the choking smoke, coughing, tears streaming down my face. I came out of the tent with only one boot on and hopped over to the end of the line in the hope that Varamini would not see me. He was, however, looking me over very closely. Then he ordered the group to hurry off on the double for morning exercises. I fell behind to pull on my other boot. Again Varamini disciplined me for lateness, and docked me another hour's sleep that night. Three days was too short a time, of course, but it did provide at least a brief personal encounter with the meaning of military discipline.

* * *

When Iraq invaded, we were certain that it was at the behest of the United States.[50] It was clear to us that Saddam would be supported by all the Western allies, and that we would have to stand alone. Waves of young volunteers marched off to fight without compulsion, out of love for their country.

Life in the rear guard had its attractions. There was the comfort of home, the warmth of the family, or maybe even marriage. There was school, and the joy of learning and studying together. There was life itself, the intense desire to live, to enjoy.

On the other side lay the front and its dangers, its bombs and bullets, the wounded and the martyred. Very few returned with their health intact. The closer you got to the front lines, the greater the danger and the more powerful the pull of life, the sweeter the scent of home.

Two forces beckoned an entire generation, one the powerful attraction of life, the other the irresistible pull of immortality. Day by day the waves of young volunteers moved closer to the call of the spirit and away from the attractions of earthly existence. They seemed drawn by an unwavering force, a force they defined as love for Imam Hossein, the model for all martyrs and warriors.[51] Material life could not resist the strength of this current. So it was that many of us felt impelled to act.

Abbas Varamini, our operations commander, was with us until the war started, when he joined the volunteer forces of the Sepah to defend the country against the Iraqi aggressors. From 1980 to 1984 Varamini served actively, rising rapidly to brigade commander. His courage under fire was legendary. In 1983, he married a college student, but even that did not keep him away from the battle front. He explained to his wife that above his love for her, he had found love of God and of his country. "A voice is beckoning me, the voice of Him who created me. I must respond," he told her.

Varamini lived with his bride for only one week. A new operation was about to be launched, and he left for the front. A year later, he attained martyrdom as he led a group of volunteers against the Iraqi invaders. Varamini never saw his son, who was named Abbas after him. Varamini was and will always be a heroic model for the younger generations in their search for a meaning in life.

It may be difficult for these younger generations to understand his message. But it is one that cannot be restricted by time, place or nationality. It belongs to all human beings. It is up to us to introduce the story of people like Varamini to the new generations, whether in Iran or anywhere else in the world. But to do so successfully, we need to find new ways to make his story theirs. This is one of the greatest responsibilities that we now face.

"Do not consider those who are killed in the way of God as dead, they are alive, yet you do not understand." The psychology of the young Iranian volunteers during the eight years of war has yet to be studied by the social sciences. The innermost cores of their lives, their convictions, their ways and their manners, have rarely been touched by contemporary literature and media. Yet the cultural lexicon of their battlefield was a unique one.

CHAPTER IX

Delta Force Down

During the pitch black night Abraheh rode his elephant, at the head of his army. He had gathered all his forces, elephants and horsemen, for the attack on God's House, his long-awaited assault on the Ka'aba. As the arrogant men swarmed across the desert, no being was aware, nor could anyone understand, except one enlightened man from the descendants of the Prophets who stood alone in midnight prayer, saying, 'O God, cherisher of the Ka'aba, You have glorified this land with Your blessings, so that in every remote corner you may be worshipped and adored. Then guard this land Yourself, for this house belongs to you.' […]

And thus it was that God sent the 'Ababeel,' birds with stones of clay aimed at the aggressors. And they were demolished like so many crushed leaves.[…] And God willed that the Ka'aba remain unharmed, so that it might remain a source of inspiration and as a model for mankind.

Excerpts from a message by the students after the Tabas incident.

CERTAIN EVENTS IN HUMAN HISTORY throw a sudden light on all that precedes and all that follows. Like brilliant comets they brighten the darkest night and leave behind them a luminous trail. The incident at Tabas was such an event. It brought the capture of the U.S. embassy and the hostage taking into sharp focus.

The bipolar world order that prevailed in the 1980s had enveloped the oppressed countries of the world in an "East or West" straight jacket. Suddenly, seemingly out of nowhere, the Islamic Revolution in Iran proposed an alternative solution, upsetting all prevailing power balances and casting all previous certainties into flux.

Less than a year after the fall of the shah, the taking of the hostages seemed to prove to the world that the idea of "American leadership" was superficial, and could not prevail against the faith and determination of ordinary people in their millions.

All of a sudden, the powerful tools of imperialism stood revealed as utterly ineffective. At Tabas, the awesome military machine of the West, long a source of fear and subordination, was to mount a show of force. Such was the intention. But instead, the total failure of the machine unmasked the decidedly less-than-invincible nature of the American military juggernaut.

On Monday, April 21, 1980, a team from the International Red Cross visited the hostages. In the light of the events of the next few days, it took little to convince us that their real mission was to confirm the location of most of the hostages within the embassy compound. My diary mentions Thursday, April 24, as a busy day of routine work. But I went on to note that certain feelings I had later that evening made the night memorable.

I took part in our evening prayers as usual, but with a feeling of suspense I'd never experienced before. It was as if something was about to happen. Some of the others had experienced the same feelings, only stronger.

"Do you smell something fishy like we do?" they asked. "It's just a feeling, more like a sixth sense. It's as if we can smell the Americans, right up close."

It was Thursday, the night we usually recite the *Kumail Du'a*, a prayer that is an expression of devotion to God as the ultimate protector. It is the prayer of Imam Ali as taught to Kumail. Now, on that night, it was as if we too were praying to steel ourselves for a combat we sensed was coming, but could not see, could not hear. The prayer continued well after midnight. We recited the final parts of the prayer together, aloud. "O God whosoever draws aim against us, aim against him, and whosoever schemes against us, then plot against him. For you are the light of those who are lost in the fearsome darkness…"

It turned out that many of us had the same intuition that night. But no one was afraid. As I looked out over the embassy compound from the upper floors of the central building hours later, I remember noticing two or three women guards on patrol in the darkness, beneath the trees of the "jungle." If our seizure of the embassy had not been daring, I thought to myself, then what was?

* * *

Early next morning I was scheduled to go hiking with a group of friends; it was to be my first outing in months. Tehran is famous for the magnificent backdrop of snow-covered peaks that mark its northern limits. The mountains are a favorite recreational destination for thousands of Tehranis who like to spend their Fridays—the Iranian weekend—clambering up the rocks that mark the foothills of the Alborz range. And like many of our fellow citizens, mountain climbing was more than simple recreation. Not only was it a physical challenge; it was a mental and spiritual one as well.

Just the kind of challenge that suited the young people of my generation. For us, the experience was like our long fight to bring down the shah, who once towered above Iran like the very mountains we so enjoyed climbing. But, step by step, we had reached the summit. The tyrant was no more. That was what the climb symbolized for us.

The months of voluntary captivity in the embassy had meant foregoing this favorite weekly activity, our only real recreation. Though we had complete freedom to leave at any time, and some of the students did, a majority of us were determined to see things through to the end.

I awakened before dawn, feeling refreshed after the extraordinary prayer ceremony of the night before, and slipped out of the embassy at 5:00 a.m. on Friday, April 25, to meet the group at 6 o'clock. By 8 o'clock we were well ahead of schedule, moving steadily up the steep, rock-strewn foothills of the mountains.

212

At noon we stopped for a meal of water and dates for energy. Several hours later we reached our destination: Tehran lay at our feet, and beyond, the distant dry hills and the desert. It was already late in the afternoon when we turned back toward the city. But we could not find the trail. By now, darkness was creeping up the mountainside. We realized we had lost our way. Our leader could not find the way back and we had only one flashlight. It was well after nightfall when we stumbled back into the city exhausted, thanks to a horse that led us back to the village of Darakeh, our starting point. I phoned an uncle to ask him to pick me up. It was 11 o'clock.

"Did you hear the news?" he said breathlessly when he arrived. "The Americans have attacked."

"You're joking."

"I'm serious. They landed in the desert. Then came a sandstorm, one of their C-130s burned, two helicopters crashed."[53]

Gradually what had happened began to sink in. I asked him to rush me to the embassy.

In the compound, the atmosphere was very different from the day before. Everybody was talking about the event with a mixture of excitement and foreboding. "It happened during the exact same hours that we were reading the prayer, and since it was Thursday, many people were praying," was on everyone's lips.

Mohsen later recalled that as he was sleeping late that fateful night, someone had telephoned to tell him that the Americans had failed in a rescue attempt. Half asleep he had picked up the telephone and said "We categorically deny any such false news." He had fallen to sleep again when the same person called back. "There is news that the Americans have attacked Iran." Still half asleep and annoyed by the insistence of the caller, he had denied the report. "But mister, the radio has just announced the news. Maybe you have been asleep!" the voice had finally exclaimed. At that point Mohsen realized that something serious had happened.

Meeting in an emergency session, the Central Committee had already decided to divide the hostages into groups of four and disperse them to cities throughout the country. Some students had opposed the idea, arguing that the Americans had agents in Iran who might have a backup rescue plan. They might be monitoring developments around the embassy itself, endangering the security of students and hostages alike.

Others argued that since the operation had failed, any pro-American elements in Iran would be in disarray, and organizational contacts broken off. They would hardly be in a position to carry on, much less put an alternative plan into operation on short notice. This was the analysis that eventually won out, and the correct one, as events showed.

Still, when each team and its group of hostages were sent off to their respective cities, no one could rule out the possibility of attacks on the cars if the passengers were recognized. For this reason, most of the driving was done after dark.

We moved rapidly. By Saturday morning 46 hostages had been relocated. But carrying out the plan proved both dangerous and difficult. We could not allow the removal and relocation of the Americans to become known. Security—theirs and ours—remained a paramount factor.

Never, despite all our contingency planning, had we foreseen such an eventuality. Arranging to house, feed and provide security for our involuntary guests was a logistics nightmare. The student teams were given the responsibility for the hostages in each city. They immediately contacted friends to inform them and prepare suitable temporary housing, for a few days at least. Some of the Americans were transferred to safe houses in North Tehran and in other parts of the capital. Others were dispersed to cities across the country.

By calling on our network of friends, fellow-students and supporters in Tehran, we quickly located vehicles to transport the hostages. It was only after they had departed, well after midnight on Friday, that we had an opportunity to sit down and analyze what had happened.

Some of us speculated that the Republican Party may have used its influence in the United States military to tamper with the airplanes and helicopters, causing them to malfunction and ultimately fail. The disaster, for which Jimmy Carter took full personal responsibility, certainly did place the Democratic administration in an untenable position only a few months before the election.[54]

But when we thought it through once more, we concluded that both parties were united in their basic principles and goals. It was unlikely that one group would take action that would undermine America's already tottering prestige for short-term political advantage. The Islamic Revolution had struck a first blow. Then came the hostage taking of November 4. Now, in less than a year, a third humiliation had occurred. It appeared as though America had nowhere to hide.

In fact, we concluded, neither the Republicans nor any other human factor alone had changed the course of events. The fiasco at Tabas was the result of multiple causes which meant little taken singly, but collectively led to one of the most abject failures an American government has ever encountered. We never doubted that divine intervention had saved Iran and thwarted the aggressive superpower.

Imam Khomeini was later to put it eloquently, "Those sand particles were divinely commissioned. They had a mission: to destroy the aggressor's planes." The Imam's statement was a clear reference to the Qur'anic account of the attack of Abraheh, the ruler of Yemen, in the "Year of the Elephant" (the year of the birth of Prophet Mohammad, 570 A.D.) on the House of God, the Ka'aba.

(Viewing Mecca as a rising commercial and political rival, Abraheh had marched to destroy the city's central attraction, the House of God, in hope of shifting the seat of power to Yemen. He mobilized a battalion of elephants trained in warfare and driven by experienced soldiers. But when a flock of birds attacked each elephant and driver with pebbles of clay, as the Qur'an calls them, the entire invading army was destroyed. The parallel between these two events, a full fourteen centuries apart, carried an unmistakable message for us.)

The Imam's account went farther in terms of its ideological weight. American idolatry, the doctrine of the infallible West backed by science and technology and an exclusive reliance on human-centered values that ultimately depicted God and religion as relics of the past, had been briefly brought face to face with the fact of its weakness.

Tabas was a signpost, a place where supernatural forces, probability and bad luck as they called it, or divine intervention as we considered it, converged; a powerful reminder to twentieth-century man that his mastery of science and technology in the form of military force is not all-powerful. This is acutely true in the face of the infinite forces of nature, as they are called in the West, or the workings of God, as we believe.

Long-term planning had gone into the operation at Tabas. Its creators drew on the experience of previous successful hostage rescue teams; they carried out full-scale Delta Force simulations, prepared detailed analysis of meteorological, geographical, political and military data, and enjoyed unlimited budgetary resources. Yet they failed.

In his message marking the occasion the Imam laid bare the complex network of American schemes in the region: there were tribal insurrections in Kurdistan encouraged by a curious amalgam of pro-American leftists; there was unrest in the universities, also strongly influenced by leftist groups linked, according to the documents we had pieced together, to the United States; there was Iraqi military provocation on Iran's borders. The effect, we were convinced, was to divert the attention of the people and the government from the hostages and the possibility of a rescue raid.

During the Tabas operation, Iranian military officers loyal to the shah such as Col. Bagheri, rendered faithful service to the Americans. Three days before the attack, the colonel had ordered that all anti-aircraft missiles be removed immediately from air bases in Tehran, Mashhad and Babolsar under the pretext of sending them to the western border. He was perfectly aware the air force had sufficient quantities of the same weapons in its warehouses, and that their presence in key locations such as Tehran and Mashhad was indispensable.

Two days later two boxes of documents from the site of the incident and from the wreckage of the helicopter were brought to the embassy for our inspection. We had, by then, acquired a nationwide reputation for deciphering and piecing together even the most mutilated scraps of evidence. They included flight plans, some scorched by fire, and reports; detailed maps of Tehran and environs, pinpointing the location of the embassy and several churches, as well as a detailed description of the operation itself. We also found sensitive information on flight plans, contacts in Iran, and the ultimate objectives of the operation.

The abandoned helicopter, which had been left undamaged, would have certainly contained additional vital, high-priority information. It had probably been the command post. The Iranian air-to-ground missile that destroyed it and all the remaining documents it contained, ostensibly "by mistake" 48 hours later, was no accident. For that, we had Col. Bagheri to thank as well. This lead helicopter most probably held a full list of connections and sources, Iranian[55] and foreign, who were to link up with the Delta Force and provide logistic support for the invaders.

The Carter administration must have feared the embarrassment that would follow exposure of the documents relating to the operation. After the Tabas incident the U.S. government was overcome by a deep sense of frustration and futility from which it never recovered. The Democrats, who owed their popularity to a history of support for human rights and social welfare programs were now facing a trial in the court of world opinion that seriously endangered their reputation. The resignation of Secretary of State Cyrus Vance, followed by a chain of hostile criticism, made matters even worse for the authors of the fiasco, primarily the president himself, and his National Security Advisor Zbigniew Brzezinski, the plan's chief advocate.

How, too, could we forget the letter? Two weeks before the incident, in early April, we had received a written message from a person, clearly well informed, who claimed to sympathize with the revolution. Such messages were not uncommon during the embassy occupation. We often received telephone calls, telegrams and letters warning us of plots, coups and imminent danger. Most we quickly put aside as rumor. We believed that the hostages were well protected, and that security was tight. Though we had taken the letter seriously enough to forward it to the Revolutionary Council, we had forgotten it completely.

It was not until after the events at Tabas that we remembered our anonymous informant, and retrieved the original of the letter from our files. The complete text was then published in several Tehran dailies.

The author of the letter had lived for several years in Tehran, had come to detest the shah's regime and understood the suffering of the people. He had made up his mind to write to inform us of behind-the-scenes developments. His information had been obtained from an Israeli intelligence officer, he wrote. He went on:

(1) The National Security Council is involved in devising a military plan for rescuing the hostages in Tehran. According to this plan, which will be implemented both within and outside of Iran, a special force will be drawn up in cooperation with the Mossad. On October 22, 1979, a mutual meeting with Ezer Weizman (the Israeli Defense Minister), the American ambassador in Tel Aviv and the American military attaché discussed details of Israeli cooperation in this plan. It was decided to recruit officers and planners from the Entebbe airport operation as well. The members of this group include men from the elite 82nd Airborne Division of the U.S. Army, stationed at Fort Bragg, N.C. They will be sent to Cyprus (Acrolimni) via West Germany and then to Israel.

(2) Another plan has also been drawn up for toppling Ayatollah Khomeini's government, under Carter's direct orders. Intelligence services in the region and Mideast are advised to plan for operations that could undermine the Iranian regime. [This attempted coup d'état occurred two months later and was aborted.][56]

William Miller has met with the ambassadors in Turkey, Iraq, Saudi Arabia and Israel, as well as CIA officers, informing them of an imminent American attack in the Persian Gulf.

Groups of discontented Iranian SAVAK and military officers are organized, guided and even trained by the CIA for these purposes. CIA and Pentagon officials travel under cover to Iran to establish contact with counterrevolutionary groups such as Forqan and pro-West groups in the army. They are also arranging to smuggle arms for rebellious grouplets in various locations of Iran. Israel, Egypt and Turkey have agreed on co-operating in these terms. Turkey has provided exceptional facilities for American intelligence services at its borders. The secrecy and confidential nature of Turkish cooperation is vital for their security for they fear that the Islamic Erbakan Party[57] might react negatively.

Since I fear that this letter may be lost I will send several copies. For obvious reasons, I cannot give my name or title but I consider myself to be one of your sympathizers.

Although we never were able to establish the identity of the author of the letter, its precise and detailed information proved convincing in the light of real events. It was clear to us that our anonymous sympathizer had provided us with more than information and insight; he had given us a detailed, credible analysis of events that was later born out by facts. Particularly telling was the section on U.S.-Turkish-Israeli cooperation. Then secret, in the late 1990s it was transformed into a formal strategic alliance which many Iranians feel is directed against Iran.

* * *

From the early hours of the next day, I began tracking international and domestic reaction to, and analysis of, the incident. My general impression was that the Americans had felt a strange sort of apprehension of what might happen, but still chose to go ahead. This same sense of unease pervaded everything they said and did, even weeks after the fiasco.

They realized that their actions had worsened the situation, particularly for the hostages who had been dispersed to uncomfortable locations and in conditions of privation in various cities. But in Iran, you could feel a new sense of confidence and calm, from the students to the government. The outcome of Tabas reassured us that despite its military superiority, the United States were doomed to defeat.

The charred bodies of the eight American servicemen were immediately sent home, although in the state of foreign aggression Iran was facing, we would have been within our rights to act otherwise. But we felt that the Americans had learned a lesson. The lesson later proved to have been short-lived.[58] But our youthful expectations had, temporarily at least, been reinforced.

I could not attend the press conference that marked the event. A small group of us was hard at work in the document center trying to decipher the encoded words and messages inscribed in the helicopter log-books.

The death of eight American servicemen, who must have sincerely believed they were serving the interests of their country, was naturally a source of concern for us. We resented that their lives had been sacrificed to the incompetence of the Carter White House. We had always prayed that the hostage-taking episode would end in favor of Iran, without bloodshed. Not a single hostage was harmed or injured during 444 days of captivity. The only American deaths were those in Tabas, and at their own hands.

Hojjatoleslam Mousavi Khoeiniha summed up the affair this way, "Tabas stands as a milestone in human history. It is a manifestation of divine intercession for a good end. It is a divine signal to awaken the Americans; may they abandon their arrogant and oppressive ways, may they realize they have no superiority over others, particularly when it comes to believers who have truly given their heart to God. And it carries a lesson for us: power and force in and of itself do not justify anything. That kind of arrogance will cause its possessor to deviate, whoever he may be. We must not be defiantly proud of this victory, but we should thank God for his endless blessings and kindness to us."

I cannot know how the history books will finally judge what happened at Tabas, but I hope they convey enough objective information to let the reader or the student judge for himself, on the basis of what actually occurred. Tabas taught many a lesson, yet many lessons remain to be learned from this enigmatic event.

CHAPTER X

SETTLEMENTS, CONCESSIONS AND SAFE DELIVERY

ON THE EVE OF OUR FIRST ANNIVERSARY, the "Den," as we called it, was no longer the center of the furious activity it had known in the early months. Only one quarter of the students who had made the compound their home during the first six months still remained. Since the hostages had been dispersed throughout Iran, and then returned to other locations in Tehran, a majority of the students had accompanied them. The embassy compound itself now actually housed only four hostages.

The documents section remained active, but at a lower level than before. Groups of students were still at work classifying and translating documents as well as reconstructing the shreds. Live televised exposures had ended, however. All planning now focused on the long term publication of the documents in book form.

Though we only granted interviews and meetings on exceptional occasions, the students were in constant demand as speakers in cities far and near from Iranians anxious to hear the inside story of the embassy takeover.

The majority of the women and many of the men who remained were involved in guarding the compound. Those who handled public relations and worked on the documents no longer resided in the embassy. They came only a day or two a week to fulfill their responsibilities.

During the final months, we decided to move the hostages back to Tehran. They and their guards were facing an increasingly difficult situation, especially in the more remote cities where security, logistics and the comfort of the hostages left much to be desired. Thirty-three hostages were taken to other locations since, after the Tabas incident, we no longer considered the embassy secure.

In spite of the difficult circumstances, we tried to maintain an acceptable level of services for the hostages. They were never entrusted to the custody of anyone else. Imam Khomeini had insisted that the students must take care of hostages until the Islamic Consultative Assembly, the Majlis, determined their fate.

So we had the responsibility of holding the Americans and planning for their needs and security up to the very last minute. Even though in the final months it was announced that the hostages had been transferred to the care of the government, the authorities asked us to continue to ensure their actual physical custody.

In these circumstances, our Central Committee decided that the most fitting way to celebrate the first anniversary of the takeover of the Den of Spies would be to invite the Iranian people to enter the embassy compound and have a look for themselves. The buildings would be closed, of course, and no one would be allowed to enter them. This would mean a three-fold increase in the number of guards as well as careful monitoring. But, considering the handful of hostages on the premises, we concluded that no serious threat existed. Several students were assigned to serve as guides for the visiting groups, showing them around the premises and pointing out the role and importance of each different section or building.

A few days before the anniversary we issued a communiqué inviting different groups of people—school children, teachers, workers, and government employees—to visit the compound.

That day, we were almost overwhelmed by the waves of people who poured through the gates from early morning until dusk to support us and visit the compound they had heard so much about. One large group of school girls arrived wearing head scarves similar to those worn by front-line fighters in Iran as well as Palestine, each carrying a flag bearing the words "Allah-o Akbar."

Their march through the compound was as spectacular as it was stirring.

Our student guides led them from one end of the compound to the other, from the "dome" that housed the sophisticated satellite and communications devices used for espionage against Iran as well as the then Soviet Union, to the vicinity of the Chancellery, explaining the importance of the secret documents we had seized.

Most of our young visitors were brimming with inquisitiveness and curiosity about the CIA's complex systems and methods.

Individuals or entire families also came. Some preferred to visit the compound on their own without any guide. At one point I was strolling through the "jungle" when I noticed a middle-class family led by a father who, from a distance, appeared to be very self-assured in his claims. Quietly I approached to listen what he had to say.

Among the trees, holes had been dug for burning dried leaves in the fall. Whether this had been done by an embassy gardener or by the students, I cannot recall. But now the family had gathered around the hole as the father explained knowingly, "Do you see this hole in the ground? Look how black and charred it is. Do you know what the Americans did here? They used it as a dungeon to torture and burn people."

I couldn't help myself; I laughed in surprise. My laughter caught the father's attention.

"Who are you to laugh so rudely?" he asked in irritation.

"I am one of the students," I replied. "Your imagination is excellent, but please don't make claims you cannot back up."

I explained the actual reason for the holes and even showed them the leaves that we had gathered. After setting matters straight, I invited the family to join a guided tour of the compound.

Most of our visitors, including many young people, were extremely well informed on the political issues surrounding the embassy seizure. The quality of their questions indicated that they were keenly aware of the role of the American Embassy in undermining the revolution. The political insight and maturity of the majority of the people who had responded to our invitation was a source of great satisfaction for us. Once again, we felt vindicated in the action we had taken.

Later in the evening began the difficult job of asking people to leave. Although we repeatedly asked people not to picnic or sit on the lawn, some families were still camped there as dusk fell. First we used a bullhorn to ask the people to leave, then we began searching.

In the northern section near the chargé's residence I noticed a shadow moving across the lawn. I cautiously approached, only to find a very old woman stumbling along in the dark. When I asked her why she was still there, she told me she was looking for the washroom. Surprised, I told her there was no washroom here; she must be mistaken. She stubbornly insisted that there was a drinking fountain as well.

"I have been here dozens of times for demonstrations and for prayers. I know this place very well," she insisted.

"But my dear, this is not Tehran University. This is the American Embassy," I told her. She must have been too old to make the distinction.

She had come with a group of demonstrators from her neighborhood. They had not properly explained to her where they were going. Tehran University was the site for Friday prayers as well as mass meetings and demonstrations. The University campus, with its many buildings and tree-shaded lanes, was similar in certain respects to the embassy grounds. After taking her to the washroom in the chargé's residence, I led her out of the compound and hailed a taxi to take her directly home.

Early on in the occupation, we had set up a lost-and-found department, where children or belongings lost during demonstrations could be left off to be claimed later. We reactivated it for our first anniversary open-house. It was our responsibility to find the families or owners after the ceremonies. That day, I remember, a young girl about five years old was found wandering alone in the compound. She had come with her family but somehow they had become separated. When I asked her to explain how she had gotten lost she piped up in a cheerful voice: "But I'm not lost. As you can see, I'm found. It's my mommy and daddy who are lost." She remained our guest for a few hours before her parents came to pick her up.

* * *

Imam Khomeini considered the question of the hostages a national issue. It was, he insisted, up to the elected representatives of the people to make the final decision on their fate. This meant none of the country's sharply differing political factions could derive either credit or benefit from the outcome.

After Iran's first parliamentary elections under the Islamic Republic, in July, 1980, the Majlis was convened. Its first task was to draft the rules, regulations and procedures governing legislative action. Then the deputies' credentials had to be approved, a process that took a total of 47 full-day sessions and lasted nearly two months.

During those days we received reports of confidential meetings at which the fate of the hostages had been discussed. We knew that certain people, including some of Bani Sadr's aides, were involved in casual contacts with the Americans and their European counterparts. However we were confident that nothing could be done before the Majlis reached its final decision.

On September 14, during its 48th session, the Majlis Commission on Foreign Affairs proposed that the matter of the hostages be brought before the full house. Over the next five sessions the deputies discussed what kind of decision should be taken, but the debate was overshadowed by constant Iraqi provocations along its border with Iran, and on several occasions it had to be postponed.

Two days later fifteen deputies petitioned the speaker, Hojjatoleslam Ali Akbar Hashemi Rafsanjani, to defer discussions about the hostage issue. "During Vietnam peace talks in Paris the U.S. was constantly bombing Vietnam as a coercive tactic. Now they presume they can use the same tactics against us. The Americans have supported and encouraged Iraq to attack us," they stated.[59]

In fact, the Iraqi invasion had opened a new chapter in the life of the Iranian nation and in our lives as well. It was a time of testing for those who claimed to believe in independence, freedom and the principles of the revolution. Now, the time to prove their willingness to sacrifice for the newly born Islamic Republic had come. Via its Iraqi proxy, the entire Western world, with its endless supplies and vast military resources, was confronting the Islamic Revolution. Now the challenge took the young generation to the battle fronts to defend their dignity with their bare hands if need be.

The Americans and their Iraqi hirelings had based their decision on accurate calculations and hair-trigger timing. Post-revolutionary Iran, in its youth and inexperience, had already faced scores of attempts to undermine its existence. The country was naturally vulnerable to any organized military attack on its borders.

The Iraqis had anticipated that the campaign would be an effortless one.[60] In the event of any negligible resistance, the abundance of material and logistical support from the Western allies would more than overcome any shortages. Logically and logistically speaking Iraq would be the undisputed victor. So confident was Saddam Hussein in his swift victory that the Iraqi government had printed maps of Iran's oil-rich southwestern province of Khuzestan, giving its cities Arabic names and drawing a new border.

That, however, was not how things turned out. Once again the Americans had miscalculated, as they had when the shah was toppled, and as they had during the hostage affair. They had overlooked Iran's spiritual strength and underestimated its human and military resources. Before their very eyes the Iranians expelled the Iraqis from their land and held the upper hand throughout the war in spite of a Western military and economic blockade.

More than 60 percent of Iran's university students, not only those involved in the embassy takeover but throughout the entire country, joined up as volunteers to serve as specialists or to fight on the front lines. The women were just as active in behind-the-lines and cultural support.

It was against this emotionally-charged background that a final decision on the hostages was delayed until October 2. On that date the

Majlis appointed a special commission. This seven-member commission was given the responsibility of devising a pragmatic plan to end the impasse. The commission was also forbidden by majority vote from any direct negotiation with the American side, which did not close the door on indirect contacts, as we were later to learn. Its final decision would become binding only after approval of the Majlis.

This debate touched off a flurry of renewed interest, not only among the students, but among Iranians at large. I remember distinctly how we used to carry pocket radios in order to listen to the live broadcast of the Majlis proceedings during our daily guard hours in the Den. Then we would go over the speeches of each and every deputy with a fine-toothed comb.

I was particularly struck by the fact that most of the deputies began by proclaiming their intention to bring the hostages—the spies as they called them—before a national or international tribunal.

During his historic message to Iran's pilgrim's to Mecca, however, the Imam had recommended that the Majlis free the hostages if the Americans met four conditions. Only if these conditions were not met were they to face trial.

"I have stated several times that the taking of hostages by our combative Muslim students was a natural reaction to the afflictions imposed upon our nation by America and that this matter may be resolved only with the return of the wealth of the deceased shah, the abandonment of all American claims against Iran, a pledge of political and military non-interference, and the unfreezing of Iran's assets," he stated.

The speech showed that the Imam was now convinced that the occupation of the Den of Spies and the hostage taking had already had a potent impact on world public opinion. To prolong the situation would be worthwhile only if the hostages were released after our conditions had been explicitly met.

The Special Commission brought its proposal before the full Majlis on October 26. I remember listening to that session from a radio in the Chancellery building. Scores of international reporters had gathered in the Majlis to listen to the debate. Not surprisingly, the plight of 50 hostages was a top priority for global media and international bodies, while the massacre of hundreds of civilians by Iraqi missiles in border cities had gone all but unnoticed during the past days. This brought a quick reaction from the deputies, who voted unanimously to postpone debate on the Commission's plan in response to the bombing of the western Iranian city of Dezful.

On November 2, forty-eight hours before the presidential election in the United States, the Commission's proposal was again brought before an open session of the Majlis after two sessions held behind closed doors. The plan was based on the conditions laid down by Imam Khomeini in his address to the pilgrims. Its details were discussed and put to a vote after minor amendments. Then, in a unanimous decision, the Majlis approved the plan that laid down the guidelines for government action.

Political observers took due note of the delicate timing of the Majlis decision and its implementation by the government. Whether by coincidence or by design, it proved detrimental to both the Democrats and the Republicans. The plan was announced only two days before the American election, leaving Carter no chance to use the settlement to rescue his floundering campaign. His inability to deal with the crisis was obvious to all American voters.

On the other hand, working out the details of the settlement were to take so long that the hostages were finally released during the early hours of Reagan's term, which robbed the Democrats of any political gain during their last days in power. But the release of the hostages was nonetheless an achievement of the other party, so the Republicans had few political gains to boast of.

Several analysts were later to claim, on the basis of the circumstantial evidence available at the time, that this delicate timing was the result of a precise plan which aimed at shifting the power balance in the United States in favor of the Republicans. Such speculation, fueled by the fabrications of president Bani Sadr, whose influence had begun to wane, took the form of a political scandal in the U.S. which became known as the "October Surprise." It was later to surface again in the form of the Iran-Contra and the McFarlane affairs.[61]

During the Majlis sessions, many deputies raised the question of optimal timing for the debates and resulting legislation. The first time speaker Hashemi Rafsanjani brought up the hostage question, a group of deputies protested that the Majlis had more important matters to attend to.

We also heard rumors that a particular Majlis faction had claimed that since the United States presidential elections were directly influenced by the Majlis's decision, they should not only bear this fact in mind but also make the most of it.[62]

In one open session some of the deputies proposed to up the ante and pressure the Americans, in order to obtain other advantages such as strategic spare parts for military equipment purchased by the shah's regime. Foreign news services claimed that an American military plane loaded with spare parts was waiting in Stockholm. Other deputies opposed the idea, insisting that they were not interested in gaining credit from the Americans. "But credit is the exact word that the Imam used in his speech," another replied in direct reference to Imam Khomeini's statement.

The implication was basically that any deal done with the Americans, even beyond the official Majlis proposal, would not be considered contrary to the interests of Iran or to the Imam's doctrine, although it might encounter sharp criticism on the home front. In other words, even if a particular faction actually concluded a deal with the Republicans, this would not weigh heavily against them in Iranian political or judiciary circles. The American half in any potential secret deal faced a different predicament: such a deal was unauthorized and in many respects illegal.[63]

The tactics of the Majlis speaker and certain deputies in delaying or speeding up the decision-making process and the subsequent timing of the settlement with the Algerian government have been seen by some as clear evidence of a clandestine deal with the Republican party. Even though the odds against such an arrangement are considerable, many prefer to believe that considering the Imam's insistence on obtaining credit from the Americans, some people in authority may well have carried out precisely such an operation. Subsequent events such as the

McFarlane arms deal leading to the notorious Iran-Contra scandal lend credence to such speculation.

These rumors became so persistent that in the Majlis, deputy Mohammad Khazaie openly denied them in the November 2 session. "The only reason for any delay in this matter is the regular process of Majlis legislation," he asserted.[64]

Each leading political figure had his own particular position. Many, including most of the students, hoped that Carter would be defeated in the elections—not because they preferred Reagan but because they saw it as a show of force by Iran's Islamic Revolution. During the shah's regime, all significant political personalities, including the top leaders, had to be approved by foreign embassies, and particularly the Americans. Now the process had been reversed; we had a say in American politics. Many also looked forward to Carter's defeat, seeing it as the realization of Imam Khomeini's assertion that "Carter should leave."

Others, like the late Prime Minister Mohammad Ali Rajai'e were so firm and uncompromising in their stand against the U.S. that it is very difficult to imagine any deal concluded behind the scenes without their consent. Rajai'e believed that the hostage question had turned into an troublesome affair which had to be swiftly resolved in the greater interest of the country.

Abolhassan Bani Sadr, then President of the Islamic Republic, had made it clear in government sessions that he preferred to see the Democrats remain in power. This ambitious politician actually seemed to prefer one party over the other, while the majority of Iran's intellectuals and officials believed otherwise. In essence both U.S. parties were staunch secular capitalists on the national level, and imperialists on the global level. Synchronized in strategies, they differed mostly on tactics, changing roles with the consent of one another only to secure their absolute authority over the American people and, in terms of economics and culture, over much of the world.

Bani Sadr, we were convinced, was actively trying to strike a deal with Carter's men while another faction may well have preferred to play the Reagan card.[65] In any case, Bani Sadr's secret contacts with the CIA could conceivably have continued during the ensuing months. As the embassy documents indicated, a long-term approach to Bani Sadr had been evaluated as positive by the CIA. And though the same documents pointed to several Iranian political figures, none was as powerful and influential as Bani Sadr, who was then at the inner core of the Islamic establishment.[66] This means that the possibility that he was in direct or indirect contact with the American administration, possibly through the CIA, during these crucial episodes, cannot be ruled out.

His conspicuous preference for the Democrats made him in our eyes a likely candidate for involvement in a deal in which they ultimately proved the losers in a tug-of-war with their Republican opponents.

* * *

The conditions as laid down by the Majlis were finally implemented by the government of Prime Minister Rajai'e. A working group headed by Behzad Nabavi was set up. It was to sound out the Americans through Algerian mediators. In fact, the American response, giving consent to the basic framework, had already been received through unofficial parallel channels such as the Vatican and the Palestine Liberation Organization.

Now the details of the settlement had to be approved by both sides. Any change in the plan would require a new approval process by Iranian authorities. The result was intensive shuttle traffic back and forth between Washington, Algiers and Tehran.

The government made several decisions on the actual method of implementation. It agreed to pay all outstanding debts on long term loans and to return all assets securing those loans. In this way Iran avoided paying high interest rates, and at the same time was able to abrogate all economic links with the United States. It also accepted that an international arbitrator or court would rule on questions arising from the long term implementation of any agreement, as well as the settlement of any claims.

Based on Iran's conditions, the Algerian government, with the agreement of the American side, finally came up with a plan of action. An initial transfer of sufficient assets to an escrow account in the U.K. would be the signal for the release of the hostages.

We students were never informed of, involved in or consulted on the implementation process. It was only after all the arrangements had been completed that Ahmad Azizi and Behzad Nabavi asked for a meeting with our leaders to discuss the details of the release of the hostages. At that meeting, they asked us politely what we thought about the agreement. But since everything had been decided, we only smiled in response.

* * *

Amir Abbas Hoveyda had been prime minister to the shah's regime for more than a decade. He and his cabinet were notorious for their incompetence, their bureaucratic mentality, their corruption and outright theft. Among his many properties was a large villa adjacent to Sa'adabad Palace in northern Tehran. It was there that the American hostages were housed during their final days in Iran.

As the day of their release drew near we gradually allowed the hostages more access to information. Their initial reaction to the news of their impending freedom was one of disbelief and cynicism. Many believed Carter did not think their lives were important, and that he would do nothing to bring about their release.

I was not in immediate contact with the students during the final days. I had been appointed to the editorial board of an English-language Tehran daily newspaper; since the universities were closed I spent most of my time there. One afternoon one of the brothers telephoned me and told me that they needed my assistance. The matter was totally confidential, he said. When I arrived at Hoveyda's villa I met the students who explained what they intended to do. How different the atmosphere was from the first days of the embassy takeover!

The following morning, acting on the students' plan, I met Katherine Koob and Elizabeth Swift, the only two remaining women hostages. I told them their freedom was imminent, that the Majlis had reached a decision and that the Americans were now holding up the process. They did not believe the news and were particularly despondent. I talked with the brothers about the matter; we decided to provide them with English-language newspapers. Next morning we bought copies of Tehran's two dailies, *Kayhan International* and *Tehran Times* from the newsstands. It was only then that Koob and Swift actually believed what we had told them. To say the attitude and morale of all the hostages had perked up substantially would be an understatement.

Once the final release arrangements had been completed, Algerian doctors were asked to visit and check the health of each hostage. A large room in Hoveyda's palace was set aside as a makeshift clinic. An examination bed with all the necessary medical equipment was provided. The hostages were led to the room one by one. Their blood pressure, pulse, temperature, pupil contraction and other vital signs were examined and recorded.

We made a point of asking the doctors to check their bodies for any signs of physical abuse. Many of the hostages, particularly those directly involved in espionage activities, were so skeptical about their imminent release that they constantly asked the Algerian doctors whether all the hostages would be released or not.

They asked the doctors these questions in urgent whispers which we ignored, despite our agreement that they not converse. Now that our conditions had been met, little else mattered.

Predicting the hostile propaganda that was sure to follow, we decided to tape a video interview with each of the hostages before their release. I was asked to perform the task—to finish the job, in a manner of speaking. Each interview lasted between three and four minutes.

The questions concerned the hostages' health, their treatment, how they spent their time and the quality of their food. They were pointedly asked if they were harassed or persecuted during their confinement.

Of all the hostages I interviewed that day, I most clearly remember the behavior of Mike Metrinko, one of the CIA agents. He stalked into the interview room and declared point blank that he was not willing to be interviewed by a woman. I quickly responded, "It's an honor for you, as a spy, to be interviewed by a Muslim woman! I'm doing what I choose to do. Otherwise, I would refuse to interview an American spy!"

Metrinko was perhaps the strangest of all the hostages; his secretive personality and unconventional behavior irritated Iranians and Americans alike. He preferred solitary confinement and took no part in any of the religious ceremonies we had arranged for our charges. Needless to say, he was not interviewed that day.

We breathed a sigh of collective relief, and gave deep thanks to God that not a single hostage had been injured or harmed during their 444 difficult and precarious days of confinement. It was a matter of pride for us that we had succeeded in completing such a demanding task in a highly charged political atmosphere and under extraordinary international pressure with harmony and competence. We had embarked upon the embassy takeover as students. Now we released the hostages as young adults, with a new sense of maturity.

* * *

Finally, the day had come. The hostages were taken from Hoveyda's palace by buses under student guard to Mehrabad airport where an Algerian Airways jet was waiting on the tarmac. There they were handed over to the Algerian officials at the foot of the stairs leading to the aircraft. The count was complete. The hostage episode had ended, 444 days after it had begun.

The next morning's headlines in Tehran's daily newspapers read: "America Bows to the Nation's Conditions; Hostages Released."

Meanwhile, political tensions between Bani Sadr and his supporters (the self-styled "People's Mujahideen" who had by then launched a campaign of political assassination and bombing public places in the hope of securing power), and the followers of the Imam were growing sharper. Most of the opposition factions, including the Iran Liberation Movement, were seriously criticizing the Majlis and the government for the terms of the settlement. They had been opposed to the takeover and the confrontation with America from the very first, but now they were attempting to reshape public perceptions of what had happened and their role in it.

During the final stages of the event, we students experienced the entire gamut of emotions and opinions. Many of us were reluctant to support the manner in which the government had implemented the Majlis's conditions. Others approved the overall strategy, but had reservations about the specific details.

Generally we felt that as long as the Imam and the Majlis were informed of the process and had given their consent, nothing contrary to the interests of the people would be signed. The key to this attitude of confidence and trust lay in the personality of Imam and his style of policy making.

I personally believed that the we had made the best of the circumstances and that the gains heavily outweighed any possible losses. It seemed clear to me that once the Majlis' conditions were implemented, bureaucratic complications and limitations on both sides, particularly with respect to the bankers who settled the financial matters, would make matters difficult and complex. But all things considered, I felt that we had done well. We had accomplished something vitally important: we had shattered the image of American superiority in the world.

The students, most of whom were now dispersed throughout the country, with many at the battle front while others had returned to their classes, were summoned to a final gathering in the Den of Spies.

We had often talked among ourselves about the destiny of our group as a student movement. Throughout the fifteen months that we 300 students worked together in the embassy we had established a well organized system where each person was relatively well identified and recognized for his or her individual merits and capabilities. Each one of us had gradually found his or her place in the organization. It was not surprising that some of us felt that we had the potential to establish a coherent organization focused on the very principles for which we had taken action in the first place.

One group of students believed that we should establish an official organization or political party to be called "Muslim Students Following the Line of the Imam." Others had serious doubts about such a course of action. We were wary of following in the footsteps of political organizations which had gradually deviated from their original goals and objectives and ended up acting against the interests of the country for the sake of their narrow agendas. The Muslim Students Following the Line of the Imam had won the unconditional confidence of the people at a time when most other groups had displayed little more than insincerity. The movement was a sacred one, but could anyone guarantee the future? In addition, those opposed to the idea argued that the group had never been brought together with this objective in mind. We had joined forces for one reason alone: to fulfill our obligation to the revolution and the nation. Nothing more. Our movement was sacred, sacred in the sense that we had no worldly motivations. We never sought to secure power for ourselves, or fame, or any political gain. On the contrary, our utopian aspirations centered on the prosperity and welfare of our fellow countrymen.

We debated the question in two or three general sessions. Students took turns speaking, for and against. Those who advocated setting up an organization were in the minority. Ultimately most of us were convinced that the best thing for our movement would be to announce its dissolution. One last communiqué was drafted explaining our final decision: "We shall join the nation on the battle front, in the reconstruction of our country, in the lecture halls…" it read. "The students were the children of this nation from the start; they never were a separate entity. Now that they have accomplished their task they will return."

Epilogue

TODAY, 21 YEARS LATER, a clearer understanding of how the capture of the American Embassy shaped events in our country has begun to emerge. Along with it, new questions have also arisen. Do we, the former students, see things in a different light today than we did then? Has time distorted our judgement or dimmed our memory? Did the ideals we supported so fervently back then, survive?

These questions strike to the very heart of modern Iranian political life and to our role in it. In order to understand and respond to them one must look closely at the realities behind Iranian politics and public opinion, and examine the dynamics of the Islamic Republic through a lens altogether different from that through which the international media and Western observers have, for the last 21 years, viewed our country.

While this book, because of its focus, can only touch on some of these questions, it points clearly to the connection between the takeover in 1979 and the reform movement that emerged in 1997. Was it mere coincidence, the play of destiny, or a logical, predictable sequence of events? Whatever the case, no one can deny that both of these historical watersheds share common participants, and that the reform movement has been identified as the natural outcome of the takeover, even though on the surface they would seem to contradict one other in tone as well as intention.

While today it is widely acknowledged in Iran and abroad that the reform movement is democratic in nature, that it promotes the values of pluralism and openness, very few realize, let alone acknowledge, that the Islamic Revolution led by Imam Khomeini was in fact the beginning of a new process of political development and democracy in our country. The Revolution ousted a dictatorial, monarchical regime and established, on the basis of a referendum and a series of regularly-held elections, the first Islamic Republic of its kind.

Although initially, full democracy and political development were unable to flourish due to foreign pressures, to the war with Iraq, and to the establishment of a political monopoly by Iran's conservative faction, the teachings and philosophy of the Imam pointed to a democratic system based on the contemporary concepts of accountability, justice, transparency, and fundamental freedoms as guaranteed by the Constitution.

The conditions that prevailed during those years, and the conservative political faction that dominated the Iranian political world after the death of the Imam combined to block the full implementation of the Constitution. Elected local municipal councils, political parties, freedom of expression for the opposition and a just system of accountability were some of the provisions of the Constitution that had been ignored, delayed or suppressed.

The recent reform movement set out to reach those objectives while conforming to a legal framework and promoting respect for the law as an integral aspect of its campaign. The result has been a serious political conflict, as power is transferred from a conservative "right" to a reformist "left," each with its own particularities, complexities and internal divisions. As the reformers searched for their direction, and learned their political limitations, many were arrested and sentenced to prison terms.

World media, and the self-styled Western experts who are called upon to explain events in Iran, reacted with surprise when this forward-looking reform movement emerged from within the very heart of the Islamic Revolution. Suddenly, or so it seemed, Iran was rife with change. The old images were no longer adequate to describe a new reality: that of a sophisticated, democratic, yet religious government.

Political life in Iran has always been described in the West as unpredictable. I have often felt that this was due, at least in part, to the difficulty Westerners experience in understanding Islam. What has happened in our country since May 23, 1997, is certainly no exception.

But there is another factor which the West has ignored.

Iranians to this day are deeply attached to their history and to their national identity. They have never forgotten their country's contribution to world civilization. When they chose Islam 14 centuries ago, it, along with national pride and the thirst for advancement and progress, became the bedrock of our sense of who we are and where we stand in the world.

Unseen by the experts, hidden from the view of a narrow-minded and short-sighted international media establishment, Iran has been carrying on a debate with itself. The debate focuses on the compatibility of religion and democracy, and on our right, as Muslims, to advocate a just economic and political order for our society. Many, perhaps most, Iranians see in President Khatami a man who believes that Islam and participatory democracy can become one, and create a social environment in which human development, individual freedom and dignity can flourish.

One of the most important contributions to the awakening of public involvement in the affairs of the country has been the explosion of a free, combative press. Once represented by the lonely voice of *Salâm*, the daily published by Hojjatoleslam Mousavi Khoeiniha, Iran's independent press flourished in the first two years following the election of President Khatami. Courageous publishers, editors and journalists braved censure, censorship, imprisonment and the closure of their newspapers by the conservative forces that still dominate Iran's state institutions.

In the summer of 1999, *Salâm* published classified Information Ministry documents outlining plans drafted by a certain Said Eslami, who was soon thereafter to die in captivity, allegedly by his own hand. Immediately after publication of the documents, *Salâm* was closed. The action touched off widespread unrest.

In early March, 2000, Sa'id Hajjarian, who was such a popular lecturer during our impromptu courses in the U.S. Embassy compound, was shot and critically wounded in broad daylight as he was arriving to attend a meeting of the Tehran city council, democratically elected for the first time the year before. Though the would-be assassins were tried and sentenced, their motives were never adequately explored.

And, following the parliamentary elections of February 18, 2000, sixteen daily and weekly newspapers were closed by the country's judiciary, depriving the public of its right to the free exchange of informed opinion. However, the Sixth Majlis, in which the pro-reform forces now enjoy a 75% majority, convened on May 25, 2000.

If recent Iranian history can teach us anything, it is that these clashes, rifts and tensions are part of an intense, accelerated learning process. There have been setbacks; qualified candidates have been disqualified. But in one ballot after another, citizens have demonstrated their determination to support those who stand for reform.

At the same time, the conservative groups who looked upon post-revolutionary Iran as their own private garden, have been slowly learning that their attitudes are no longer appropriate to the needs of the day, if indeed they ever were. Every incident that reveals a lack of sincerity on their part has further undermined their support among the public.

Radical pressure groups, extreme right wing conservatives, terrorist groups in exile and some Western political commentators have pointed to a rift between the Supreme Leader, Ayatollah Khamene'i, and President Mohammad Khatami. Mr. Khamene'i has, however, repeatedly supported the president and his policies, while Mr. Khatami has continued to stress his unity with the Leader.

The civil society that is taking shape in Iran today is unique in several ways—the religious backbone of our society and the religious commitment of those who lead the reform movement set it apart from the secular movements that exist in many other countries.

The experience that Iranians built up in carrying out an anti-imperialist revolution has helped sustain morale and confidence, even in adversity. Despite severe economic difficulties due to both internal factors and outside sanctions, living standards for a majority of the population have improved. Key indicators such as life expectancy, literacy, and significant advances in education have demonstrated that the political and executive structures of our country are relatively competent. This in turn has given the people confidence that they can rely on their own resources for social and political development.

The reform movement has set out to anchor basic civil and political freedoms within the context of the constitution of the Islamic Republic. In doing so, it has opened new space for debate. Today, in towns and villages, in homes and offices and mosques, Iranians are discussing such basic issues as freedom of expression, morals and values, tolerance, good governance, women's rights, and pluralism. Never in its long history has our country experienced such openness.

Islamic Iran is a young country, and its younger generation has high expectations. As the reform movement deepens and spreads, it can understand and accommodate this new generation and its concerns. We are caught up in a delicate balancing act: while the basic principles of the Islamic Revolution—which made the reform movement possible in the first place—will remain unaltered, we must also bend to the requirements of changing times. But I am convinced that the flexibility inherent in Shi'a jurisprudence will allow the system to arrive at a dynamic equilibrium between tradition and modernity, freedom and morality, consistency and change.

The U.S. Embassy takeover took place during the last years of the bipolar international system that emerged from World War II. Direct and indirect intervention by the two superpowers—the U.S.A. and the U.S.S.R.—were commonplace throughout what once was called the "Third World." But the Islamic Revolution in Iran transformed a once-devoted ally of the West into a "rogue state" that insisted on taking orders from none other than God.

In those circumstances, safeguarding the revolution and thwarting efforts to undermine it was the only possible approach. We looked on with amusement as the international agreements and conventions that had given the green light to the oppression of the Iranian nation were seen critically only after the students detained 52 Americans. From our point of view, the double standard we had exposed was reason enough for the action we took.

But though our action had, as Imam Khomeini put it, smashed an idol, and brought about a change of attitudes throughout the region, the same idol has reconstituted itself, and is still exerting a powerful influence on the lives of billions. We owe our independence and freedom today to those moments of clarity during the takeover and resistance against the West, and during the war against the aggressors, and also to the perseverance Iranians have demonstrated as they rebuilt the nation and set out to restore a civil society.

Two decades later, we have traded the bipolar world of the Cold War for a new world order ruled by a single superpower which pursues its policies under the guise of globalization while at the same time daringly rejecting international conventions.

Seen against this background, it should come as little surprise that the students of 1979 are in the vanguard of a reform movement that intends to put the revolution back on track, to secure freedom and democracy within the framework of Iran's Constitution.

One of the most important objectives of this movement is to ease tensions in foreign relations, and to build solid and enduring economic, cultural and political relations with the world around us. Economic and cultural links with many nations, including the United States, have already begun to take shape, and may well flourish in the future.

The restoration of normalized political relations may take much longer. Though the American government has admitted some of its responsibility for the subversion of our national life in the past, very little has changed in practice. If Iran's Islamic Revolution taught us nothing else, it showed us how to resist the demands of a superpower. The reform movement to which we are committed will prove to be no exception.

Twenty-one years have passed since we stormed the gates of the U.S. Embassy on that fateful day in November, 1979. Since then we have learned many lessons. We have tried to understand how our youthful enthusiasm was often misunderstood outside Iran, and how it was manipulated by certain groups inside the country. Surely the conclusions we reached have helped shape the movement that we have become a part of, particularly its focus on freedom of expression and the creation of an Islamic civil society. That we, as a movement, have chosen pacifist resistance to violence is no accident.

My deepest hope is that this book will, in the end, have provided readers in the West with an alternative view. Not only of the events which shook a country and shocked the world, but of the misunderstood qualities of the Islamic Revolution as, at last, they emerge into the full light of day.

Barriers still stand between us. But the way is now open to understanding and dialogue among equals.

Tehran, June, 2000

Appendix A

Letter from John Graves, public relations officer,
United States Embassy, Tehran
to R. T. Curran, United States International Communications Agency

EMBASSY OF THE
UNITED STATES OF AMERICA
Tehran, Iran

October 4, 1979

CONFIDENTIAL

OFFICIAL-INFORMAL

Mr. R. T. Curran
Director for North African, Near Easter
and South Asian Affairs
United States International Communications Agency
Washington, D.C. 20547

Dear Ted:

At the end of my second month in Tehran, it should be useful
for me, and perhaps for you also, to try to sort out where I
think we are now and what we should do in the next six months
to promote U.S. interests in Iran.

The Revolution: As I see it, the revolution which suddenly
found itself victorious last February was essentially a
revolt against privilege. The forces opposing the Shah were
a disparate lot -- Shi'a traditionalists, Westernized
democratic liberals, socialists, Marxists -- who coalesced for
one purpose only, to oust the Shah. These disparate groups
could never, however, have mustered the force to face down
the Shah without the fanatical backing of the masses who
were fired up by the charisma of Khomeini. In addition to
opposing entrenched privilege, many who fought the Shah were
profoundly upset by rapid change and Western (especially
American) influences which permeated Iranian society and in
the view of many were undermining traditional values and
institutions.

In brief, the revolution was against privilege and rapid
Westernization. I believe it is essential that we keep
this firmly in view as we go about trying to promote U.S.
interests by entering into ongoing communication processes
with influential Iranians. There are, of course, specific
communication tensions, but the deep-seated tensions stemming
from revolt against privilege and Westernization underlie
most of the other limited tensions we may address.

CONFIDENTIAL

244

Appendix B

CIA documents relating to SD/LURE (Abolhassan Bani Sadr) discovered in the embassy

S C R E T 040807Z SEP 79 STAFF

CITE TEHRAN 54117

TO: IMMEDIATE DIRECTOR

WNINTEL RYBAT LPGAMIN SDLURE

     1. FOLLOWING IS RUTHERFORD'S REPORT OF SECOND MEETING HELD WITH SDLURE/1 ON 3 SEPTEMBER. (COMMENT: ALTHOUGH RUTHERFORD WAITED FOR SUBJECT ONE HOUR AT LATTER'S RESIDENCE ON 2 SEPTEMBER, SDLURE/1 (L/1) TELEPHONED THAT HE WOULD NOT BE ABLE TO MAKE IT AND SUGGESTED CHANGING TO NEXT DAY.)

     2. L/1 HAS BEEN MAINTAINING A BUSY SCHEDULE SINCE HIS RETURN TO IRAN LAST FEBRUARY. BETWEEN ATTENDING DAILY SESSIONS OF THE ASSEMBLY OF EXPERTS, MEETINGS OF THE REVOLUTIONARY COUNCIL AND PUBLISHING HIS PAPER, HE IS NORMALLY WORKING UNTIL AFTER MIDNIGHT ON A REGULAR BASIS. HE BROKE AWAY FROM A MEETING ON THE DRAFT CONSTITUTION TO MEET WITH RUTHERFORD FOR TWO HOURS ON 3 SEP AND PLANNED TO RETURN TO PARLIAMENT IN THE AFTERNOON TO CONTINUE THE DISCUSSIONS ON THE CONSTITUTION.

     3. SUBJECT HAS NOT BEEN ABLE TO REVISIT PARIS SINCE HIS RETURN IRAN. TWO OF HIS CHILDREN CONTINUE TO STUDY IN PARIS. ASKED ABOUT HIS APARTMENT THERE, HE INDICATED THAT HE STILL RETAINS IT BUT HOPES TO TERMINATE IT BECAUSE OF THE FINANCIAL BURDEN. HE AND THE MEMBERS OF HIS FAMILY IN TEHRAN ARE LIVING WITH THREE MARRIED SISTERS WHO OCCUPY THE THREE APARTMENTS AT CHANAS STREET LOCATION.

     4. IN DISCUSSING THE CENTER OF POWER IN THE REVOLUTIONARY GOVT OF IRAN, SUBJECT STATED THAT POWER RESIDES IN THE HANDS OF COUNCIL, THE REVOLUTIONARY PROSECUTOR AND IN THE KOMITEHS. ACCORDING TO HIS EXPLANATION, THE KOMITEHS ARE PRIMARILY CONCERNED WITH LOCAL MATTERS BUT, NONTHELESS, ARE CAPABLE OF PROPOSING SPECIFIC STEPS OR ACTION BY THE OTHER ELEMENTS OF POWER. ALTHOUGH INCLUDING THE PRESENT CABINET AS A HOLDER POWER, SUBJECT NOTED ONCE AGAIN THAT IT TAKES ACTION ON RELATIVELY UNIMPORTANT MATTERS SUCH AS THOSE CONCERNING EDUCATION, HEALTH, ETC.

     5. SUBJECT WAS EITHER UNABLE OR UNWILLING TO NAME A LIKELY SUCCESSOR TO BAZARGAN WHENEVER HE STEPS ASIDE.HIS RESPONSE WAS THAT " WE SHALL HAVE TO WAIT AND SEE."

Appendix C

May 5, 1980

In the Name of God, the Merciful, the Compassionate.

His Excellency Pope John Paul II,

I received your letter which expressed concern over the strained relations between the Islamic Iran and the United States. I express my gratitude for your good will and would like to inform you that our combatant and noble people regard the severance of relations as a good omen; they have made merry, illuminated and celebrated the occasion. I thank His Excellency for praying God, the Almighty, on behalf of our combatant nation. Still, I ask His Excellency not to be concerned over the eruption of new, poor relations and greater hazards mentioned in that letter, since Iran's Muslim nation welcomes any predicament which may arise by the severance of ties, and is not frightened of the more serious hazards warned of in that letter.

The truly dangerous day for our nation is when (foreign) relations similar to those preferred by the former traitor regime are resumed, which, God willing, shall not happen.

Considering His Excellency's spiritual influence among the Christian believers, I ask His Honor to warn the U.S. government of the consequences of its oppressions, cruelties and plunders, and advise Mr. Carter, who is doomed to defeat, to treat nations desiring absolute independence of global powers on the basis of humanitarian principles. He should be advised to observe the guidelines of Jesus Christ and not to expose himself and the U.S. Administration to defamation. I pray God, the Almighty, to grant prosperity to the oppressed worldwide and rupture the hands of the oppressors.

Ruhollah Mousavi Khomeini

NOTES

FOREWORD

1. James A. Bill, *The Eagle and the Lion: the Tragedy of American-Iran Relations*, (New Haven: Yale University Press, 1988), 295.

2. Said Amir Arjomand, *The Turban for the Crown: The Islamic Revolution in Iran*, (New York: Oxford University Press, 1988), 139.

3. *New York Times*, April 16, 2000: 1.

4. Jean-Pierre Digard, Bernard Hourcade, Yann Richard, *L'Iran au XXe siècle*, (Paris: Fayard, 1996), 173: "L'existence en son sein d'une tendance «tiers-mondiste», «de gauche», opposé au clergé traditionnel, à «droite» rappelle combien it serait erroné de vouloir réduire la République islamique à une quelconque théocratie médiévale, à un califat, et a quel point elle reste marquée par la révolution populaire qui l'a fondée."

5. Interview, Tehran, February, 2000.

6. Fred A. Reed, *Persian Postcards: Iran After Khomeini*, (Vancouver: Talonbooks, 1994), 225.

7. George Bayley, "Television War: Trends in Network Coverage of Vietnam 1965-1970," *Journal of Broadcasting* (Washington, D.C.) Spring, 1976. Quoted in *Le Monde Diplomatique*, avril 2000: 27.

CHAPTER I: IN THE BEGINNING

8. For a discussion of the role of Dr. Shariati in the Islamic Revolution, see Hamid Algar, *The Roots of the Islamic Revolution*, (Toronto: The Open Press, 1983).

9. These suspicions were justified. In the days immediately prior to the collapse of the Pahalavi regime, in January 1979, General Robert Huyser was dispatched to Tehran with instructions to organize a military coup. The shah's army had disintegrated so thoroughly that the plan had to be dropped (Bill, 254).

10. "Israeli intelligence…played a major part in the creation and operation of SAVAK." (Bill, 98). Relations between Iran and Israel, though clandestine, were close. At a meeting between Henry Kissinger and the shah in Zurich, on February 18, 1975, "the monarch agreed to provide the Israelis with additional Iranian oil if they acceded to Kissinger's retreat plan from Egyptian oil fields in the Sinai."

    See also the memoirs of former General Hussein Fardoust (*The Rise and Fall of the Pahlavi Dynasty*, translated and annotated by Ali Akbar Dareini, [Delhi: Motilal Banarsidass Publishers, 1999]), teams of SAVAK operatives were sent to Israel for special training. Israeli instructors, specializing in interrogation techniques, later came to Tehran to train Iranians.

11. Personalities assassinated during this period included Ayatollah Morteza Mottahari and Ayatollah Mohammad Mofatteh, two outstanding religious scholars who played a pivotal role in familiarizing the younger generation with an authentic version of Islamic thought presented in simple, attractive language.

On June 28, 1981 within six months of the release of the hostages, a powerful bomb demolished the headquarters of the Islamic Republican Party. Officially, 72 people, including Supreme Court Justice Ayatollah Mohammad Hossein Beheshti, died in the explosion.

In August of the same year President Mohammad Ali Raja'i and Prime Minister Mohammad Javad Bahonar met a similar fate. In 1983, the *New York Times* revealed that the American government had been secretly funding the MKO (Mujahideen Khalq Organization), led by Massoud Rajavi. Robert Woodward in *Behind the Veil*, his book about former CIA director William Casey, writes that the Reagan administration's CIA director was obsessed until his death with covert operations aimed at the assassination of Imam Khomeini himself. This stood in strange contrast to oft-repeated American claims that United States policy forbade attempts on the lives of foreign heads of state or government, a policy honored much more in the breach.

By 1985 more than 1,000 officials of Iran's government met death by assassination that most Iranians saw as instigated by outside forces. The present Leader of the Islamic Revolution Ayatollah Seyyed Ali Khamene'i and former President Hashemi Rafsanjani were gravely wounded in attempts against their lives in 1981 and 1980 respectively.

12. It was widely believed in Iran that ethnic uprisings undertaken by the Kurds of Kurdistan Province were provoked and financed by the U.S.S.R. as well as by Iraq, that the Arabs of Khuzestan Province were similarly provoked by Iraqi agents, and that the Baluchis of Sistan-Baluchistan Province and the Turkomans in and around Gorgan (Mazandaran Province) were encouraged by the Soviet Union. The Bazargan government was concerned enough about these developments to seek assurances from the United States that Washington was not fomenting ethnic unrest along Iran's borders.

Documents uncovered in the U.S. Embassy pointed to U.S. involvement in all these events, with assistance from the military regime which had taken power in Turkey in 1980.

Given the massive financial and logistics support so readily made available by Saudi Arabia and Kuwait when Iraq actually invaded Iran on September 22, 1980, it may be assumed that the royal families, with eyes closed and pockets open, helped to foment ethnic unrest inside the country, willy nilly enticing Saddam Hussein to attempt in August, 1990, to capture one of the geese that laid the golden eggs.

13. Hojjatoleslam Mousavi Khoeiniha, a leading Islamic theologian, was an intimate associate of the late Imam Khomeini. Like many of the Imam's companions, he had fought against the regime of the shah and against its foreign-instigated policies. Mr. Khoeiniha is a man of wide-ranging intellect, with a strong commitment to Islam and is considered to have particular insight into the Imam's world view. A three-term Member of Parliament, appointed as Attorney General by the Imam, he was, until its closure by the authorities in July, 1999, publisher of the daily newspaper *Salâm* and a member of the Rohaniyoun Mobarez party. Mr. Khoeiniha had often been referred to in American and British papers as the "Red Mollah," a consequence of his having allegedly studied in the Soviet Union. It was an example of the crude media inventions through which the West claims to "know" Iran. Mr. Khoeiniha neither studied nor traveled in the former U.S.S.R.

14. The jewel-encrusted Peacock Throne had been stolen from India by the adventurer Nader Shah (ruled 1736-1747) and appropriated by the Pahlavi family as a dynastic symbol.

15. The Americans had reason to be concerned about security. The decision to allow the deposed shah into the United States for medical treatment touched off sharp reactions among American diplomats in Tehran. James Bill quotes Barry Rosen (soon to become a hostage) as saying: "Despite many strong reasons for preserving our dignity by welcoming the shah, I was utterly opposed to it. [...] Sooner or later we had to acknowledge that our support of the shah had been badly conceived and managed" (Bill, 326).

CHAPTER II: CAPTURING THE IDOL'S DEN

16. Mehdi Bazargan, who had likened his government to a knife without a handle, had proven indiscreet in his fledgling government's relations with the United States. "Under siege and surrounded by enemies...a number of the moderates believed U.S. support to be essential" (Bill, 292). Their naiveté proved to be their undoing.

17. Immediately after footage of the meeting was broadcast in Tehran, some two million angry demonstrators took to the streets of the Iranian capital, shouting "Death to America!"

CHAPTER III: SETTLING IN

18. Khomeini, Ruhollah, *Tafsir Sura Hamd*, (Tehran: 1982).

19. "Fatima acts as a halo for the visages of all of the oppressed who later become the multitudes of Islam. All of the usurped, extorted, oppressed sufferers, all of those

whose rights have been destroyed and sacrificed by pressure and force and have been deceived, had the name of Fatima for their slogan. [...] It is most difficult to speak about the personality of Fatima. Fatima is the woman that Islam wants a woman to be. The concept of her visage is painted by the Prophet himself. He melts her and makes her pure in the fire of difficulties, poverty, resistance, deep understanding and the wonder of humanity."

20. The impact and the quality of the revelations contained in the embassy documents is discussed at length in James Bill's exhaustive study of U.S.-Iran relations. "These documents then became a powerful political tool used by the revolutionary extremists to bludgeon the moderates, who were now demonstrated to have had close associations with American intelligence officials" (Bill, 286).

21. The White Revolution was announced in January, 1963. A disguised privatization scheme devised to satisfy the Kennedy administration, it called for land reform, the sale of public enterprises, electoral representation for women and the creation of a literacy corps. Most Iranians saw it not as the "Revolution of the Shah and the People" but as that of the shah against the people. Massive anti-government demonstrations, led by Ayatollah Khomeini, broke out six months later in Qom, repressed at the cost of thousands of lives. (See Bill, 147-148).

22. Two of the hostages released—a man and a woman—may have been CIA agents.

23. *A Compilation of the Messages of the Muslim Students Following the Line of the Imam*, (Tehran: Publications of the Muslim Students Following the Line of the Imam, 1981), 53-56.

24. Former hostage Barry Rosen, who appeared in a debate focusing on the dialogue of civilizations with former student hostage-taker Abbas Abdi on CNN in November, 1998, had earlier concluded: "...the entire episode was closer to defeat for both sides, which no amount of celebrating could turn into its opposite" (Bill, 302).

CHAPTER IV: SORTING OUT THE DOCUMENTS

25. "Known in the intelligence cable traffic as SD/PLOD/1, Amir-Entezam was highly regarded by American officials," writes James Bill (290). He, along with other senior officials of the Provisional Government, had been extensively briefed by CIA agent George W. Cave in August and October, 1979. (Cave was later to play a central role in the Iran-Contra scandal in 1985-86.) The October briefing took place only one week before the shah was admitted to the United States. At the meeting, the Iranian side expressed concern about upheavals in Kurdistan, which they were convinced were being fomented by the CIA via the Iraqis. The Americans replied that they were committed to a stable Iran, and that the oil keep flowing.

Among the members of the Provisional Government, Amir-Entezam was probably the strongest supporter of closer ties with the United States.

26. The Mujahideen Khalq Organization (MKO) was founded following the mass demonstrations of 1963, as a radical amalgam of Marxist and Shi'ite ideas. In 1972, during the visit of U.S. president Richard Nixon to Iran, the organization carried out a campaign of political assassinations and bombings. The group's eclectic political and religious outlook earned it the mistrust of the Shi'a clerical establishment as early as 1975, when its Marxist orientation became clear. Although the MKO liked to suggest an affinity with the ideas of Dr. Shariati, it described his thought as a "petty bourgeois understanding of Islam." Shariati himself dismissed the group as confusing agitation with action. In 1981, one week after the dismissal of Abolhassan Bani Sadr from the presidency, the organization launched an attempt to overthrow the Islamic republican regime in a series of terror bombings, street battles and assassinations that quickly escalated into a near-civil war.

    The MKO was crushed, and its leader, Masoud Rajavi, fled Iran in company with deposed President Bani Sadr. The organization regrouped in Europe, primarily France, which finally expelled it. It then transferred its activities to Iraq, where it is jointly funded and supported by Saddam Hussein and the CIA. Despite being labeled as a "terrorist organization" by the United States State Department, the MKO operates an office in Washington D.C., and enjoys substantial high-level political support in several Western countries.

27. Thomas Ahern was CIA station chief in Tehran at the time of the embassy takeover. After a brief occupation of the United States Embassy in February, 1979, the entire CIA detachment had been airlifted out of Iran. Agents began to return in the summer of 1979. Then chargé d'affaires and later hostage Bruce Laingen had at that time warned his superiors of the serious danger of a CIA presence in Iran (Bill, 290).

28. Guy Rutherford was also known as William Foster. His real name was Vernon Cassin, an experienced CIA agent who had been stationed in the Middle East since the mid-1950s. He was involved in "an abortive attempt to rearrange the political system of Syria in 1956," becoming station chief in Amman, Jordan, before moving into deep cover positions in the region. "Because of the sensitivity of Cassin's mission, [in Iran, he] was to be provided with 'watertight coverage' with a twenty-four hour emergency telephone contact number. [...] The Central Intelligence Agency's brazen attempt to recruit and to buy information from Bani Sadr backfired badly when the embassy documents exposed the entire escapade" (Bill, 287-288).

CHAPTER V: NEGOTIATION IMPOSSIBLE

29. Gary Sick, *All Fall Down: America's Encounter With the Iranian Revolution*, (New York: Random House, 1985).

30. Pro-Israeli members of congress had, in the aftermath of the fall of the shah, argued that the Iranian revolution demonstrated "Arab instability" and underlined the "strategic importance" of Israel to the United States. The wife of then-Senator Jacob Javits, a staunch supporter of Israel, was actually on the payroll of the Iranian government (Bill, 365).

31. "Abu Jihad," or Khalil al-Wazir, was assassinated in Tunis on April 16, 1988, during an assault on his residence by an Israeli sea-borne commando led by Ehud Barak, currently Prime Minister of Israel.

32. Hansen, a Republican congressman from Idaho, was defeated in a reelection bid in 1984, following conviction and sentencing on charges of false income tax disclosure.

33. Belief in the Twelve Innocent Imams is one of the central pillars of Shi'a Islam. The Twelve Holy Imams, descendants of Ali ibn Abu Talib, son-in-law of the Prophet Mohammad, fourth Caliph and first Imam, are considered by the Shi'i not only the Prophet's successors in a legislative or administrative capacity, but as partaking of the spiritual dimensions of the prophetic mission. The last of the Imams, the Mahdi, or Redeemer, is believed to be in occultation, and will return to the world at the day of judgment to establish a regime of divine justice.

34. Harold Saunders, *American Hostages in Iran: The Conduct of a Crisis*, (New Haven and London: Yale University Press, 1985), 73-143.

35. Abolhassan Bani Sadr was elected the first President of the Islamic Republic in January, 1980, with a 70% majority.

36. Saunders, 121.

37. Ruhollah Khomeini, *Sahife Nour*, Vol. II, 98.

38. Saunders, 136.

CHAPTER VI: HOSTAGES AND STUDENTS—LIFE ON THE INSIDE

39. Though the occupation and hostage taking were widely regarded as being in violation of international law and norms, Francis Anthony Boyle (*World Politics and International Law*, [Durham, N.C.: Duke University Press, 1985]:189), argues that the seizure of the diplomats could be viewed as a legitimate exercise of Iran's right of self defense under Article 51 of the U.N. Charter. "[...] viewed from the Iranian perspective, the American diplomats were justifiably seized and detained in order to forestall another decisive and perhaps fatal coup d'état sponsored by the United States government operating in explicit violation of international law."

40. Details of the location of the hostages in the embassy may have been revealed to U.S. intelligence prior to the April rescue mission by the cook, who on a flight from Iran

to Turkey found himself seated next to a CIA operative. See Paul B. Ryan, *The Iranian Rescue Mission: Why It Failed*, (Annapolis: Naval Institute Press, 1985), 35.

41. Where decisions of these bodies may run counter to American interests, the United States simply disregards them, as in the case of the mining of Nicaraguan ports during the U.S.-sponsored Contra counterinsurgency. Where the very nature of a body or instrument might endanger those interests, as in the case of the International War Crimes Tribunal, the Treaty to Ban Land Mines, the Nuclear Weapons Test Ban Treaty, or the Kyoto Treaty on Climate Change the United States withholds recognition or ratification. NATO, on the other hand, remains quite popular with the American political establishment.

42. On September 8, 1978, martial law had been imposed in Tehran and 11 other Iranian cities, following weeks of unrest. That evening, troops had fired on a dense crowd of demonstrators in Jaleh Square, in the historic center of the capital. The resulting massacre touched off a series of strikes and protests that sped up the pace of revolutionary developments.

43. *444 Days: The Hostages Remember*, compiled by Tim Wells, (New York: Harcourt, Brace, Jovanovich, 1985).

CHAPTER VII: MEDIA WARS

44. After the fall of the shah, the Tudeh Party supported Khomeini, and succeeded in infiltrating the new Islamic bureaucracy. A Soviet diplomat and KGB officer in Tehran who defected to Great Britain in 1982 provided the British with a list of Soviet agents operating in Iran. The information was made available to Iranian authorities who arrested more than 1,000 Tudeh members, including party leader Nouredin Kianouri. In 1983, 18 Soviet diplomats were expelled from Iran.

45. Robin Woodsworth Carlsen, *Crisis in Iran: A Microcosm of the Cosmic Play*, (Victoria, BC: Snowman Press, 1979).

46. The students encountered pressure from many Iranian political groups to be included in the list. The MKO pleaded several times, but was each time turned down. They felt that the group and its leader, Massoud Rajavi, lacked sincerity. Subsequent events were to bear out their apprehensions.

47. Ayatollah Hossein Ali Montazeri, who had been reconfirmed as successor in 1985, was relieved of his position in March 1989, and assigned to virtual house arrest in Qom. Montazeri had sharply criticized the regime, its conduct of the eight-year war against Iraq, and called for a general amnesty for political prisoners. His treatment can be viewed as a barometer of the Islamic regime's ability to tolerate dissenting opinion.

48. Ayatollah Ali Khamene'i, today Iran's Supreme Leader or Guide, was, at the time, a member of the Revolutionary Council. He was elected President in October, 1981, following the assassination by bombing of Mohammad-Ali Raja'i, and appointed Leader in June, 1989, one day after the death of Imam Khomeini.

CHAPTER VIII: WITHIN THE WALLS

49. Sa'id Hajjarian, an engineering graduate, continued his studies in political science. He worked in the Ministry of Information in the first years of the Islamic Republic. Later, he went on to become one of the leading strategists in the campaign that brought Seyyed Mohammad Khatami to the presidency of Iran in 1997. He was subsequently elected to the Greater Tehran municipal council, and was editor-in-chief of *Sobh-é Emrouz* (This Morning), the leading reformist daily. On March 12, 2000, he was shot by a gunman apparently linked to a violent anti-reform faction within the security services. He survived the trauma and has returned to active politics.

50. The Iraqi invasion, which began on September 22, 1980, was supported by all permanent members of the United Nations Security Council with the exception of China.

51. Hossein, son of Ali and third Imam, died a martyr's death against overwhelming force in the battle of Karbala in 680 A.D.

52. Qur'an; 1:154

CHAPTER IX: DELTA FORCE DOWN

53. A team of 90 specially trained volunteers from the Pentagon's anti-terrorist Blue Light Unit and 90 Air Force crew invaded Iranian territory aboard eight RH-530 Sea Stallion helicopters and six C-130s. Halfway over the desert, two of the helicopters experienced mechanical troubles in the midst of a sandstorm. One was forced down while the other was able to return to the U.S.S. *Nimitz* in the Persian Gulf. The remainder of the aircraft landed in the vicinity of Tabas, an oasis town in the central Iranian desert. Another helicopter malfunctioned and broke down, effectively aborting the mission. As the Americans began their escape one of the helicopters collided with a C-130. Both aircraft exploded, killing eight Americans.

    After refueling at Tabas, the original plan was for the helicopters to fly to a mountain hide-out east of Tehran prepared and equipped with vehicles and facilities provided by Ali Eslami and a team of pro-monarchists. The C-130s were to leave Iran and later return to a separate landing site outside the capital. The troops would drive to Tehran "under cover," attack the embassy and free the hostages. The helicopters would land in the embassy compound or an adjacent stadium to lift the Americans to a nearby air strip where they would board the waiting C-130s and leave Iran.

Had the American commando force managed to reach Tehran, American and Iranian casualties would certainly have been heavy. James Bill quotes assault team leader Charlie Beckwith as saying: "When we went into that Embassy, it was our aim to kill all Iranian guards—the people holding the hostages—and we weren't going in there to arrest them" (Bill, 301).

The details of the operation remain to this day little known in the United States.

54. "It remains for future historians to decide to what extent Carter's approval of the raid derived from his humanitarian concern for the hostages' safety...and from his need, in an election year, to 'do something'..." (Ryan, 46).

Immediately following the Tabas fiasco (April 1980), a Special Operations Review Group chaired by Adm. J. L. Holloway III issued a Rescue Mission Report. The report, says James Bill, "clearly softens criticism." Ryan notes that the Review Group limited its efforts to the technical and military aspects of the debacle.

55. One of the Iranian traitors was a certain Ali Eslami, a bazaari who had prepared a hideout and vehicles near Garmsar. He escaped to the U.S. shortly before the operation. Documents show he had cooperated with the CIA before the takeover.

56. Gary Sick states that two coup attempts were foiled by Iranian security forces: one in June, the other on July 10, 1980. (*October Surprise: America's Hostages in Iran and the Election of Ronald Reagan*, [New York: Times Books, 1991]).

57. The Refah Partisi (Welfare Party), founded by Dr. Necmettin Erbakan, favored friendly relations with Turkey's eastern neighbor. Dr. Erbakan visited Iran in 1996, as prime minister of a coalition government that was later overthrown by the Turkish military.

58. American columnist Jack Anderson on August 18, 1980, revealed that the Carter administration had planned to "invade Iran with a powerful military force." The allegations proved mistaken, argues Gary Sick. The plan was really a second rescue mission (Sick, 25).

CHAPTER X: SETTLEMENTS, CONCESSIONS AND SAFE DELIVERY

59. Proceedings of the Majlis Shoura Islami, *Discussions on the Hostage Issue*, (Tehran: Majlis Publications, 1981).

60. Iraqi forces invaded Iran on September 22, 1980. Speaking at a press conference held inside Iranian territory, Saddam Hussein promised to hold a second press conference one week later in Tehran.

61. The *October Surprise* thesis was propounded by former U.S. Naval Captain Gary Sick, at the time Zbigniew Brzezinski's deputy on the National Security Council. In his book *October Surprise*, Sick claims that a series of major meetings involving William Casey, former CIA director and head of the Ronald Reagan presidential

campaign, and an Iranian delegation headed by a leading Shi'a cleric, took place at the Hotel Ritz in Madrid in July and August, 1980, "where the outline of an agreement was struck, and again in Paris, in October, where the terms were made final." (Sick, 11).

"Unbeknownst to the Carter administration, a rival foreign policy would be concocted by representatives of an opposition political party whose higher obligations to their country would be sacrificed on the altar of ambition." (Sick, 36).

62. Iran's then-foreign minister Sadeq Qotbzadeh stated on August 16: "We have information that the American Republican Party, in order to win the upcoming election, is trying very hard to delay the resolution of the hostage question until after the American election." (Sick, 89).

63. Political factions in the United States apparently shared this outlook, argues Sick. "Did William Casey, without the knowledge of the United States government, travel to Paris during the period of October 15-20, 1980, and there meet Iranian and Israeli representatives to arrange the release of the U.S. hostages to the Reagan-Bush forces in return for promises of military equipment? The answer, it appears, is yes." (Sick, 155).

64. Proceedings of the Majlis Shoura Islami, *Discussions on the Hostage Issue*, (Tehran: Majlis Publications, 1981). In the complex world of Iranian politics, denials are often interpreted as confirmation of allegations.

65. Gary Sick writes that "the Republicans feared that Carter himself would launch an 'October surprise' that would win the election" (Sick, 11).

66. James Bill quotes Javad Mansouri, "an important member of the Islamic Republican Party deeply involved in the embassy takeover" as saying: "Embassy documents prove that Bani Sadr has committed high treason. Is there a place in the world where a man proved to have committed high treason is President" (Bill, 288).